Trade Unions in China

Dr Pringle's book is an extremely useful contribution to the important and rapidly developing discussion on the future of worker organisation and trade unionism in China. Based on extensive fieldwork and research on the ground, he clearly demonstrates that whilst the ACFTU can be viewed in many ways it is not an unchanging monolith. Perhaps even more importantly his conclusions help to demolish the stereotype of Chinese workers as simply passive actors in the development of their own and the global economy.

Brendan Barber, *General Secretary, Trades Union Congress*

The transition from a command economy to a capitalist market economy has entirely altered the industrial landscape in which Chinese trade unions have to operate. This book focuses on how the All-China Federation of Trade Unions (ACFTU) is reforming under current conditions, and demonstrates that labour unrest is the principal driving force behind trade union reform in China. Presenting case studies where reform has been largely inspired by the pressure of worker activism from below, the book examines three crucial areas of trade union activity – collective bargaining, labour rights and trade union direct elections – against the background of China's turbulent industrial relations history.

As well as exploring the principal direction of trade union reform, which has been to channel disputes into juridical forms of dispute resolution sponsored by the state, the book also highlights key examples of more innovative experiments in trade union work. These represent a clear break with past practice and, crucially, have been recognized by both the union and Party leaderships as models for future trade union policy and practice. The book provides both a timely reference point and highlights the road to effective trade union solidarity.

Tim Pringle has been researching labour relations in Asia since 1996 with particular attention to China. He has lived in China and Hong Kong for twelve years, and his previous publications include *The Challenge of Transition: Trade Unions in Russia, China and Vietnam* (Palgrave), with Simon Clarke.

Routledge Contemporary China Series

1 **Nationalism, Democracy and National Integration in China**
Leong Liew and Wang Shaoguang

2 **Hong Kong's Tortuous Democratization**
A comparative analysis
Ming Sing

3 **China's Business Reforms**
Institutional challenges in a globalised economy
Edited by Russell Smyth and Cherrie Zhu

4 **Challenges for China's Development**
An enterprise perspective
Edited by David H. Brown and Alasdair MacBean

5 **New Crime in China**
Public order and human rights
Ron Keith and Zhiqiu Lin

6 **Non-Governmental Organizations in Contemporary China**
Paving the way to civil society?
Qiusha Ma

7 **Globalization and the Chinese City**
Fulong Wu

8 **The Politics of China's Accession to the World Trade Organization**
The Dragon goes global
Hui Feng

9 **Narrating China**
Jia Pingwa and his fictional world
Yiyan Wang

10 **Sex, Science and Morality in China**
Joanne McMillan

11 **Politics in China Since 1949**
Legitimizing authoritarian rule
Robert Weatherley

12 **International Human Resource Management in Chinese Multinationals**
Jie Shen and Vincent Edwards

13 **Unemployment in China**
Economy, human resources and labour markets
Edited by Grace Lee and Malcolm Warner

14 **China and Africa**
Engagement and compromise
Ian Taylor

15 **Gender and Education in China**
Gender discourses and women's schooling in the early twentieth century
Paul J. Bailey

16　**SARS**
Reception and interpretation in three Chinese cities
Edited by Deborah Davis and Helen Siu

17　**Human Security and the Chinese State**
Historical transformations and the modern quest for sovereignty
Robert E. Bedeski

18　**Gender and Work in Urban China**
Women workers of the unlucky generation
Liu Jieyu

19　**China's State Enterprise Reform**
From Marx to the market
John Hassard, Jackie Sheehan, Meixiang Zhou, Jane Terpstra-Tong and Jonathan Morris

20　**Cultural Heritage Management in China**
Preserving the cities of the Pearl River Delta
Edited by Hilary du Cros and Yok-shiu F. Lee

21　**Paying for Progress**
Public finance, human welfare and inequality in China
Edited by Vivienne Shue and Christine Wong

22　**China's Foreign Trade Policy**
The new constituencies
Edited by Ka Zeng

23　**Hong Kong, China**
Learning to belong to a nation
Gordon Mathews, Tai-lok Lui, and Eric Kit-wai Ma

24　**China Turns to Multilateralism**
Foreign policy and regional security
Edited by Guoguang Wu and Helen Lansdowne

25　**Tourism and Tibetan Culture in Transition**
A place called Shangrila
Åshild Kolås

26　**China's Emerging Cities**
The making of new urbanism
Edited by Fulong Wu

27　**China-US Relations Transformed**
Perceptions and strategic interactions
Edited by Suisheng Zhao

28　**The Chinese Party-State in the 21st Century**
Adaptation and the reinvention of legitimacy
Edited by André Laliberté and Marc Lanteigne

29　**Political Change in Macao**
Sonny Shiu-Hing Lo

30　**China's Energy Geopolitics**
The Shanghai Cooperation Organization and Central Asia
Thrassy N. Marketos

31　**Regime Legitimacy in Contemporary China**
Institutional change and stability
Edited by Thomas Heberer and Gunter Schubert

32　**U.S.–China Relations**
China policy on Capitol Hill
Tao Xie

33 **Chinese Kinship**
Contemporary anthropological perspectives
Edited by Susanne Brandtstädter and Gonçalo D. Santos

34 **Politics and Government in Hong Kong**
Crisis under Chinese sovereignty
Edited by Ming Sing

35 **Rethinking Chinese Popular Culture**
Cannibalizations of the Canon
Edited by Carlos Rojas and Eileen Cheng-yin Chow

36 **Institutional Balancing in the Asia Pacific**
Economic interdependence and China's rise
Kai He

37 **Rent Seeking in China**
Edited by Tak-Wing Ngo and Yongping Wu

38 **China, Xinjiang and Central Asia**
History, transition and crossborder interaction into the 21st century
Edited by Colin Mackerras and Michael Clarke

39 **Intellectual Property Rights in China**
Politics of piracy, trade and protection
Gordon Cheung

40 **Developing China**
Land, politics and social conditions
George C.S. Lin

41 **State and Society Responses to Social Welfare Needs in China**
Serving the people
Edited by Jonathan Schwartz and Shawn Shieh

42 **Gay and Lesbian Subculture in Urban China**
Loretta Wing Wah Ho

43 **The Politics of Heritage Tourism in China**
A view from Lijiang
Xiaobo Su and Peggy Teo

44 **Suicide and Justice**
A Chinese perspective
Wu Fei

45 **Management Training and Development in China**
Educating managers in a globalized economy
Edited by Malcolm Warner and Keith Goodall

46 **Patron-Client Politics and Elections in Hong Kong**
Bruce Kam-kwan Kwong

47 **Chinese Family Business and the Equal Inheritance System**
Unravelling the Myth
Victor Zheng

48 **Reconciling State, Market and Civil Society in China**
The long march yowards prosperity
Paolo Urio

49 **Innovation in China**
The Chinese software industry
Shang-Ling Jui

50 **Mobility, Migration and the Chinese Scientific Research System**
Koen Jonkers

51 **Chinese Film Stars**
Edited by Mary Farquhar and Yingjin Zhang

52 **Chinese Male Homosexualities**
Memba, *Tongzhi* and Golden Boy
Travis S.K. Kong

53 **Industrialisation and Rural Livelihoods in China**
Agricultural processing in Sichuan
Susanne Lingohr-Wolf

54 **Law, Policy and Practice on China's Periphery**
Selective adaptation and institutional capacity
Pitman B. Potter

55 **China-Africa Development Relations**
Edited by Christopher M. Dent

56 **Neoliberalism and Culture in China and Hong Kong**
The countdown of time
Hai Ren

57 **China's Higher Education Reform and Internationalisation**
Edited by Janette Ryan

58 **Law, Wealth and Power in China**
Commercial law reforms in context
Edited by John Garrick

59 **Religion in Contemporary China**
Revitalization and innovation
Edited by Adam Yuet Chau

60 **Consumer-Citizens of China**
The role of foreign brands in the imagined future China
Kelly Tian and Lily Dong

61 **The Chinese Communist Party and China's Capitalist Revolution**
The political impact of the Market
Lance L. P. Gore

62 **China's Homeless Generation**
Voices from the veterans of the Chinese Civil War, 1940s–1990s
Joshua Fan

63 **In Search of China's Development Model**
Beyond the Beijing Consensus
Edited by S. Philip Hsu, Suisheng Zhao and Yu-Shan Wu

64 **Xinjiang and China's Rise in Central Asia, 1949–2009**
A history
Michael E. Clarke

65 **Trade Unions in China**
The challenge of labour unrest
Tim Pringle

Trade Unions in China
The challenge of labour unrest

Tim Pringle

Routledge
Taylor & Francis Group

LONDON AND NEW YORK

First published 2011
by Routledge
2 Park Square, Milton Park, Abingdon, Oxon, OX14 4RN

Simultaneously published in the USA and Canada
by Routledge
711 Third Avenue, New York, NY 10017

*Routledge is an imprint of the Taylor & Francis Group,
an informa business*

© 2011 Tim Pringle

The right of Tim Pringle to be identified as author of this work has been asserted by him in accordance with the Copyright, Designs and Patent Act 1988.

Typeset in Times New Roman by Sunrise Setting Ltd, Torquay, UK
First issued in paperback 2013

All rights reserved. No part of this book may be reprinted or reproduced or utilised in any form or by any electronic, mechanical, or other means, now known or hereafter invented, including photocopying and recording, or in any information storage or retrieval system, without permission in writing from the publishers.

British Library Cataloguing in Publication Data
A catalogue record for this book is available from the British Library

Library of Congress Cataloging in Publication Data
Pringle, Tim, 1959-
 Trade unions in China: the challenge of labour unrest/Tim Pringle.
  p. cm.
 Includes bibliographical references and index.
 1. Zhonghua quan guo zong gong hui. 2. Labor unions–China.
 3. Industrial relations–China. I. Title.
 HD8732.C485 2011
 331.880951–dc22   2010050594

ISBN: 978-0-415-72835-5 (pbk)
ISBN: 978-0-415-55958-4 (hbk)
ISBN: 978-0-203-83104-5 (ebk)

For Simon

Contents

List of illustrations		xii
Acknowledgements		xiii
Abbreviations		xiv
	Introduction	1
1	Industrial relations in the People's Republic of China	11
2	Labour unrest in the state sector: the rise and demise of decent work with Chinese – and some Russian – characteristics	56
3	From victims to subjects: the long march of migrant labour	87
4	Experimental pragmatism I: collective consultation in Xinhe town	114
5	Experimental pragmatism II: trade union rights centre in Yiwu	133
6	Trade union elections: from dependency to democracy?	160
7	Constraining capital in the era of globalization	183
	Notes	189
	Bibliography	194
	Index	210

List of illustrations

Figures

1.1	Comparison of employment structure, 1978 and 2006 in percentages	42
3.1	Rural–urban migrant workers, 1989–2006	89
4.1	Number of enterprises by workers employed in Xinhe	124
5.1	Changes in the industrial structure of Yiwu city (per cent)	138

Photograph 3.1   Migrant workers on the school run   90

Tables

1.1	FDI in China: 1988–1995	29
1.2	Urban citizens' responses to the statement 'the problem of labour-capital conflicts is increasingly serious'	46
3.1	Labour disputes registered for arbitration, 1996–2006	100
3.2	Top six provinces for recorded labour disputes going to arbitration	104

Acknowledgements

This book would not have been possible without the guidance, support and friendship of Professor Simon Clarke who supervised my PhD. The fieldwork for the case studies owes a great deal to the research skills of Professor Xu Xiaohong. The analysis and interpretation of all data are the sole responsibility of the author.

Abbreviations

ACFTU	All-China Federation of Trade Unions
ACWF	All-China Women's Federation
AFL-CIO	American Federation of Labor and Congress of Industrial Organizations
ALII	Asian Legal Information Institute
BFAWU	Bakers, Food and Allied Workers Union
BWAF	Beijing Workers Autonomous Federation
CASS	Chinese Academy of Social Sciences
CCC	China Commodities Cities Group Company Limited (Zhejiang)
CEDA	Chinese Enterprise Directors Association
CEO	Chief Executive Officer
CLB	China Labour Bulletin
CLEC	China Labour Education Centre
CLNT	China Labor News Translations
CLSY	China Labour Statistical Yearbook
COE	Collectively-Owned Enterprise
COHSE	Confederation of Health Service Employees
CPC	Communist Party of China
CPCCC	Communist Party of China Central Committee
CPPCC	Chinese People's Political Consultative Conference
CSR	Corporate Social Responsibility
DUA	Department for Urban Administration
EPO	Establishment of Primary Organizations
ESRC	Economic and Social Research Council
ETI	Ethical Trading Initiative (UK)
FDI	Foreign Direct Investment
FEER	Far Eastern Economic Review
FIE	Foreign-Invested Enterprise
FMC	Factory Management Committee
GFTU	Guangzhou Federation of Trade Unions
GLF	Great Leap Forward
GMD	Guomindang

GUF	Global Union Federation
HRM	Human Resource Management
HRW	Human Rights Watch
HKCTU	Hong Kong Confederation of Trade Unions
ICEM	International Federation of Chemical, Energy, Mine and General Workers' Unions
ICFTU	International Confederation of Free Trade Unions
ICO	Institute of Contemporary Observation
IHLO	International Hong Kong Liaison Office
ILO	International Labour Organization
ITUC	International Trade Union Confederation
JCPC	Jinhua City People's Congress
LCCC	Labour-Capital Consultative Conference
LCL	Labour Contract Law
LDAC	Labour Dispute Arbitration Committee
LFF	Liaoyang Ferroalloy Factory
LMAL	Labour Mediation and Arbitration Law
LNGO	Labour Non-Governmental Organization
LPCOD	Law on the Prevention and Cure of Occupational Diseases
LSC	Labour service companies
MNC	Multinational corporation
MoC	Ministry of Civil Affairs
MOLSS	Ministry of Labour and Social Security
NFTU	Ningbo Federation of Trade Unions
NGO	Non-Governmental Organization
NPC	National People's Congress
OECD	Organisation for Economic Co-operation and Development
OHS	Occupational Health and Safety
PLA	People's Liberation Army
PRC	People's Republic of China
PRD	Pearl River Delta
PSB	Public Security Bureau
SEZ	Special Economic Zone
SFTU	Shenzhen Federation of Trade Unions
SOE	State-Owned Enterprise
SWC	Staff and Workers Congress
SWRC	Staff and Workers' Representative Congresses
TNC	Transnational Corporation
TVE	Township and Village Enterprise
USSR	Union of Soviet Socialist Republics
VTUF	Village-level Trade Union Federations
WAF	Workers Autonomous Federations
WFTU	Wenling City Federation of Trade Unions
WRC	Workers' Representative Conference
WSC	Workers Support Centres

WTO	World Trade Organization
XFTU	Xinhe Federation of Trade Unions
XWSMA	Xinhe Woollen Sweater Manufacturers Association
XWSTU	Xinhe Woollen Sweater Sector Trade Union
YFTU	Yiwu Federation of Trade Unions
YHFTU	Yuhang Federation of Trade Unions
YICT	Yantian International Container Terminals Limited
YWLRC	Yiwu Workers' Legal Rights Centre
YYFTU	Yuyao City Federation of Trade Unions
ZJWD	*Zhejiang Workers' Daily*
ZCCCG	Zhejiang China Commodities Cities Group Company Limited

Introduction

Throughout the period of economic reform, mainstream opinion of the All-China Federation of Trade Unions (ACFTU) has been largely negative in the developed countries. The most important criticism is that the ACFTU does not meet ILO standards of independence due to its constitutional and legally enshrined acceptance of Communist Party of China (CPC) leadership. Although the Chinese government signed the International Covenant on Economic, Social and Cultural Rights in 1997, it entered a reservation to the clause in Article 8 pertaining to freedom of association. Thus, the ACFTU's monopoly status has remained intact and its response to the transition from a command economy to a market economy has been largely top-down. It has played a key role in drafting laws and regulations that both construct and constrain the organization's role in a still evolving industrial relations system based on labour law and contracts. The consequences of the absence of competition for membership and influence from alternative trade unions are seen in the slow rate of reform to its traditional modus operandi and weakness at enterprise level. The picture of an anaesthetized and compliant trade union is complemented by lingering stereotypes of passive Chinese workers stealing jobs from all and sundry in a global race to the bottom.

However, beginning in 2003 – by my estimation – there has been a thaw in the relationship between the former International Confederation of Free Trade Unions (ICFTU) and the ACFTU. The defrosting continued following the merger between the ICFTU and the World Confederation of Labour to form the International Trade Union Confederation (ITUC) on 1 November 2006. Further impetus came after the Change To Win federation's split from the AFL-CIO. Even though Change To Win is not an affiliate of the ITUC, its initiative of dialogue with the ACFTU has encouraged a moderate rethink in the AFL-CIO itself. In December 2007, the ITUC voted to seek engagement with the ACFTU based, according to General Secretary Guy Ryder, on 'clear policy objectives'. Given that approximately one quarter of the global working class is Chinese and that China is the favoured destination of global foreign direct investment, the ITUC's change of direction is profoundly significant. At the research level, it opens up opportunities for research on Chinese trade unions and will add weight to the significance of the results.

China's industrial relations policies between 1949 and the mid-1980s ensured stable employment for the urban working class. Although the political environment

2 Introduction

was frequently rocked by campaigns such as the Anti-Rightist Movement, the Hundred Flowers and the Great Leap Forward during the 1950s and the Cultural Revolution of the 1960s, the state went to considerable efforts to ensure that these campaigns did not impinge on industrial production.[1] At least in part, some of the aforementioned campaigns were either a response to labour militancy or a desire to forestall it in order to maintain industrial peace and ensure production targets were met. Nevertheless, working class militancy as expressed through strikes, the refusal to meet quotas and production targets, absenteeism, a disregard for factory rules and petty sabotage were an important feature of pre-reform industrial relations (Sheehan 1998: 2–3). While the demands raised by workers in these struggles often, but not always, resonated with the demands of industrial workers anywhere – for higher wages, improved safety, etc. – their class character was muddied by the political environment in which they took place. All of China's four Constitutions to date have been based on the revolutionary notion that the working class, led by the CPC, is the leading class, in effect the ruling class. As 'masters' of state-run enterprises, the nature of any collective class action by workers in pursuit of improved pay and working conditions was consequently far from straightforward.

The economic reforms are officially recognized as beginning in 1978 when the Third Plenum of the Eleventh Party Congress gave approval to land distribution reforms pioneered in the provinces of Anhui and Sichuan on the initiative of farmers themselves. Since this historic decision, the economic reforms have had a profound effect on the structure, composition, geography and demography of the Chinese working class. As government policy edged the country into a period of transition from a command economy to a market-orientated economy – described by the CPC since 1992 as a 'socialist market economy' – the position and political influence workers have been able to impose collectively on society has been subject to contradictory pressures. On the one hand, state-owned enterprise (SOE) restructuring has put paid to the command economy status of urban workers as 'masters of the enterprise' – despite constitutional reassurances to the contrary – along with the economic benefits and privileges that came with this comparatively privileged political position. At the same time, the return of private capital, rapid urbanization and China's expanding role in the global economy has increased the potential collective power of workers exponentially. Since 2003, we have seen glimpses of this potential in the increasingly effective militancy of migrant workers in South and East China as they have pushed up pay rates for skilled labour and government-fixed local minimum wage levels. As the ITUC's policy shift towards engagement with the ACFTU suggests, the implications of these transformations in the world's largest working class go way beyond China's borders.

Up until the mid 1990s, the changes descending on the urban working class were, generally speaking, of a gradual nature. Power over hire and fire, wages and contracts granted to SOEs – previously referred to as state-operated (*guoying*) – managers during the 1980s were employed sparingly as local governments and industrial leaders sought to avoid labour unrest (Liu Aiyu 2005: 86). As the influence of private capital grew, the competition dictated a major restructuring that began with small- and medium-sized enterprises. Membership of the World Trade

Organization (WTO) in late 2001 has propelled the restructuring process towards almost all SOEs.

A major political event, the mass lay-off of tens of millions of workers, was a consequence of different pressures. But the most important were the migration of tens of millions of migrant workers into off-farm employment; and the continuation and consolidation of the policy of encouraging foreign direct investment as a motor for development, especially in the manufacturing sector. The policy of mass redundancies from SOEs was known as *xiagang* in Chinese. Literally translated into English the term means 'to step down from one's post' which awards it a voluntary inference that is not accurate in this case. *Xiagang* facilitated a still-ongoing rebalancing of the relations of production in favour of private capital. The state has resorted to various euphemisms to encourage the traditional urban working class to accept the traumatic transformation imposed on them. For its part, the ACFTU, through the pages of *Workers' Daily*, exhorted skilled workers and low-level managers to 'jump into the sea' of enterprise and commerce (*xiahai*) and blue-collar workers to 'liberate their thinking' (*jiefang sixiang*), reject irrational egalitarianism and practise self-reliance.

As private and foreign capital became the engine of China's growth, the rural internal migrant workers who facilitated this realignment faced very high levels of exploitation. Known as *nongmin gong* or literally peasant workers, they retained their rural status and were excluded from many of the citizen rights enjoyed by urban workers. The practice of drafting in migrants from the countryside to work on urban infrastructure projects was not new in the People's Republic. But the migration of peasants to work in private enterprises in which they were subjected to capitalist labour relations was very new. The strangeness of the factory system to these new arrivals and the high degree of state management over their temporary transfer from the countryside acted as constraints on their capacity to defend their rights at work. And anyway, these rights weren't given full formal legal status until the national labour law was enacted in 1995. This was followed by an increase in labour disputes between labour and private capital that has continued ever since. Indeed, by 2005, migrant workers' actions were providing the greatest incentive to the ACFTU to improve its representative performance and even beginning to win important hikes in both the minimum and average wages.

The responses of both the traditional urban working class and their recently arrived, yet still separated, rural brothers and sisters to the issues confronting them in China's industrial workplaces have been determined by various factors. Structure, composition, history, geography and demography have all conditioned how workers react to exploitation. Of equal weight are the policies of the state itself: the absence of freedom of association; the state's prioritizing of employment creation before 'decent work'; restrictions on residential rights that have excluded off-farm workers from full urban citizen rights even as they have retained the right to land; an expanding but monitored and supervised civil society; an incomplete legal system for governing industrial relations; a restricted media and the fact that China remains a one-party state in which the organization of class interests beyond the structures permitted by the CPC is still, to all intents and purposes, politically inconceivable. Combined with the country's sheer size and diversity, this array of objective and subjective factors suggests that it is not possible to speak of a unified working class response to either the restructuring of SOEs or the imposition of 'primitive accumulation' on migrant workers from the countryside in the private sector (Xu Xiaohong 2003: 55). Some commentators have drawn the conclusion that Chinese workers – indeed Chinese society – are as disparate as 'grains of sand' and that this by default precludes any effective collective influence on government and society.

Yet, a growing body of research suggests that a generalized scenario of disempowerment is far too simplistic. The absence of independent trade unions does not automatically preclude working class influence on most aspects of the government's labour relations policies, including wages. Hobsbawm reminded us that '[M]en live surrounded by a vast accumulation of past devices' and over the last 27 years of reform, and especially since the Fifteenth Party Congress in 1997, Chinese workers have drawn on 'the most suitable of these, [so as] to adapt them for their own (novel) purposes' (Hobsbawm 1998: 44). In China, workers have in the main pursued what are often referred to as 'bread and butter' issues that by no means directly challenge the current political status quo: better wages, wages on time, pension rights, dole payments and health and safety issues. Very rarely, demands for union recognition have surfaced, more often than not cautiously couched in China's labour traditions.

Over the past five years, there have been two important developments: firstly there is a slight and ongoing shift in the labour market in favour of workers due chiefly to labour shortages, demographic trends, a discernible change in the central government's agricultural policies – itself due to farmer unrest over tax burdens and land access issues – and the consolidation of the rise of new geographic areas of economic growth such as the Yangzi River Delta. Crucially, there has been a growing sense of rights awareness and collective strength, particularly among migrant workers. Secondly, workers have been able to make use of the tension between central government laws and regulations, and local government's need to maintain stability in an environment of increased rights awareness, labour shortages and higher expectations among the second generation of migrant workers. An interview with a trade union official in Zhejiang province corroborated views from entrepreneurs in the same area that there was a quantitative and qualitative difference in the workplace attitudes among the younger migrant workers that has not been lost on labour activists. The current generation is far more 'aware of the labour law and the rights they should have under this law' (LNGO staff, interview, Shenzhen, 6 January 2006). Moreover, their long-term ambitions have changed. Many have 'no intentions of going back to the land if they can possibly avoid it' (LNGO staff, interview). Changes in the labour market – at least until October 2008 and the onset of global recession – and the accumulated bank of knowledge of the factory system by migrant workers have produced improvements in wages, working conditions and general standard of living, as well as new strategy and tactics to pursue such goals. While China's 'new factory proletarians, rural labourers, miners and others of the sort' have not yet fully learnt 'how to run a trade union' (Hobsbawm 1998: 46) and the process of doing so is slowed by political restrictions, we can see how the myth that reduces Chinese migrant workers to unthinking workhorses 'that don't need or want days off' is indeed just a myth.[2]

How then does the traditional state-run trade union respond to the changing complexities of industrial relations in general and labour unrest in particular? The unions have been under considerable pressure to stabilize labour relations and slow the rise in collective labour disputes. In response to unrest, central and local governments and at times investors have looked to the ACFTU to becalm the situation (Howell 2003; Taylor *et al.* 2003; Clarke and Pringle 2009). In response, the ACFTU has embarked on a number of almost exclusively top-down strategies in attempts to increase its credibility among workers by forging a direct link between labour rights, trade union activity and social harmony. These include: membership campaigns beginning in 1999; the theoretical inclusion of off-farm migrant workers in the formal working class since the 14th Trade Union Congress in 2003; participation in law-drafting and trial implementation of regulations on collective bargaining and collective wage consultation; case intervention at the levels of mediation, arbitration and the courts; the direct election of trade union officials and committee members at enterprise level etc. As essentially a government institution, the ACFTU has played a major role in the field of labour law-drafting. In 1988, the organization even made a serious attempt to have the right to strike included in the revision of the Trade Union Law being drafted at the time. Although in this instance its efforts failed, the impact of the ACFTU on law-drafting has continued and deepened as the relatively pro-worker Labour Contract Law (2008) has demonstrated. At the same time, these well-documented top-down policies have not excluded less well-known local initiatives and, some argue, have even created space for them. In this book, I present three case studies and draw on information from one more to demonstrate that the ACFTU does not only engage in top-down strategies and that locally initiated pilots form an important part of its policy development, especially in the area of responding to labour unrest.

The context for this dialectic of labour unrest and trade union reform has three aspects. The first is that, constitutionally, China remains a 'socialist state under the people's democratic dictatorship led by the working class' (Constitution 1982). As far as the CPC is concerned the creation of a 'socialist market economy' and the social relations that have emerged have not altered this basic circumstance and, as a consequence, it remains deeply concerned with its legitimacy. Despite the passage of time, the CPC is still keenly aware of modern Polish history and the role of Solidarność in bringing about the downfall of the previous regime. More recently, the role of foreign-funded non-governmental organizations (NGO), labour-orientated and otherwise, in the so-called 'colour' revolutions of Georgia and the Ukraine has given rise to similar anxieties.

The second aspect pertains to the nature of China's transition. The depth of the reforms was illustrated in speeches by the former President and Party Secretary General Jiang Zemin in 2000 and 2001 in which he awarded Chinese entrepreneurs and managers a dramatically expanded ideological space for the pursuit of profit. As decisive political moments in China's transition, the speeches recognized that the allocation of China's resources was no longer solely the prerogative of the state. Continuing political control was ensured in Jiang's exposition of his theory of the Three Represents, which argues that the CPC has the capacity to represent the interests of all the 'progressive' actors in society. While my research is not intended as a transition study, least of all one that risks 'presenting too laudatory a narrative of China's "successful" turn to capitalism' (Lee Ching-kwan 2007: xi) both these contextual aspects demand a thorough review of labour relations in the former command economy and how the working class influenced them. My review draws on recent research that has shed a questioning light on the view that workers remained largely passive players in the arrangements and relationships of pre-reform industry. Following this exploration of the historical working class, its traditions and its more recent 'unmaking', I review the development of labour unrest in the private sector over the reform period. Throughout, I use the role of the ACFTU as both an anchor and reference point for my research.

The third contextual aspect for this work is the emergence of 'space' in which Chinese civil society currently operates and, more to the point, where it comes from. Globalization has given increased impetus to the argument that representative parliamentary democracy is a 'natural' result of trade and the engagements that trade brings. The argument is often cited by western governments and TNCs to justify doing business with states in which democratic institutions are either lacking or in their infancy. In China, it is often assumed that the appearance of a prosperous middle class will lead to demands for democratic channels of participation in political life. While not a focus of my project, the authenticity – or lack of it – of this argument is rendered relevant by my contention that it has been primarily workers' self-activity that has pushed the barriers of social participation, not the market.

Methodology

This book started out life as an inquiry into the changes the economic reforms and political adjustments were bringing to China's rapidly expanding working class. During the late 1990s my discussions with academics such as Simon Clarke (sociology), Chang Kai (labour law) and economists Xu Xiaohong and Martin Hart-Landsberg had heightened my awareness of the scale and global relevance of the transformation of China's working class. As such my PhD research, upon which this book is based, posed four questions: the extent of working class unity in China; the extent of the development of labour protests; regional differences in labour relations; and the existence, or otherwise, of a correlation between workers' protests and pay and conditions. However, during the course of my early reading, discussions and conversations with trade unionists, workers and academics, there was invariably an 'elephant in the room' that would sooner or later make its presence felt. The elephant's name is the All-China Federation of Trade Unions. My reading of secondary sources also led me to realize that, while there are excellent studies on the structure and nature of the ACFTU (some, such as Harper's work, dating back to the 1960s), far less research has been carried out on the organization's response to a rapidly evolving industrial relations map. I concluded that one reason for this dearth is the school of thought which holds that the absence of freedom of association and the political constraints on the ACFTU dictate that it has not responded, indeed cannot respond, to the transformation of China's economy. Yet my reading and research suggested otherwise. Moreover, my work as a research fellow at the University of Warwick on an ESRC-funded research project into trade unions in Russia, China and Vietnam afforded me comparative insights into the results of my research that directly inform the main argument of this book: that class struggles between workers and employers are the principal catalyst for trade union reform in China.[3]

Chapters 1 to 3 are based on Chinese and English academic resources, literature surveys and Chinese media reports. These secondary sources are supplemented by extensive fieldwork which includes interviews with workers, trade union officials, labour NGO staffers, lawyers and journalists in Shenzhen, Hong Kong, Guangzhou, Beijing and Hangzhou and north-east China between 2000 and 2009. During this time, I was resident in Hong Kong but spent, overall, more than 14 months on the mainland conducting fieldwork.

Chapters 4 to 6 are built around the results of our research in Zhejiang and Guangdong. This research was conducted either as part of my PhD research or under the aforementioned ESRC project. Working with experienced labour researchers who enjoy close links and excellent access to the ACFTU has been a profound learning experience to which this book is indebted. Nevertheless, I should stress that any mistakes in the interpretation of the data are mine and mine alone. The fieldwork itself involved in-depth interviews with enterprise-, county- and city-level trade union cadres, labour bureau officials, enterprise managers and workers. Also conducted was one evaluation of the attitudes of 60 Guangdong-based enterprise-level trade union cadres attending courses on labour and trade union law; and two assessments of employer and worker attitudes to the process and results of trade union elections. The latter exercises involved, respectively, 144 workers and 23 employers in a prosperous Zhejiang town. Prior to, during and following the research period, I supplemented the supervised research with in-depth interviews with trade union officials and factory managers conducted by myself and triangulated by press reports and conference papers. I would be the first to admit that the conclusions I draw in Chapters 4, 5 and 6 are tentative and more research is required. At the same time, the research has enabled me to demonstrate that the underlying dynamic of these experiments in trade union innovation has been labour unrest and the search for industrial harmony rather than a sole dependence on law and edicts from above. I believe that this conclusion, along with the evidence provided to support it, is of considerable value to the development of the labour movement in China and how external agencies might react to it.

Ethical consideration

Experience has taught me that anonymity is of key importance to individuals and groups that do not enjoy the status required to afford protection against employers or China's rules on censorship and social research. I have applied this lesson whenever I judged it necessary. My research has deliberately avoided delving into the sensitive topic of freedom of association in favour of concentrating on what is possible in actually existing conditions.

Structure

My central argument departs from conventional assumptions about the ACFTU and Chinese labour in three respects. First: although the trade union maintains a monopoly on formal union organizing in China, this does not equate to an absence of tactical divergence with regard to workers' rights and interests. Second: the variety in union approaches to its work is not a result of edicts and regulatory commands from the centre, but the product of pilot projects at the local level. Third: the stereotype of Chinese workers as passive victims of capitalist globalization and authoritarian government does not fit the reality of industrial relations in China. In fact, it is increasingly sophisticated labour unrest that is providing the primary impetus for local pilots in trade union work.

I have structured my argument as follows. Chapter 1 provides an account of the historical development of Chinese industrial relations from 1949 to the present day. There are two basic models spread over five periods. The command economy model is dominated by the concept of the *danwei* or work unit. Rooted in pre-liberation heavy industry, *danwei* authority was not limited to production alone but to the overall management of urban working lives and the spaces in which they were lived out. In this scenario, the traditional union encouraged workers to meet production targets, administered workplace benefits, arranged holiday functions, sporting and leisure events and occasionally represented individual workers in minor disputes with factory management. The heyday of the *danwei* dated from 1957 and the completion of nationalization until 1986 when new regulations pertaining to labour contracts signalled the beginning of the end of lifetime employment.

The roots of the socialist market model can be found in the early years of the new republic when the CPC based its early urban reconstruction programmes on the coexistence of private capital and socialist labour. The underlying assumption that, in the right conditions, the two sides are compatible with industrial relations in a workers' state re-emerged in the reform era. I have divided – as far as possible – the post-command-economy years into three stages: early reform, the post-Southern Tour period, and the years following WTO membership up to the present day. I trace the development of the socialist market model of industrial relations via regulatory expansion, contracts, formal dispute mechanisms based in law, and the changing role of the union as it recovered from its near collapse during the Cultural Revolution era.

Chapter 2 is the first of two chapters on labour unrest. My intentions in these chapters are twofold. First, to shatter the myth of passivity equated with workers in the People's Republic of China (PRC) despite the work of Chen Feng, Yu Jianrong, Anita Chan, Chris Chan, Elizabeth Perry, Jackie Sheehan and others. And second, to demonstrate the impact of labour unrest on industrial relations in general and trade union policy in particular. Chapter 2 is an historical survey of unrest in the republic's early years and its development in the state sector following full nationalization. The large-scale workers' demonstrations in 2002 in north-east China are often seen as the climax of traditional state sector labour unrest. My explanation of the failure of SOE workers and their trade union to defend up to forty million jobs between 1997 and 2002 is based on their removal from the source of power and leverage: production. Unlike the private sector, there was very little political space for the ACFTU to organize any alternative to the huge job losses that came with SOE restructuring and privatization. Politically, the union was hamstrung by its legal obligations to the Party. Practically, as witnessed by the dramatic rise in unemployment in the West during the 2008–2009 global capitalist crisis, trade unions can do little to fight redundancies no matter where they occur.

Chapter 3 shifts the focus to labour unrest in the private sector and how this has produced pressure on the ACFTU to improve its representative capacity. This pressure comes from above and below. An increasingly militant workforce has concentrated senior Party minds on industrial relations and these leaders have consequently instructed the union to play its part in a wider project for social harmony. In this sense, we can see – perhaps somewhat ironically – how labour unrest has actually increased the political status of the ACFTU in the Chinese political system.

These chapters provide the backdrop for an array of union pilots and models, and I devote the following three chapters to three examples. In Chapter 4, I focus on an experiment in collective bargaining in a small town that was later held up as an example of how Chinese regulations on collective consultation can produce a 'win–win' situation. Our research demonstrates that while the conclusion of a sector-level collective wage table based on work processes in the garment sector was a remarkable achievement, it was not the result of a regulatory framework imposed from above. Instead, it was a spontaneous reaction to local conditions led by 'trailblazing' (*chuangxin*) individuals in the local union who were able to compel employers' accountability to their employees by drawing on state authority.

In Chapter 5, I examine the establishment of the ACFTU's first labour rights centre. This was a contested process that owed its eventual success to the local trade union's strategy of forging alliances with a wide range of local players. Wider social resources were opened when the county-level city union went beyond the traditional union 'fence' and registered its rights centre as a social group (*shehui tuanti*) with the Ministry of Civil Affairs. This breakthrough is conceptualized as the 'socialization' (*shehuihua*) of union work.

In Chapter 6, I examine the national experiment to improve the capacity of enterprise-level cadres via the direct election of trade union chairpersons and committees. The chapter surveys the recent history of trade union direct elections prior to a detailed examination of two local case studies in which different electoral procedures were applied. The difference between the two experiments lies with the constraints or otherwise on candidature. I argue that while it is clear that the ACFTU remains averse to risking direct elections as an *immediate* response to labour unrest, elections are nevertheless both a response to militancy and the subsequent pressure on the union to become more representative.

In Chapter 7, I place the conclusions of my research in the context of changing global and national conditions such as the financial crisis and the ITUC's new policy towards the ACFTU. I argue that despite the trauma of the global capitalist crisis that temporarily reduced Chinese workers' capacity to pursue their interests and consequently keep up the pressure for reform, there is still much work to be done both at the practical and research levels if we are to see the emergence of an effective global trade union movement.

1 Industrial relations in the People's Republic of China

This chapter summarizes the history of China's labour relations since 1949, the year the CPC defeated the Guomindang (GMD), established a new government and embarked on a programme of economic reconstruction. In contrast to the land reform in the countryside where enforced redistribution was deemed the most effective way of restoring production to a war-ravaged agriculture, urban areas were distinguished by a period of compromise in which the need to create jobs was prioritized over practically all other considerations. Over thirty years later, the spectre of unemployment and accompanying economic stagnation was to play a similar role as the unemployment crisis of the late 1970s and early 1980s became 'the initial impetus to labor policy change' (Ngok Kinglun 2008: 45).

If employment creation has been a major economic concern of the CPC since it won power, stability at work has been a consistent political concern. Although the addition of 'Chinese characteristics' via the thoughts of Mao, Deng, Jiang and Hu has at times made it difficult to perceive Marx's influence on CPC theory and practice, the Party has nevertheless remained cognizant of Marx's central idea on change: the collective power of the working class. This chapter examines how various industrial relations regimes in China have been developed on the basis of both exploiting and containing this power. It is an extraordinary journey imbued variously with revolutionary excitement, chaos, triumph and trauma.

The organization of the chapter is relatively straightforward. I have employed labour and the unions as anchors to a basically historical approach split into four broad sections: the *danwei* era, the early years of reform, the socialist market economy and developments since China became a member of the WTO in 2001.

Industrial relations under the command economy

The danwei

The institutional core of industrial relations in pre-reform China was the urban work unit known as the *danwei*. Lü and Perry offer a useful five-part functional definition of this institution: power over hire, fire and transfer; communal facilities such as housing, dining halls, cars and health clinics; independent accounting; an urban purview; and existing in the public sector (Lü and Perry 1997: 5–6). From an industrial relations perspective, I would add three main characteristics: stability via enforced low labour turnover rates; a top-down administrative remuneration system based on wages, bonuses and high levels of welfare; and the ideological integration of the interests of managers and managed.

Individually, none of these characteristics is specific to a command economy, Chinese or otherwise. Dore conceptualized Japanese industrial relations as an 'organization-orientated system' that offered lifetime employment in exchange for workers' loyalty to a given enterprise (Dore 1987: 30). In the circumstance of a developing country, the total remunerative packages in a large key (*zhongdian*) *danwei* were high (Lü and Perry 1997: 3; Weil 1996: 35). In fact 'workers real wage levels in 1970 represented a thirty-five per cent rise above those of 1952' (Lee Ching-Kwan 2000: 42), permitting comparisons with the Scandinavian model, albeit cautious and qualified. In Soviet Russia, Clarke explained how the term 'labour collective' (*trudovoi kollektiv*) was used to refer to 'the whole workforce of the enterprise – from manager to cleaner' (Clarke 2006: 31). This ideologically inspired integration of interests resonates with the Chinese word '*zhigong*' which, during the command economy era, generally referred to all the staff and workers of a work unit regardless of managerial authority or the lack of it. Indeed, continued use of the term *zhigong* in post-reform Chinese statistics has hampered the reliability of data on wages and working conditions.

Writing on the former Soviet Union, Clarke located a material basis for the common interest of managers and workers in the absence of capitalist-style compulsion on managers to reduce costs and intensify the rate of work. As a consequence, managers and workers at an enterprise had a shared interest in the negotiation of a slack production plan and ensuring that the targets contained therein were not overfulfilled (Burawoy *et al*. 1993: 15–17, 26). In the People's Republic of China, the picture was complicated by an overabundance of labour and the leverage over working conditions this allowed Chinese managers – especially during campaigns such as the Great Leap Forward and in some phases of the Cultural Revolution – as opposed to the USSR's chronic lack of skilled workers that in turn awarded Soviet workers considerable advantage at enterprise-level negotiations.

The *danwei* in China was as much a political and social undertaking as it was a productive unit. It has even been described as a 'small city' (O'Leary 1998: 54) able to meet all the basic social and welfare requirements of urban living and into which 'individuals are born, live, work, and die' (Naughton 1997: 170). The capacity to provide comparatively high standards of living in a developing economy, i.e. in conditions of scarcity, required the power of the state to ensure that the always-precarious integration of the interests of urban residents was not upset by peasants moving to the cities and demanding a share of the metropolitan cake. To this end, the state developed a rigorously implemented system of restrictions on residence known as *hukou* based on the division of town and country. Beginning in the late 1950s, *hukou* regulations successfully underpinned *danwei* exclusivity until well into the reform era (see Chapter 2). Put another way, the danwei's durability relied on strictly enforced boundaries that kept peasants out of *danwei* membership and the privileges that came with it. Thus, state power and control became the mainstay of the *danwei* system, enabling it to fulfil comprehensive social, political and productive functions (Naughton 1997: 167). The obvious agency to deliver this power and control was the CPC itself. The Party was directly involved in the administration of industrial relations in the *danwei* era and, as we shall see, its withdrawal presented the trade unions with a major crisis of legitimacy.

There is a range of views on the implications of the Party's dominant role in *danwei* management and labour relations. Although You Ji premised his conceptual approach on the research of Walder's 'communist neo-traditionalism' and Womack's 'work unit socialism' – both of whom argued that control in urban China could not be reduced to fear of a totalitarian state alone – he nevertheless characterized *danwei* relationships as a condition of totalitarianism that has since been undermined by the autonomy that market reforms and privatization have brought to SOEs. You Ji's totalitarianism has its origins in the 'Party's monistic control' of enterprises developed during the political campaigns and worker recruitment drives of the early 1950s (You Ji 1998: 32–3) during which 'workers "active consent" gradually gave way to passive submission to a powerful "new class" of cadres' (You Ji 1998: 17). He also traced a direct relationship between the increasing presence of party cells in enterprises and the decline in union power at primary level. Beginning in October 1951, following a fierce debate over whether or not the state's interests were separate from those of trade unions, the ACFTU leadership was purged and 'more direct party control started to take root in shop-floor politics in the wake of the clampdown on the unions' (You Ji 1998: 35).

As union autonomy began to fade, the *danwei*'s capacity to provide access to consumer goods and welfare services in a time of general scarcity strengthened the hand of factory cadres over workers (You Ji 1998: 13). In exchange, the urban working class apparently accepted political controls and monitoring by party cells in enterprises. It was this allocation of economic benefits in return for acceptance of political constraints which, according to some scholars, partially accounted for a 'relatively high level of social order' (Lü and Perry 1997: 3). Citing Korzec, Warner frames the arrangement as a deal, a 'social contract' between the CPC and the working class that 'fed, housed, hospitalised and generally cosseted the "vanguard" of the working class' (Warner 2000: 3). On the other hand, Lee argues that the arrangement did *not* imply worker passivity in return for Party largesse. She points to blue collar wage hikes, the capping of enterprise managers' salaries at 10 to 30 per cent above those of skilled workers and the requirement for them to participate periodically in shop-floor labour as evidence of workers' enhanced position vis-à-vis managerial cadres (Lee Ching-Kwan 2000: 42). Moreover, Sheehan's new history of Chinese workers has demonstrated that intermittent outbreaks of working class militancy continually reinforced the CPC's anxiety over working class power (Sheehan 1998). She contends that, far from the existence of a 'social contract',

> conflict, often originating from economic grievances, but quickly developing into a political dispute as a result of the dominance of the Party within

enterprises, has been a far more common feature of industrial life in China than is generally recognised.

(Sheehan 1998: 2)

I will return to the central question of labour unrest in Chapter 2.

Walder's concept of 'communist neo-traditionalism' emphasized the complexity of the relationships that workers formed within a *danwei* in order to survive and improve their lot. His definition of the term makes use of two descriptive elements. The first refers to the absence of market forces, and of bargaining between worker and *danwei* in determining wages and conditions. Under communist neo-traditionalism, employment in a *danwei* cannot be reduced to a purely economic activity solely for the extraction of surplus value in return for wages. It also carried a welfare role with a 'value in itself' (Walder 1986: 11). As such, the *danwei* is not just an economic entity but also a (state) agency for the delivery of a range of social services that, as we have already seen, were not available to those outside the *danwei* system. Walder's second descriptive element referred to the institutionalized dependency on which this arrangement rested. The absence of non-Party affiliated institutions within the *danwei* – and wider society – forced workers into a dependent relationship producing three characteristics that, in Walder's view, distinguished industrial relationships in the *danwei* from those of Western enterprises: dependency on the enterprise for goods and services (including wages); on the Party and its auxiliary organizations – such as the trade unions – for representation; and on the supervisors for personal promotion and increased access to non-pecuniary forms of remuneration – a larger flat, for example – that came with it (Walder 1986: 8–14). Xu also uses notions of dependency to conceptualize *danwei* relationships and designated the period from 1957 to 1978 as the second stage in the post-liberation development of industrial relations during which the *danwei*'s 'urban purview' and 'public sector' attributes reigned supreme. He characterized the period as one in which 'the capitalist class was abolished, labour-capital relations were wiped out, and "labour" as a subjective entity lost all significance. The free independent labourer was extinguished as [China] entered [a period of] socialism' (Xu Xiaohong 2003: 15).

But, as I have already suggested, theories that focus on the *danwei* as the source of complex relationships inducing layers of dependency and the disappearance of the 'free labourer' have not gone unchallenged in the literature. While certainly important to our understanding of labour relations in the command economy, these theories tend to rely on somewhat stereotypical notions of received passivity and dependence resulting from 'simple Leninist imposition from above' or even as the 'reflection of any alleged cultural propensity toward an unquestioning obedience to authority' (Perry 1997: 43). In contrast, by homing in on the traditional Chinese concerns with geographical origins, Perry has argued that while household registration (*hukou*) certainly restricted a tradition of 'urban sojourning', the victory of the CPC and consequent political campaigns did not miraculously replace native-place identity and affiliations with class identity and the dependency that Maoist interpretations of class interests tended to imply in practice. For Perry this was too clean and simplistic a break with the past and '[P]lace-based divisions of rural and urban residence or collective sector employment versus a job in a state-owned unit constituted equally significant socioeconomic distinctions in Maoist China' (Perry 1997: 43–4).

As we shall further explore in Chapter 2, the actions of *danwei* employees themselves demonstrated that it was hardly the case that China's urban working class was simply persuaded or repressed into acquiescence by a combination of welfare and state control. Indeed, as is currently the case, the ebb and flow of working class militancy was a major influence on the political status of trade unions, despite their overall subordination to Party leadership and near elimination during the Cultural Revolution.

Danwei stability

Whether awarded, negotiated or won, the superior conditions enjoyed by the 'privileged minority of the urban industrial workforce' (Perry 1997: 44) were real and even had a colloquial name: the 'iron rice bowl'.[1] Basically, this referred to the high level of job security and the absence of labour markets, both of which contributed to very low labour turnover rates. For example, in 1979 there were 22,000 'quits and fires' of state employees representing just 0.03 per cent of the labour force (White 1993: 44). Naughton emphasizes the lack of general mobility – both geographical and occupational – as a characteristic of industrial relations during the command economy era. He points out that in 1978 'death was four times as important a cause of job-leaving as were resignations or being fired' comparing this with much higher labour turnover in the former USSR where ... '[I]n 1978 in the Russian Republic, sixteen per cent of all industrial manual workers quit their jobs during the year' (Naughton 1997: 173). In fact, by tracing the economic foundations rather than the political development of the *danwei*, Naughton argues that the catastrophe of the Great Leap Forward (GLF) and subsequent famine (1958–61) provided the economic conditions for a 'completion' of the *danwei* system. The threat of hunger spreading from the rural areas to the cities and the dire need to reverse the flow of migrants into the latter as a result of the Great Leap induced the state to take full control of employment in urban areas, 'allocating ninety-five per cent of first jobs in urban areas and taking away the hiring function from the individual enterprise' (Naughton 1997: 172).

The danwei wage system

Following a post-liberation period in which the CPC accommodated private enterprise and, according to Harris, 'inequality of income was a deliberate act of policy' (Harris 1978: 96), a major wage reform was introduced in 1956 when the Soviet-inspired eight-grade wage system was implemented and remained in place until 1985. In a Chinese context, the system was perhaps symbolic of institutionalized inequalities lying at the heart of a remuneration system that was nevertheless far more egalitarian than wage systems in the West or the Soviet Union. As the name suggests, eight grades of pay were established with variations of about 30 per cent across different industries and 11 geographical areas (Harris 1978: 97). It was a highly centralized system that left enterprises with 'little or no autonomy in the distribution of wages which remained ineffective as an instrument of labour mobility' (O'Leary 1998: 57). O'Leary argues that the 'one big pot' (*da guo fan*) was part of a three-factor industrial relations policy on wages, levels of employment and working conditions that emerged out of a 'complex interaction between state, managers and employees'. However, this appears to contradict his assertion that enterprises – and by implication in a command economy, their employees – had hardly any say in the matter of wages (O'Leary 1998: 51–4). You Ji and White respectively bring clarity by explaining how the eight-grade system worked. At national level:

> First of all, an aggregate national wage bill was worked out by central planners on the basis of the State's financial situation. Then this wage bill was used to determine a national employment system quota specifying how many new workers to recruit. A central decision, taken each year, was also embodied in the bill as to whether and when wages were to be increased and by how much, and how many workers were to be promoted.
>
> (You Ji 1998: 111)

At municipal level the 'labour plan' was

> based on an estimate of the needs of enterprises and offices within the city, each of which submits its labor requirements to the labor and wages office of its superior bureau which then communicates with the municipal labour bureau. The ensuing recruitment plan draws on three sources of labor: the strategic groups under centralized 'unified allocation' who must be given priority; junior and middle school graduates from the city ... and people with jobs who want to move. The actual process of assignment to a state enterprise is handled by three agencies in concert: the enterprise, the relevant bureau's labor office, and the city labour bureau.
>
> (White 1989: 162)

The annual decision on the national wage bill would have taken into account factors such as commodity prices, production targets, the political atmosphere and the mood of workers. This in turn would have involved factory managers, Party Secretaries and the trade unions, which is probably what O'Leary meant in his description of three-way negotiations. Managers of large SOEs pulled as many strings as possible in order to channel resources to their work units, yet there was no formal bargaining process (O'Leary 1998: 52). Working class input into the process was influential but, due to the absence of freedom of association, became politicized and indirect. It was expressed via the strike waves that invariably occurred when the political climate appeared to warrant taking the risks that such action involved. For example, the strike waves of 1956–57, the Hundred Flowers movement, the first three years of the Cultural Revolution in 1966–68 and workers' participation in the 1976 April Fifth Movement (Lee Ching-Kwan 2000: 43; Sheehan 1998: 10).

A reward system ran parallel to the eight-grade wage system that linked material reward to ideological attitudes and its implementation proved it to be an effective tool of labour discipline (You Ji 1998: 111) when '[T]he national range [of wage differentials] was not wide (3:1)' (Harris 1978: 96).

There is general agreement that the wage system, along with non-pecuniary welfare entitlements, gave SOE workers a coveted social and material status. Lee maintains that in the *danwei* era 'the working class as a whole made great strides vis-à-vis the peasants, the bourgeoisie and intellectuals in terms of political status, wages, welfare and employment security' (Lee Ching-Kwan 2000: 42). Weil argues that the material benefits urban workers enjoyed as a result were considerably beyond those of workers in other developing countries (Weil 1996: 34). However, there is divergence with regard to the relative degree of workers' material benefits and wage levels. For example, Hussain highlights 'a combination of low wages with surplus labour and lifetime employment' as one of the three salient features 'originally embedded in the post liberation economic and political structure' (Hussain and Zhuang 1998: 58).[2] For Harris, the confusion lay in the high proportion of non-pecuniary benefits in the overall remuneration system (Harris 1978: 96), which was certainly the case on the eve of reform. In 1979, average annual take-home pay was 717 yuan while government and employer subsidies were worth 879 yuan, representing 122 per cent of remuneration. Subsidies covered subsidized housing,[3] labour-related insurance, medical cover (including dependants), non-staple food allowances, winter heating and home-leave travel. On top of these state-employer obligations, the government also provided education, medicines, transportation and staple foods (Cieri *et al.* 1998).

Managing the danwei

In the four years following Liberation, the new regime implemented a mixed economy policy and there was no immediate campaign for the nationalization of industry. In the private sector, expectations had been raised by the new political arrangements, producing a wave of strikes from workers and anti-capitalist rhetoric from some enterprise-level party and trade union cadres who were accustomed to working underground in confrontational circumstances. In Shanghai, for example, the civil war period of 1946–1949 produced a politicization of urban workers that apparently 'eased the city's transition to the Communist era' (Yeh Wen-hsin 1996: 62) and certainly helped to put capital on the back foot. However, the Party moved quickly to dampen workers' enthusiasm and declared an industrial relations strategy that was 'of benefit to both labour and capital' (*lao-zi liang li*). This was aimed at restraining both sides in order to facilitate a period of reconstruction following Japanese occupation and the civil war. Nine months after the CPC took power, and facing a restive working class, Mao delivered a speech in which he emphasized a spirit of compromise. He spoke of the need to 'rationally coordinate the industry we already have, as well as practically and appropriately improve public-private relations and labour-capital relations ... [and] improve relations with the national bourgeoisie and not be overly aggressive' (Mao Zedong 1950).

The institutional expression of this policy was the 'labour capital consultative conference' (*lao-zi xieshang huiyi*) that on the surface seemed to be 'weighted in favour of labour' (Sheehan 1998: 19). However, in almost eerie resonance with collective consultation of more recent years, it was not hard for employers to take advantage of trade union inexperience.

During negotiations with private employers, the lack of experience of cadres representing workers' interests often showed. The capital side appears to have been much better prepared and more effective than were the cadres and workers' representatives on the labour side, who, for example, found themselves unable to dispute capitalists' assertions about their finances and what constituted a reasonable level of profit at an enterprise as they had not worked out their own figures beforehand (Sheehan 1998: 20).

In the existing nationalized enterprises, there was a mix of gradual political change and a continuation of management norms built up in republican China (Yeh Wen-hsin 1996: 60–88; Perry 1997: 46) and from the CPC-controlled liberated areas (Lü Xiaobo 1997: 21–41). The Factory Management Committee (FMC) and the Workers' Representative Conference (WRC) were introduced via regulations aimed at improving management accountability and democratization (Sheehan 1998: 20). The WRC was the forerunner of the Staff and Workers Congress (*zhigong daibiao dahui*) run by the trade union (Sheehan 1998: 21). These institutions were unable to head off workers' increased criticisms of management, party and union cadres (Sheehan 1998: 27) and the period from Liberation until 1953 was marked by strikes in both the private and public sectors.

Meanwhile, the Party employed political movements and campaigns to cement its power and prepare the way for the First Five-Year Plan. These included the Democratic Reform Movement aimed at 'changing bureaucratic capitalist enterprises into socialist (state) enterprises and changing old democratic – private – enterprises into new democratic ones' (Sheehan 1998: 37); and the three- and five-anti campaigns aimed at corrupt tax-dodging capitalists, wasteful bureaucracy, gang bosses, counter-revolutionaries, etc. The plan was launched in 1953, and signalled that while politics remained central, production took precedence over all else – a strategy that contributed to the eruption of a massive strike wave in the mid 1950s taking the Party completely by surprise (see Chapter 2).

The period 1953–1957 witnessed almost total nationalization in years of relative industrial calm following the ACFTU's 7th Congress in 1953 – at least until mid 1956. During this period, the FMCs and WRCs matured into permanent management committees as the *danwei* institution took up its position at the core of urban life. There was a brief experiment with Soviet-style one-man management, abandoned in 1955 in favour of the *lao san hui* or three committees that formed the 'basic institutional structure at enterprise level' in a 'dual system' of both Party and management control (Warner and Zhu 2000: 23). Politically, Mao set a course for socialism, but proceeding at a steady clip.

The general line or the general task of the Party for the transition period is basically to accomplish the industrialization of the country and the socialist transformation of agriculture, handicrafts and capitalist industry and commerce in ten to fifteen years, or a little longer. This general line is a beacon illuminating our work in all fields. Do not depart from this general line, otherwise Left or Right mistakes will occur.

(Mao Zedong 1953)

The 'dual system of control' was a sometimes tense division of labour in which the Party Committee oversaw the *danwei*'s political and ideological functions while a general manager chaired the FMC and ran production. Following earlier struggles over the role of trade unions, discussed in the next section, the representative role of the unions was dramatically curtailed, reducing union work to the not inconsiderable administrative task of overseeing social and welfare matters and encouraging production via socialist competition and exhortation (Clarke and Pringle 2009: 87).

In practice, it was often the case that 'the same person shared the positions of Party Secretary and General Manager at the same enterprise' (Warner and Zhu 2000: 23). Moreover, the failure of one-man management and growing presence of enterprise-level party cells and members meant that Party Secretaries 'controlled the overall political and production agenda while directors carried out the daily administration of the decisions reached by party cells' (You Ji 1998: 36). In short, the Party Committee was the committee that counted in most enterprises and Mao personally advocated 'that all major issues must be first discussed by party committees and then executed by directors' (Zhang Zhanbin 1988: 78–79 cited in You Ji 1998: 37).

The role of trade unions

The CPC had been instrumental in setting up China's first national trade union body in 1925. In the years that followed, both the GMD and the CPC struggled for leadership of Chinese labour by setting up their own unions and occasionally working together or with the few relatively independent occupation-based unions and associations. In the climate of the time both parties followed Sun Yatsen's argument that the presence of foreign imperialists on Chinese soil made it imperative that trade unions were part of a wider political struggle for liberation. But in 1927, the right wing of the GMD seized power and immediately set about destroying communist influence in the increasingly militant labour movement. Guillermaz states that 13,000 trade unionists were executed and a further 25,000 died in the fighting (Guillermaz 1972: 226). This effectively ended collaboration between the CPC and GMD over labour issues at the national level as well as any systematic attempt by the CPC to rebuild effective trade unions on a national basis. This is not to say that communist organizers were entirely absent from the urban areas and indeed the ebb and flow of the urban labour movement between 1927 and 1949 broadly reflected the wider national picture and balance of class forces as a whole. Following the bloody events of 1927, labour organizing entered what Perry calls a 'conservative interregnum' (Perry 1993: 88) that gave way to a 'radical resurgence' from 1937 up to liberation in 1949 (Perry 1993: 109) during which time labour protests became increasingly common and CPC influence grew accordingly. Nevertheless, the unions generally had a 'skimpy industrial spread and a limited "proletarian" base' (Ng Sek-Hong and Warner 1998: 17) and this 'weakened their ability to make demands on the party' (Lee Lai To 1986: 30 cited in Ng Sek-Hong and Warner 1998: 17). The ACFTU's 6th Congress in 1948 reaffirmed democratic centralism as its organizational principle perhaps wary that a less severe approach to internal trade union decision making would lead to a repeat of past struggles and alliances with guilds and home-town organizations.

During the Congress, the ACFTU decreed that workers would be organized on an industrial and geographical basis rather than along occupational lines. Ng and Warner find that the one-way nature of the trade union transmission belt that consequently developed between party and class in post-liberation China has its roots in pre-liberation conditions and that 'the historical legacy of the pre-1949 period and the difficulties of organizing nationally led the CPC to use the ACFTU essentially as a one-way link between Party and "masses"' (Ng Sek-Hong and Warner 1998: 17). Thus we can identify a tradition of CPC-affiliated organizers in China's working class, but their strategy and tactics, especially with regard to workplace representation, was never far from national politics. As such, there was no practice of effective representation and indeed this trade union function actually declined once the *danwei* system entrenched itself. This reductionist process was not confined to the realm of ideological debates at high level, though these did take place. Post-liberation labour unrest and worker militancy gave substance to the debates over the role of unions that were also accompanied by, on the one hand, ACFTU leadership purges and on the other, concessions to workers. Finally a wave of repression was introduced after temporary and contract workers spearheaded a strike wave during 1956–57 that gave vent to anger at being 'left out of the new *danwei* system … [and being] denied the privileges that came with permanent employment at large state enterprises' (Perry 1997: 49).

As both minister of labour and acting head of the ACFTU, Li Lisan was given the responsibility of drafting labour policy and regulations for the new government (Perry 1997: 45). Perry argues that the results of his work, which included a Trade Union Law (1950) and Labour Insurance Regulations (1951), 'were a defining element of the emerging *danwei*' (Perry 1997: 45) and as such Li and his comrades such as Liu Shaoqi, Chen Yun and Zhou Enlai deserve much of the credit for the generous provisions awarded to the new 'masters of society', or at least some of them. This generosity, combined with his views on the need for trade union autonomy to defend it, no doubt helped get Li sacked as head of the ACFTU for 'economism and syndicalism'. Although an eccentric figure whose flamboyance tended to arouse the suspicions of party purists, Li was not isolated. In fact, his reputation and popularity among skilled workers and the potential power base this represented probably hastened his departure from the union movement. Indeed, during his tenure, primary level union cadres in both state-owned and private enterprises took a 'more independent line, siding with workers in defence of their interests in the enterprise' (Sheehan 1998: 36).

Nevertheless, despite two trade union crises in the first half of the 1950s, a combination of labour unrest, the regime's rhetoric and the state's policy of gradually moving towards 'collectivist relations of production' rendered the unions a definite force in labour relations at least up until the introduction of one-man management. Sheehan cites union participation in management decisions as *'mandated by workers*' (Sheehan 1998: 50 – author's italics) being curtailed by the rolling out of one-man management on a national scale in April 1954 (You Ji 1998: 36). As a consequence, there was widespread disappointment among workers following nationalization and this sense of disappointment was fed by perceived and actual bureaucratization and dissatisfaction with the performance of both Party and union cadres at enterprise level. The strike wave of 1956–57 was the result. At the 8th Party Congress in 1956, Li Lisan's successor, Lai Rouyu, outlined the confusion in the ranks, reinforced the parameters of the renewed debate over trade unions and spelt out the union position:

> Some people seem to think that because the working class wields state power, the State as a whole will safeguard the interests of the working class, and the trade unions have lost their function as protector of workers' interests. This view is wrong. The reason is that classes have not yet been completely eliminated in our country, while various bureaucracies continue to manifest themselves among us and it will take us time to overcome them. Under these circumstances, the material interests and political rights of the mass of workers and employees are not safe from damage by the bureaucracy.
> (Lai Rouyu 1956 cited in Maitan 1976: 38)

Lai is clearly advocating a continued representative function for trade unions despite full scale nationalization. His argument was both strengthened and weakened by the appearance of autonomous workers' organizations. On the one hand, this expression of working class independence alarmed the Party into taking the unions seriously and, on the other hand, angered senior Party leaders fearful of a workers' power base beyond their control. The parallels with 1989 and the Workers Autonomous Federations (WAF) are clear. Perhaps a parallel with the 2003–2008 period may also be drawn when strikes have emerged as the workers' weapon of choice and the ACFTU has come under intense pressure to improve its representative performance. But to return to the mid 1950s, the unrest led to a crackdown on expressions of autonomy outside the unions and the gradual clawing back of the financial gains extracted by workers from enterprises during the strike wave of late 1956 and early 1957. The Anti-Rightist Campaign was launched in the summer of 1957. Next came the Great Leap Forward, with its emphasis on reducing unit costs and dramatically improving production as epitomized by the 'unthinking optimism of slogans like "produce more, more quickly, better and more economically"' (Maitan 1976: 45). Lai and some in the unions continued to press for increased powers of worker participation and, by implication, union influence at *danwei* level. Their efforts bore no fruit in the new political climate that was hardly conducive to further debate. Indeed, it is probably fortunate for Lai Rouyu that an early death from ill health prevented him from meeting the wrath of Red Guards during the Cultural Revolution of the following decade. They proved too much for his predecessor Li Lisan, who committed suicide in 1967 (Perry 1997: 46).

The years following the 8th Congress saw the overall fortunes of the trade unions rise and fall – even skirting with total prohibition during one phase of the Cultural Revolution. But their role at the welfare rather than business end of the *danwei* and acceptance of Party leadership was cast pretty much in stone for the remainder of the command economy era. During the period 1957–1978, the primary functions of the trade unions were to maintain labour discipline, encourage production and administer a large part of the state's housing, social and welfare apparatus, the benefits of which were delivered via the *danwei* as a means of stimulating labour motivation and maintaining political control. As such, the trade unions were primarily an instrument for controlling the working class, although they did play some protective role in the workplace, representing individual workers in the event of disputes over such management failings as the miscalculation of wages, pension entitlements or illegal punishment by the employer. In theory, they were also supposed to enforce the protective clauses of relevant labour regulations and to maintain minimal standards of health and safety at work. In practice, these tasks were often sidelined as increasing production overruled all other considerations. Overall, the role of the trade unions was to harmonize the interests of labour and management rather than to represent the interests of their members in opposition to management. The traditions and practices built up as a consequence have profoundly constrained trade union work since the introduction of the market economy in the reform era.

Trade unions and the 'ten lost years'

The prohibition, to all intents and purposes, of formal trade union activity renders the Cultural Revolution period of 1966–1976, and the following two-year build up to the formal introduction of market-orientated reforms, beyond the scope of this book. Nevertheless, the Cultural Revolution was an important period for the Chinese working class. In essence, the event was a power struggle that focused on China's rate of progress towards 'communism' and who should lead it. It began with Mao's astonishing appeal to students to 'Bombard the Headquarters'[4] as he launched a struggle to regain control of the Party – lost following the Great Leap Forward – and eradicate its leadership in the summer of 1966. Less than a year later, growing and largely unforeseen working class participation in the Cultural Revolution prompted a response from the People's Liberation Army (PLA) as 'troops moved into factories and rural communes to supervise industrial and agricultural production' (Karnow 1984: 297). As the balance of power between armed 'conservatives' and 'rebels' ebbed and flowed, China edged towards civil war. Eventually, Mao pulled back and threw his weight behind the army and tripartite Revolutionary Committees made up of cadres from the Party, army and leaders from Red Guard organizations. On the surface, the committees represented a compromise between struggling factions during the tumultuous and violent upheavals of 1966–68, and were established as new organs of power at all levels of society, including in the factories (Schram 1973: 101; Howe 1973: 245). The factions included provincial-level workers' organizations such as the Red Flag Army of Harbin whose members were drawn from 'industrial and transport workers fighting for shorter hours and a better wages system' (Maitan 1976: 150). In practice, the Revolutionary Committees were largely dominated by army personnel fluent in Maoist rhetoric but under orders to ensure that some sort of order was returned. Militancy was at least partially deflected by periodic participation in struggle meetings against individuals deemed as having capitalist sympathies or of supporting others who did. The army's response to autonomous workers' associations such as the Red Flag Army was 'to dissolve these organizations and jail their leaders' (Maitan 1976: 150) as the 'more "economistic" aspects of the mass movement proved equally unacceptable to the central authorities' (Sheehan 1998: 136). Despite the fiery speeches accompanying their arrival, the Revolutionary Committees were ultimately an expression of the army's authority, commitment to order and above all the maintenance of production. Although they sometimes included former union cadres, the committees rendered enterprise-level unions superfluous, even 'reactionary', in the new stage of 'socialism' and at the 9th Party Congress in 1969 a new party structure was established that virtually ignored trade unions.

These were grim times for the trade unions, their cadres and sections of the working class in general. On the other hand, it was also at a time when, at least in the earlier phase of the Cultural Revolution, workers took 'advantage of the unprecedented opportunity presented to them by the lifting of party controls on organizations' (Sheehan 1998: 136). Indeed, the first three years of the Cultural Revolution was a period that 'many workers retrospectively saw as a high point of democratization and freedom of expression and organization in enterprises and wider society' (Sheehan 1998: 137–8). Like workers, the students whom Mao had originally turned to during the opening shots of the Cultural Revolution also suffered a reverse in fortunes after enjoying exceptional initial freedoms. Millions of them had taken advantage of free travel and time off from class to 'link up' (*chuanlian*) and exchange revolutionary experiences all over the country. Beginning in 1968, they were ordered to return home and their revolutionary fervour was subsequently redirected to rural areas where millions were sent to 'learn from the peasants' whose poverty, and at times hostility, rendered the experience traumatic for many of the 'sent down' youth.

The 9th Party Congress marked the end of the struggle phase of the Cultural Revolution and, on paper, set the stage for a 'revolution in mass-management' (Sheehan 1998: 138) in which there was no role for trade unions. In reality, the following years were marked by extreme Maoist rhetoric that heaped 'ubiquitous praise for the superiority of the working class' while subjecting workers to the 'same autocratic rule as the rest of Chinese society' (Sheehan 1998: 138). Yet echoes of the early years of this extraordinary period still emerge in conversations with workers. During a discussion in 1997, 25 years after the fall of the Gang of Four, exiled labour activist Han Dongfang expressed opposition when SOE textile workers in Mianyang employed Cultural Revolution tactics and 'airplaned' their factory director through the streets during a dispute over wage arrears. On the other hand, a laid-off miner in Shulan told me that he owed his position as a permanent worker to a strike at his mine in 1968 and went on to say, during a long bus journey over dreadful roads in November 2001, that 'another Cultural Revolution would stop those bastards up there in the offices from shutting the place [mine] down – and improve these fucking roads!' (*nong hao zhege ta ma de lu!*).

On the eve of reform

By 1978, the Chinese economy was under severe strain with unemployment rapidly emerging – or rather re-emerging – as a major systemic challenge for both Party and government. Deng's return to power had added impetus to the movement of former Red Guards back to urban areas, putting further pressure on the government to create jobs – in 1978 the official figure for urban unemployment was 5.3 per cent (White 1989: 154).[5] Moreover, the reformers' case for the gradual opening up of urban labour markets was strengthened by the presence of 'semi legal rural immigrants whose numbers have swelled in recent years' (White 1989: 154). By 1982, Chinese experts were estimating rural surplus labour to be approximately 35 per cent of total rural labour (White 1989: 154). Spurred on by rising unemployment and a stagnating economy, reformers' arguments crystallized on the need to introduce economic reforms in order to raise productivity. They argued that labour mobility was an essential component of policies aimed at revitalizing Chinese industry which, according to China's reform economists, was

> too rigid and bureaucratic, constraining the flexibility of the economy, perpetuating poor labor production, and retarding technical change. Changes were necessary, they argued, to increase the flexibility of movement of the labor work-force, give management more power over their work-force labor, and to break the iron rice bowl of the state workers. Specifically, they have argued that the degree of direct administrative control over urban labor has been excessive, rendering the economic actors themselves – both managers and workers – inert.
>
> (White 1989: 155)

The programme for growth and development was originally labelled the 'Four Modernizations', and formally announced in 1977. Aimed at industry, agriculture, science and technology and defence, this ambitious plan continued the Maoist habit of exaggerating China's capacities in order to achieve the unachievable. As Deng consolidated his return to power, he began scaling down the goals of the Four Modernizations and shifted the emphasis to institutional reforms that would facilitate the 'genuine process of economic transition' that was to unfurl during the 1980s (Naughton 1995: 5).

Industrial reform

Phase one 1978–1992

There was no blueprint for economic reform. The process took a step-by-step approach that Deng summed up with the Chinese metaphor meaning 'to cross the river by feeling for the stones', or, as Naughton put it, 'the strategy of not having a strategy'. Yet the Party-state was far from 'muddling through' (Lindblom 1959: 79–88). Once the political battle for a course of economic reform had been won, and announced at the landmark Third Plenum of the 11th Congress of the CPC in December 1978, the road ahead was signposted by a combination of pilot projects, provisional regulations and eventually the passing of an Enterprise Law (1988), a Trade Union Law (1992) and, for the first time, a national Labour Law (1995).

The first phase of economic reform is generally referred to as the period of the 'dual-track system' (Liu Aiyu 2005: 77). Naughton emphasizes the 'co-existence of a traditional plan and a market channel for the allocation of a given good' and that dual-track refers to the 'coexistence of two coordination mechanisms and not to two ownership systems' (Naughton 1995: 8).

Expanding enterprise autonomy placed profit retention at the heart of the first stage of industrial reform (Liu Aiyu 2005: 77). Beginning in 1978, the policy was piloted by Zhao Ziyang, who later became CPC General Secretary and famously wept when visiting hunger-striking students in Tiananmen Square in 1989 saying 'we have come too late'. The pilot initially focused on six enterprises in Sichuan province and was followed up with similar pilots conducted in Yunnan province and Beijing (Yao Kaijian and Chen Yongqin 2003: 223). The Sichuan pilot quickly expanded to cover 100 enterprises which, at the time, transmitted 92 per cent of their profits to the central government, with the remainder ploughed back into the company (6.5 per cent). Some of this was shared out among the workforce as an annual bonus (Liu Aiyu 2005: 77). 'Marking the beginning of nationwide urban reform' (Naughton 1995: 99) the State Council issued five regulations that summed up the experience of these pilots and gave the go ahead for their wider application. By June 1980, 6,600 profitable SOEs were implementing a profit-retention system and exercising autonomy over production planning, marketing, capital utilisation (*zijin yunyong*) and employees' welfare and bonus funds. Naughton argues that, following this initial push in the direction of autonomy, the state then pulled back and switched to a more conservative policy in 1981. Liu puts this down to concerns over fiscal shortages at the Treasury arising from a decline in profits handed over to the state (Liu Aiyu 2005: 78), while Naughton, pointing to the link between enterprise autonomy and the reliability of the price system, argues that it was the reformers' unsuccessful attempt to 'rationalize prices and financial relations' that underpinned a fairly dramatic drop in the pace of reform.

This led him to characterize the period 1979–1983 as a 'classical policy cycle ... in which a phase of energetic reform policy was followed by a phase of cautious retrenchment' (Naughton 1995: 97). The upshot was that in spring 1981 an alternative system to profit retention was piloted entitled *ying kui bao gan*. Liu explains the difference:

> Enterprises taking responsibility for their profits and losses (*ying kui bao gan*) is profit retention (*lirun liucheng*) in another form, but the system underlying it is different. The ratio of profits retained under the profit retention system is based on the previous year's actual achievements. On the other hand, the system of taking full responsibility for profits and losses is on the basis of consultation and planning. The amount of profits handed over to the centre is the average sum of monies extracted by the central government over the previous three years.
>
> (Liu Aiyu 2005: 78)

A two-year period of wrangling followed as SOE managers sought to use the new regulations issued by the State Council to consolidate their position vis-à-vis Party basic units or cells in the enterprises. For workers, it initially seemed that the high expectations of reform, which the state had encouraged, were real enough as wages climbed. By the winter of 1984, the Party's influential industrial organizations were blaming managers and the autonomy they had gained 'for loss of control over wage increases and failures in investment decisions' (You Ji 1998: 65). The power struggle between traditional management methods via the aforementioned three committees (Party, management and recently reactivated trade unions) and the reformers' case for awarding increased autonomy to the factory director continued as the latter pushed wider application of the Director Responsibility System. By September 1986 reformers were back in the driving seat when, following intense debates in the Politburo Standing Committee and the National People's Congress Standing Committee, the State Council and the Party's Central Organization Department issued three documents that later became the basis for the Enterprise Law of 1988. From now on the director was no longer under the leadership of the party committee and it was 'confirmed that an enterprise is a legal entity with the managing director as its legal representative vested with all necessary powers' (You Ji 1998: 51). Contracted labour was back – and the material conditions for a 'new form of industrial relations in the state sector' were now in place (Chan 2000: 38).

However, caution, 'crossing the river by feeling for the stones', or the 'strategy of not having a strategy' remained the name of the game. Although China's traditional employment system guaranteed permanent employment to a relatively small number of urban workers, these people had much to lose. The employment system had become entrenched to the degree that SOE workers' children were able to inherit the jobs of their parents via an arrangement known as *dingti*. The Party was sensitive to Maoist and/or conservative arguments that any attempt to dismantle the 'iron rice bowl' of permanent employment carried the risk of social unrest. A three-stage strategy of talking up the material gains that a labour market offered to workers while simultaneously introducing policies that would inevitably undermine permanent employment was launched. The first stage involved loosening the state's grip on employment allocation procedures and substituting it with a three-in-one combination of channels for recruitment and job seeking known as *san jie he* or the three-in-one combination.[6] The three avenues to employment now included: the labour bureaux that still allocated most jobs either directly or through newly established labour service companies (LSC); through one's own efforts; or to become self-employed. LSCs also began to supply labour to enterprises 'under new forms of ownership arrangements including private enterprises and joint ventures' (Hu Teh-Wei and Elizabeth Hon-Ming Li 1993: 157). This was crucial as eventually the dismantling of the iron rice bowl owed more to competition from the private sector and ensuing influx of cheaper migrant labour than administrative reforms emanating from Beijing. Beginning in 1980, labour contracts were piloted among skilled and experienced workers in Shanghai, gradually spreading across eight provinces. By early 1982, 1.6 million workers were on contracts, rising to 6.5 million by early 1983 (Liu Aiyu 2005: 81) when the policy was applied to newly recruited SOE workers hired on five-year contracts.

Stage two no doubt deepened a growing sense of insecurity and loss of political status among many SOE employees. The Central Committee released its 'Decision on Economic Restructuring' allowing mines, building sites, transport and the ports to employ internal migrants from the countryside. However, the pace remained cautious and, contrary to some newspaper reports, this was by no means a headlong rush for the cities – at least not yet. For example, clauses in a contract between a Sichuanese migrant worker and the Jingyan County Employment Service Bureau demonstrate that even as late as 1992, migration from the countryside was very carefully managed. Clauses 4.1 and 4.2 refer to good health, age restrictions and gender – must be male – of the worker. Most tellingly, Clause 4.4 states: that '[T]he family (shall have) sufficient or even surplus manpower so that when the worker leaves his hometown, his family's production in the household responsibility system would not be affected' (Liu Kaiming 2005: 31). In 1986, labour contracts were rolled out nationally via four sets of provisional regulations on hire and fire and unemployment insurance. The same caution was widely exercised despite the fact that a 'major effort was launched to restructure the employment system' to new state employees (Naughton 1995: 210). Sectors with labour shortages were 'granted a variance', permanent employment was still offered to technical school and college graduates, and a two-year period of grace was built into the new regulations.

The third stage of reforming the new employment system was one of refining the existing changes and encouraging managers to make use of it via the 'optimization of labour [force] composition' (*youhua laodong zuhe*). 'Progress' continued to be too slow for reformers like Zhao Ziyang. On the one hand, moderates such as the economist Chen Yun wanted to keep the 'bird in the cage' i.e. ensure that the market operated under the guidance of the plan. On the other hand, Zhao Ziyang was increasingly turning to 'radical ideals' (Naughton 1995: 123) that were only brought to a – temporary – halt by the tanks rumbling towards Tiananmen Square in the early hours of 4 June 1989.

Also central to the destruction of the iron rice bowl was wage reform. As early as 1977, the state began to widen wage differentials by awarding pay increases to workers in selected sectors and reintroducing the bonus system abolished during the Cultural Revolution. Bonuses increased as a percentage of overall wages throughout the 1980s despite the ceilings imposed by planners on the ratio of basic wage to bonus. In fact, the ratio leapt from 2.3 per cent in 1978 to 17.2 per cent in 1988. The wage increases in this period improved workers' living standards – no doubt easing anxieties over contracts and rural migrant labour – with the average industrial wage in SOEs and collectively owned enterprises (COEs) rising from 615 yuan in 1978 to 1,747 yuan in 1988 (Hu Teh-Wei and Elizabeth Hon-Ming Li 1993: 164). However, neither differentials nor bonuses were able to weaken the traditional working class's attachment to egalitarian principles. Bonuses could be employed as a management tool to elicit more effort from workers but had little impact on average levels of compensation. Consequently, 'workers tended to push for egalitarian distribution of bonuses' (Naughton 1995: 105) especially when planners continued attempts to restrict bonus-basic-wage ratios. Even when managers obtained the right to fire workers after 1986, thus ending on paper the institutionalized 'long-term coexistence' of both sides, the former were as reluctant to threaten the occupational security of their employees as the latter were to 'jump in the sea' (*xiahai*) of market forces and set up in business or get a job in the private sector. In short, the change in policy simply passed many enterprises by. Indeed, Liu found that 72 per cent of workers in enterprises in Shenyang and Shanghai felt that their employment security had not been threatened by the introduction of contracts and increases in management autonomy. Managers cited various constraints on dismissing workers including 'prioritising stability', 'pressure to create employment', and a feeling of solidarity even with newly hired contracted workers who 'are our brothers and sisters' (Liu Aiyu 2005: 86). These sentiments were sharpened by traditional geographic proximities when 'managers and their families usually lived in the same factory-run residential quarters along with workers and their families, who thus had many informal ways to pressure managers' (Naughton 1995: 105).[7]

In sum, while some workers and Party members may have seen the writing on the wall with the introduction of dramatic changes to industrial relations, the overall picture was not one of mass discontent in the workplace, despite the key roles workers played in the Democracy Wall movement at the beginning of the decade and the Democracy Movement at the end of it when the formation of WAFs in major cities deeply alarmed the CPC. However, while working class anger at the representative inadequacies of the ACFTU, inflation and corruption undoubtedly induced millions of SOE workers and middle managers to join enormous marches for clean government in the spring of 1989, the calls issued by the Beijing WAF for a general strike largely fell on deaf ears. The fact that the right to strike was removed from the Constitution in 1982 was not the reason why the strike calls were largely ignored. According to WAF leader Han Dongfang, the reason was simply that the WAFs did not have a strategy or indeed a capacity effectively to organize workers in the workplace.

The repression of the Democracy Movement was violent and thorough. It purged the ACFTU and arrested workers and supporters suspected of being involved in the WAFs. It also opened the door for 'conservatives', led by Premier Li Peng, to slow down the pace of reform and even reverse the direction as China entered a period of relative isolation, despite the best efforts of some foreign governments to reassure the Chinese government and foreign capitalists that it was business as usual (Liang Guosheng 1996). In truth the situation was something of a stalemate. Naughton dismisses the efforts of those wishing to roll back the reforms as little more than a hiccup. As Table 1.1 demonstrates, foreign investment continued to increase before taking off in 1992/3 when Deng's Southern Tour indicated the stalemate was over.

The international trade union movement recoiled in horror from the violence leaving the ACFTU isolated and with a new leadership vigorous in its commitment to Party leadership. On the other hand, SOE wages increased significantly in this period, indicating the willingness of the authorities to make concessions to workers as the price of social peace. Some observers have also attributed wage increases to workers actively taking advantage of the lull in reforms to push forward wage claims at a time when SOE managers were anxious to avoid labour disputes that brought unwanted attention to their enterprises (Hussain and Zhuang 1998: 43–68). In 1992, Deng's Southern Tour brought the stalemate to a dramatic end.

Trade unions in the early reform period

The reform policy was a double-edged sword for the trade unions. On the one hand, Deng Xiaoping's return to power symbolized that the dark days of attacks on the trade unions were finally off the ideological agenda. But on the other hand, the creeping commoditization of labour power not only threatened the position of workers and trade unions in SOEs, it also heralded the return of a formalized divergence of interests across China's industrial relations map: between the managed and the managers and, in the new private sector, labour and capital itself. In other words, the reforms put the trade unions back on the political agenda but with an as yet limited influence over events and no recent experience of handling

Table 1.1 FDI in China: 1988–1995

Year	FDI (US$ billion)	FDI (RMB billion)
1988	3.19	11.89
1989	3.39	12.77
1990	3.49	16.68
1991	4.37	23.24
1992	11.01	60.70
1993	27.52	158.54
1994	33.77	291.03
1995	37.52	313.33

Source: China Statistical Yearbooks cited in Wei Kailei *et al.* 2008.

opposing interests. Considering these dilemmas, Howell identified four implications that the opening up of the economy would have for the unions: first, they would need to become familiar with handling contract-based disputes chiefly by studying both national and international law; second, the unions would have to 'reconsider the balance between representing the interests of the Party and those of the union [i.e. the workers]'; third, they would have to become more confrontational if they were to defend workers against predatory, and often unrestrained, capital; fourth, they would have to learn to organize rural migrants (Howell 1998: 156–7). Thompson argues that initially at least, the institution of the Staff and Workers Congress (SWC) was the chosen vehicle to bolster the union's backbone as it negotiated its way through the changing 'web of interests' in China's enterprises and improved workers' participation in economic reforms (Thompson 1992: 233–5). Obviously anxious not to overstep the mark and risk reigniting past debates over autonomy, the tried-and-tested SWCs facilitated workers' participation even as it blocked real influence at enterprise level. Thus, at the '10th National Congress in 1983 we find the head of the ACFTU, Ni Zhifu, calling for a stronger role for trade unions within the enterprise through a strengthening of the workers' congresses' (Howell 1998: 159).

In fact, as early as 1978, Deng Xiaoping was strongly advocating that as the organization in charge of both convening SWC meetings and running its day-to-day business, the ACFTU's primary branches were ideally placed to enable workers to 'elect section heads and other junior management ... [discuss] major issues ... [and] suggest replacements of leading personnel' (Thompson 1992: 236). As Thompson and many others have commented, whether or not the SWCs were – or are – capable of exercising control over management is a moot point. Certainly the institutions were to become a strategic focal point for SOE workers fighting the legality of bankruptcies and asset transfers during the period of deep restructuring that followed the 15th Party Congress in 1997. But what of the SWCs' influence where it counted: the pace, pay and conditions of production?

In 1986, the State Council passed the Regulations on Staff and Workers Congresses in Industrial Enterprises Owned by the Whole People. This was the same year that enterprise managers were given dramatically expanded powers over hire and fire, wages and working conditions in SOEs. The new regulations were timed to provide a counterweight to the extension of management authority while neutralizing shop-floor opposition to the new arrangements. On paper, the rights of SWCs were impressive: Article 7 gave delegates the right to make suggestions on issues relating to production; examine, approve or veto company policy on wages and welfare issues; make suggestions on the allocations of housing stock; and even dismiss enterprise directors and senior management (Chinese Academy of Sciences 2009). Moreover, Article 33 of the Labour Law (1995) appeared to open up an opportunity for staff and workers to make use of SWCs to initiate and approve collective contracts even in the absence of trade unions. The article refers to private- and foreign-owned enterprises in which both SWCs and trade unions were most notable for their absence. There is no evidence that this right has been exercised with any success.

In retrospect, we can best interpret the emphasis on SWCs as an initiative aimed at heading off unrest in the state sector by presenting them as an institution that would help to strengthen unions in the private sector.[8] Howell contends that this strategy had an international dimension. The rise of Solidarność in Poland gave added urgency to the debates on improving union capacity during the early reform era as CPC leaders fretted over the potential for an independent trade union movement to emerge in China. Indeed, Howell refers to such challenges emerging in the cities of Wuhan and Taiyuan (Howell 1998: 159). The pressure for more effective unions was intricately linked to the economic reforms as union cadres acknowledged that a new type of trade unionism not so closely tied to the state was required. The potential for unrest in the state sector and the gradual increase in labour disputes was at the root of these concerns, which even found expression at the 13th Party Congress in 1987 when Zhao Ziyang and other reformers supported moves for 'greater autonomy for trade unions' (Howell 1998: 159).

At the landmark and now largely forgotten 11th Congress of the ACFTU, matters came to a head when Ni Zhifu 'called for a readjustment of the relationship between the trade unions, Party and government' (Howell 1998: 159). A *Workers' Daily* editorial described the event as a 'reforming congress, a democratic congress and a unified congress' which would have been par for the course but for the editors then going on to add some substance: 'We must persevere in adding vitality to our primary level organizations and implement the policy of transforming the unions into democratized [organizations] of the working masses (*qunzhonghua*)' (*Workers' Daily* 1988).

In the context of such a dramatic Congress – even more so in hindsight – this editorial was significant. Delegates agreed that when workers' rights and interests were infringed and normal democratic channels failed to fight the situation, trade unions had the 'right to lead workers in exposing [malpractice], reporting [violations] and adopting other legal forms of struggle' to protect their members (ACFTU 1990: 82). This ruled out strike action as the right to strike had been deleted from the Constitution in 1982. Nevertheless, the tone of determination was indicative of the debates that had gathered steam in union and Party circles during a decade of reform.

The momentum came to a halt with the Democracy Movement of 1989 and the appearance of the WAFs. While many union cadres privately agreed with the criticism that the ACFTU needed to distance itself from the Party and were genuinely frustrated with the slow pace of reform, the severity of the clampdown and the concomitant purge of the ACFTU leadership persuaded them that working within the system was the only option available. In the years immediately following the turmoil of 1989, SOE workers fared reasonably well as Party conservatives used the occasion to bring the economic reforms to a temporary halt and enterprise leaders were given room to increase wages in the state sector in a bid to ward off labour unrest at a very sensitive time. The ACFTU was subjected to intense criticism from the international trade union movement and many national union federations followed the ICFTU in spurning all contact. Yet, as we have seen, foreign direct investment (FDI) continued to arrive and pressure from the private sectors, including the township and village enterprises (TVE), continued to build up. If the ACFTU was to survive with any credibility, union reform would very soon push its way back onto the agenda.

Phase two: the socialist market economy – on the road to capitalist relations of production

Market forces had little direct impact on industrial relations in the urban sector during the first decade of reform. Senior figures such as Hu Yaobang and even Zhao Ziyang who were arguing for a more rapid transformation were frustrated by the influences of post-Cultural Revolution political caution and the endurance of traditional practices which, for the most part, acted as a constraint on the pace of reform. For example, '[E]ven changes in SOE wage policies to improve productivity and material incentives were often implemented in traditional egalitarian fashion and were not linked directly to improvements in productivity' (Gallagher 2005a: 66).

During the 'dual track' period of 1978–1992 managers were reluctant to shed 'excess' workers for fear of provoking unrest – although trends that indicated a decline in workers' status and authority (*quanli*) were also beginning to emerge (Liu Aiyu 2005: 76). Nevertheless, most people's economic situation had improved or at least remained static. Liu's data of the period demonstrates that 22.5 per cent of her working class respondents were financially richer, 21.4 per cent reported a drop in income, with the remainder reporting no change (Liu Aiyu 2005: 86). As SOE restructuring gradually deepened during the mid 1990s, workers and shop-floor management in medium and large SOEs sometimes combined in order to pressure senior factory managers as they negotiated with state bureaucrats over budgets. In contrast to 37 per cent of factory managers who prioritized market share, You Ji found that

> [A] much tighter alliance [was] formed between shop floor management and workers to protect their own interests … According to a national survey of 2,765 factory managers in 1995, answers to the question 'What is the most important thing in your management?' the biggest proportion of respondents (forty-eight per cent) answered that maximizing workers' income was their primary objective.
>
> (You Ji 1998: 140)

Liu also found that managers were reluctant to shed 'excess' workers on account of fear of provoking unrest and pressure to keep unemployment under control.

Although the contract system and the authority of managers to terminate contracts had a sound legal basis, the new power was used extremely carefully and in reality was subject to very real restraints. In recruiting new workers, managers would go through the motions of seeking employees on the open market, but in actual hiring, they continued the practice of fencing (*nei zhao*). Managers certainly didn't go looking to stir up trouble by ending employment contracts arbitrarily. The power to fire was tempered by a number of social considerations which they justified in phrases such as 'stability above all else', 'employment first and foremost' (Liu Aiyu 2005: 86).

While direct Party intervention in the enterprises declined, social stability remained a key factor on SOE managers' agendas. As late as 2001, when the sheer scale of SOE lay-offs had become clear, the traditional social obligations of the 'enterprise' lingered on – at least in the minds of trade union officials. One enterprise-level trade union chairman in a large brewery made reference to these obligations to visiting American students during a study trip organized by the author:

> The system in our state-owned enterprise is different from your factories in America. The machinery we have imported from Germany and Belgium has boosted production and we are now the third largest brewery in China, but such modernization does not mean we will lay off workers just to increase profits. [Large-scale] nationalized industry has to make money for sure, but we also have a responsibility to society and can't just lay people off – though this is also changing.
> (Trade Union Chairperson, Zhujiang Brewery, Guangzhou, 12 September 2001)

As we shall see, it was not the laws and administrative regulations paving the way for private enterprise that brought about the unmaking of the traditional working class and the securities it enjoyed. It was private enterprise itself.

The rise of township and village enterprises

Powerful entrepreneurial forces were developing alongside institutional change as private economic activity spread from the fields to rural factories in the form of TVEs. Evolving out of the pre-Cultural Revolution commune brigade enterprises (*shedui qiye*) of the 1950s, TVEs expanded rapidly during the 1980s. Formal parameters for their ownership and control were not in place until 1990 with the release of Regulations on Township and Village Collective Enterprises of the People's Republic of China issued by the Ministry of Agriculture.[9] Article 18 of these regulations placed the assets of TVEs under the ownership of 'all rural residents of the township or village'. Enterprise management could be subcontracted out via a 'managerial contract responsibility system, leasing or joint operations with enterprises of other types of ownership'. This facilitated an influx of private and foreign capital into TVEs that has increased ever since. Essentially, the 1990 regulations on TVEs restricted 'the use of revenue by community residents and government to two purposes: reinvestment and local public goods' (Che Jiahua and Qian Yingyi 1998: 5), an apparent constraint that appeared to add gusto to the TVEs' capacity for exploitation as they quickly developed a reputation for appalling working conditions.

Hussain and Stern argue that the explosive growth of China's TVEs was due, at least in part, to two 'special features' of the pre-reform era. First, a high degree of decentralization allowed local provinces considerable discretion in their economic administration which resulted in a large volume of transactions 'outside the aegis of the state supply system', and this tradition certainly seems to be true for the early development of private markets operating on the edge of national policy, as was the case of Zhejiang's Yiwu county, the location for a pilot in trade union innovation discussed in detail in Chapter 5. Second, the division of the command economy into 'semi-autarkic cells' facilitated the Chinese practice of running pilot projects in economic reform that avoided 'disruption to the rest of the economy' (Hussain and Stern 1994: 10–11). As Chapter 3 on sector-level bargaining demonstrates, the same point can be applied to trade union experiments in improved representation. Despite the absence of competition from a 'second trade union' (*di'erge gonghui*) and continued commitment to democratic centralism, labour unrest has created the space for innovation that has not led to wider disruption, or indeed, a second trade union. At least not so far!

In 1978, township enterprises accounted for 5.05 per cent of industrial output, rising to 14.2 per cent by 1993. Industrial output for village enterprises – a smaller version of the TVE – went from 4.04 per cent to 12.25 per cent in the same period (Che Jiahua and Qian Yingyi 1998: 2) and by 1993 TVEs were employing over 123 million rural workers (China Statistical Yearbook 1995: 363–4). The TVEs sparked debate inside and outside China over whether they constituted socialist enterprise or capitalist exploitation. On the one hand, they were dynamic, flexible and, crucially, demonstrated a capacity to soak up the large amounts of surplus rural labour that resulted from the dissolution of the communes. Conversely, they were much quicker to dismiss employees in times of austerity. As the government reined in access to credit in the late 1980s, TVE employment fell from 47.2 million in 1988 to 45.9 million in 1990 (Che Jiahua and Qian Yingyi 1998: 18). Viewed in this light, TVEs were presented by some as a potential model that could be adapted to other developing countries (Field *et al.* 2006: 21) and even as 'the first indigenous and competitive form of socialist enterprise' that could save socialism itself (Roemer 1994: 127 cited in Greenfield and Leung 1997). On the other hand, labour activists in Hong Kong regarded TVEs as the product of inappropriate alliances between local officials and nascent capitalists formed in order to take advantage of an unmonitored and unregulated environment for capital accumulation, ostensibly in the name of economic development. Far from being the saviours of socialism, TVEs were pushing open the door to local and foreign capitalists whose capital was facilitating rapidly expanding private control of public or community assets (Greenfield and Leung 1997). Indeed, SOE managers frequently cited them as a source of unfair competition, complaining that TVEs 'earned profits through unfair and underhanded business practices, such as disorderly competition, shoddy goods and exploitative labor practices that were often based on familial or clan relations' (Gallagher, 2005a: 140).

The 'southern tour'

Aside from generating employment and rural income, TVEs were instrumental in demonstrating that market forces were capable of producing economic growth and this added weight to the reformers' arguments. By 1992, Deng's post-1989 patience with attempts to slow the pace of reform had run out. In February, he set off on his now famous tour of the southern boomtown of Shenzhen, taking in a number of other Special Economic Zones (SEZ) and export promotion zones as his entourage swept through South China. The paramount leader's well-publicized enthusiasm for private enterprise and its dramatic transformation of Shenzhen's economic status put paid to post-Tiananmen fiscal and political conservatism at the policy level. Later in the same year, the 14th Party Congress formally sanctioned the 'socialist market economy', a formulation that was first publicly used by Deng – as far as I have been able to ascertain – in an interview in the *People's Daily* as early as November 1979. In hindsight, this shift in the political landscape was of truly seismic proportions and its implications for the future direction of industrial relations should not be underestimated. So much so that

> [B]y the mid-to-late 1990s a clearer picture of the Chinese state's conception of labor relations began to emerge as key labor legislation was promulgated and the Communist Party began to move on deep restructuring of the core public sector with the measures implemented in the wake of the Fifteenth Party Congress.
> (Gallagher 2005a: 76)

Ironically, the socialist market economy was sanctioned just as the market economy was about to lose most of its 'socialist' characteristics!

Regulating deregulation

The emerging picture was framed by two important laws pertaining to industrial relations. A revised Trade Union Law (1992) replaced the original 1950 law and China's first national Labour Law (1995) combined various regulations pertaining to different types of enterprise – based on ownership and size – and codified them into one national law that applied to all industrial workers.

Essentially, the Labour Law plastered legal form and authority onto the institutional reforms that had signalled the state's desire to dismantle the iron rice bowl during the 1980s. It took 10 years to write and involved over 30 drafts. Emulating the ILO format,[10] it created a tripartite structure of industrial governance composed of the state (Ministry of Labour), employers, represented by the Chinese Enterprise Director's Association (CEDA), and the trade unions. The reformed Trade Union Law passed two years earlier in 1992 had already reconfirmed the ACFTU as the only legal representative of the working class.

Perhaps the most striking feature of the new Labour Law was its emphasis on individual labour rights as opposed to collective class interests. For example, only three rather vague articles were devoted to collective contracts. Previously, labour relations had been guided by the 'Model Outline of Intra-Enterprise Discipline' formulated soon after liberation. Although the document has been criticized as a 'foreman's charter' (Harris 1978: 91) and was distinguished by a marked lack of labour rights, it did not prevent the Chinese urban working class from consolidating a collective form of job security via the *danwei* exclusivity discussed above.

36 *Industrial relations in China*

During the drawn out formulation of the Labour Law, the ACFTU lobbied to retain this collective identity. However, the final version devoted just three articles to that most viable institution for the expression of collective interests in the market economy – collective contracts. To be sure, the standards and range of individual labour rights covered in the law were high in comparison to other developing countries, but actual existing conditions made their implementation an unlikely prospect. In the final analysis the law was a balancing act with policy aims on one side – the regulation of the private sector and downsizing of the public sector in order to increase efficiency – balanced against the political risks of social unrest that the new industrial relations framework undoubtedly carried. Minister of Labour Li Boyong made this clear when he presented a draft of the law to the NPC Standing Committee in March 1994. He argued that

> The rights of enterprises to dismiss workers for reasons other than workers' faults will guarantee the legal rights of employers to run business independently and will give enterprises a certain edge in market competition ... [with limits on redundancies] ... necessary for China's social stability.
> (Li Boyong cited in Ng and Warner 1998: 62)

With the benefit of hindsight, and the minister's reassurances notwithstanding, we can perceive in these words a preparation for the restructuring of SOEs and the gradual exchange of *danwei* exclusivity in favour of competition. As negotiations for WTO membership bubbled away on the back burner of the Chinese polity, we can now see that the 'market competition' Li Boyong referred to was indeed global in scope. To achieve these bold goals the state needed an ideological bulwark – or bulldozer – in order to 'liberate the thinking' of the urban working class. For the latter the time to 'step down' was fast approaching.

Five years after the CPC's 14th Congress sanctioned the socialist market economy, the 15th Congress in 1997 shifted the pace of reform up a gear. During the build up to the Congress, Weil argued that China was at a crossroads in which the fate of the country would be decided. One direction led to the rolling back of market reforms and a 'radical move forward – to a revolutionary socialist society'. In the other direction lurked 'full recapitalisation and privatisation of the economy' (Weil 1996: 12). He dismissed the possibilities of a continuation of the '"third way" between socialism and capitalism' due to the irreconcilable class forces that were an already existing consequence of the economic reforms. As China's WTO membership began to look increasingly probable, the likelihood of a rolling back of market reforms disappeared. Premier Zhu Rongji argued that 'only with fewer workers can they [SOEs] lower costs, increase efficiency and survive and develop' (Zhu Rongji 1997).

Xiagang

The laying off of tens of millions of workers from SOEs during the late 1990s was a major political and economic event that represented perhaps the greatest challenge to Party credibility since the start of the reform era. The formal renunciation of the traditional social role of SOEs, consolidated over almost five decades of CPC rule, intensified the strong feelings of abandonment and betrayal that had been growing among middle-aged laid-off workers since the introduction of management autonomy during the mid 1980s (Pringle and Leung 2009). As a consequence, anxiety about the potential for widespread urban social instability arising from the Party's decision to push ahead with SOE restructuring was very high. The CPC produced a state policy that facilitated the unprecedented wave of mass redundancies at the same time as attempting to ameliorate its effects. This policy was known as *xiagang*, literally 'to step down from one's post' in English. From a policy perspective, the process was quite different from redundancy in advanced industrial economies. The crucial distinction was that the SOE retained a concrete set of obligations to laid-off employees, including a livelihood stipend that was between 30 and 50 per cent of their former wages and a formal – albeit pared down – labour relationship. Stood-down workers remained – at least on paper – eligible for various benefits such as partial medical expenses reimbursement and heating allowances and retained their employment record. The *xiagang* policy first moved on to the political and economic agenda in 1993 as the implications of Deng's tour began to make themselves felt. The State Council released the Regulations on the Placement of Surplus Staff and Workers of State-Owned Enterprises and the then Ministry of Labour launched pilot re-employment projects in 30 cities in 1994, prior to rolling out *xiagang* nationally. By the end of 1997, 11.5 million workers had been laid off. According to statistics published by the Information Office of the State Council, 25.5 million more SOE workers were laid off between 1998 and 2001 (State Council Information Office 2002). The redundancies were not evenly spread. The hardest hit areas were the pre-reform industrial powerhouse provinces of the north-east: Liaoning, Jilin and Heilongjiang – which became centres of unrest. Further south, Hubei, Hunan and Jiangxi were also badly affected, as was Sichuan in the west. By the turn of the century, the ratio of unemployed and *xiagang* workers as a percentage of the urban workforce in these provinces ranged between 8 and 12 per cent (China Labour Market Yearbook 2002 cited in HKCTU 2004: 12), although these percentages hid clusters of joblessness. By 2001, the city of Fushun in north-east Liaoning province recorded 396,596 people 'at their post', but 305,128 were 'not at their post', a 43 per cent lay-off rate, while the registered unemployment rate was only 2.7 per cent (*Liaoning Statistical Yearbook 2001*: 66–8 and 92). Definitions of *xiagang* varied considerably over time and place producing what Solinger called a 'layering of statuses' into seven categories of *xiagang* (Solinger 2001: 684–8) rendering a reliable count of unemployed and laid-off workers impossible due to 'inconsistent state statistics, flexible, disaggregating definitions, and multi-layering of the laid-off and jobless' (Solinger 2001: 688).

Acutely aware of the potential for the widespread but scattered resistance to *xiagang* to congeal into a national labour movement – or at least a movement of the unemployed – the state's *xiagang* policy also promoted re-employment (*zai jiuye*) by obliging restructuring SOEs to set up re-employment centres offering subsidised

38 *Industrial relations in China*

retraining courses, sometimes managed by the trade union. The government encouraged unemployed and laid-off workers to seek jobs for themselves, chiefly in the service industries and private sector. According to the State Council's 'Notice on Securing Basic Living Standards and Re-employment of Laid-off SOE Workers' a laid-off worker could not remain registered at a re-employment service centre for more than three years and labour relations with the original enterprise were terminated after this period. If he or she was still out of work, registration as formally unemployed was the next step in order to qualify for welfare benefits. Research conducted in the late 1990s demonstrated that it was the final termination of any labour relationship with the SOE – rather than unemployment itself – that laid-off employees feared most (Pringle and Leung 2009: 96–7). Profound pessimism with regard to job prospects within the three-year time limit was part of an overall lack of confidence in the re-employment centres and many of these places were described by interviewees as 'empty camps' (Pringle and Leung 2006: 100) as workers shunned them and their goal of acting as a conduit for severing the relationship with the *danwei*. In one survey carried out by the Beijing Academy of Social Sciences Institute of Sociology, only 52.5 per cent of laid-off workers had found new jobs within three years (Pringle and Leung 2009: 101). The obligation for downsizing SOEs to establish re-employment centres formally ended in 2003, although far fewer were set up after 2001, and the lifespan of most centres was from 1998 until 2001–2002.

Trade unions, SOE workers and xiagang

At primary level, the ACFTU generally confined itself to managing re-employment centres and explaining government policy to workers, generally by placing it in the context of overall national development. The absence of active trade union support for resistance to restructuring heightened the sense of abandonment felt by workers. According to both the Trade Union Law and the ACFTU Constitution, Chinese trade unions had – and have – a duty to educate workers to support the government's reform policy. Thus, trade union cadres, many of whom were also facing *xiagang*, often found themselves insisting that union members 'liberate' their thinking and accept the Thatcherite 'there is no alternative' argument. This institutional passivity spread into areas where trade unions could feasibly have played a more active role, such as in challenging management abuse of authority and the illegal asset-stripping of SOEs. The roots of union compliance lay in the union's dual role as a Party-led trade union. The trade union chairwoman of a large enterprise in Guangzhou proudly told me that her day job as a deputy personnel manager had allowed her to assist the company to meet its lay-off targets in the late 1990s (Chen Miaomei, interview, Guangzhou, 12 December 2005).

Despite the politically inspired attempts to soften the impact of redundancy, the effects on working class neighbourhoods were real enough and were in fact little different from the effects of widespread unemployment in full-blown capitalist societies. Many enterprises were downsizing due to economic difficulties and this obviously had a negative impact on their ability to pay *xiagang* wages and allowances. Research in the city of Chengdu found that 17.9 per cent of the women workers surveyed received no livelihood allowance from their employers after being laid off and those that did survived on less than a third of the average monthly income for Chengdu citizens. The average income in 2001 – when the survey was conducted – was 595 yuan per month while 11.6 per cent of the laid-off women received less than 100 yuan and 56.5 per cent between 100–200 yuan (Zou Zhongzheng and Qin Wei 2001: 55–60). A survey conducted by the Organization Department of Liaoning Provincial Party Committee in 2000 concluded that being selected for *xiagang* was often followed by a rapid descent into a 'hard and bitter life' as divorce rates went up, crime rose and suicide rates showed a marked increase (CPCCC Research Group 2001: 200–1). According to one ACFTU survey, workers aged between 35 and 55 were the first to be stood down and women before men was the general rule. Women made up between 60 and 70 per cent of all laid-off workers and their family responsibilities made it even more difficult for them to find new jobs. In Chengdu, Zou and Qin found that the introduction of contracts in the 1980s had not prepared women workers for the poverty of unemployment that invariably followed *xiagang*.

> The social position of former SOE women workers was profoundly weakened by *xiagang*. This group differs from other vulnerable social groups, such as migrant workers from the farms, or those urban dwellers who have never been attached to any work unit or enterprise. Far from being on the margins of urban society, these women were, prior to *xiagang*, at the core of the old production system – the masters of the country's [enterprises]'.
>
> (Zou Zhongzheng and Qin Wei 2001: 55–60)

Not everyone understood the details of *xiagang* and the inevitable regional variations in policy that came with it. A series of interviews I conducted with laid-off workers in 2001–2002 in the mining towns around Datong in Shaanxi province and Shulan in Jilin province demonstrated the challenges and, at times, confusion that *xiagang* visited on the working class. Most new jobs found via the re-employment centres offered inferior pay and conditions and taking one meant severing ties with the *danwei* and losing the social benefits that these had traditionally provided. In 2001, the manager of a re-employment centre in Shulan assured me there was 'no longer any such thing as an eight-hour day in China' (Zhang, interview, Shulan, 16 November 2001). In the coal capital of Datong, I interviewed Mr Zheng, a miner. He explained that he had been laid off and was now doing casual work – hauling goods on a tricycle. His rationale for not trying to get a job through his SOE's re-employment centre was that this would mean losing his *xiagang* status, which would not be in his interests. Firstly, it ruled out being prioritized for re-employment at the coal mine, a possibility that he had not yet excluded; secondly, he could supplement his *xiagang* wages with casual work; and thirdly, his current situation offered him more options than would a poorly paid, informal and likely part-time job 'washing dishes' in the restaurants frequented by Datong's emerging parvenu class of village-level cadres and farmers turned mine bosses.[11] For

Mr Zheng, the combination of the two irregular incomes exceeded the wages on offer from the jobs at the re-employment centre. And, as he explained, his main goal at the time was to maintain a relationship with the mine.

> He (points to another tricycle driver) took a job [from the re-employment centre] and then he got sacked after complaining about the hours (laughter among the group in general). Serves him right, he is a mouthy bastard at the best of times (more light-hearted laughter). I want to work in the mine again. I've registered at the re-employment centre but I will stick to this [tricycle work] to supplement what they give me. If there is work in the mine again, I will take that.
> (Zheng, interview, Datong, 10 April 2001)

The man pointed out by Mr Zheng later told me that aside from delivering goods with his tricycle, he also bred dogs to further supplement a means-tested state welfare payment [*zui di shenghuo fei*].[12] He said that registering as formally unemployed would exclude him from this payment.[13] After being laid off from the mine and then sacked from the job he got through the re-employment centre, his main concern was looking after his sick wife, a task rendered very difficult as he and his family no longer had access to medical services that the mine had previously provided. The black economy was his only option. 'Is breeding dogs a job? If I say it is, then maybe I will lose the welfare payment. My wife is sick and can't work and needs me at home to look after her. How can I do a normal job?' (Chen, interview, Datong, 10 April 2001).

Confusion was rife over what one was entitled to, as another tricycle delivery driver and laid-off miner explained:

> I haven't registered with anyone. I wouldn't know much about that. Sure I've read about it but if you actually try to register, it's a different story. I spent one morning in an office waiting to register but then they told me I was in the wrong office. That meant I earned no money that day. The mine doesn't do anything. They said we were being laid off (*xiagang*) but I am not sure what this means for us in practice. Nobody knows.
> (Interview, Datong, 11 April 2001)

Resistance to restructuring is discussed in the next chapter. For now it is sufficient to state that by the summer of 2002, China's combined unemployment and redundancy figures were reaching the 'critical point' (Deng 2002) that the government feared. The authorities had been seriously alarmed by events of the spring of that year, notably the protests of laid-off oil workers in Daqing that even showed signs of spreading elsewhere in China, and delayed a major conference on employment in Beijing during the summer for fear of exacerbating negative public sentiment (Qiao Jun, personal communication, Hong Kong, June 2002). Yet by the end of 2002 it was becoming clear that in policy terms, *xiagang* had achieved its goals and allowed the Party and government to ride out the resistance to restructuring. In 2003, as a new pay-as-you-go social security system began to take shape, the

Ministry of Labour and Social Security (MOLSS) released guidelines stipulating that workers laid off from their SOEs were to register directly as unemployed, a move that facilitated the growing practice of one-off redundancy payments known as *mai duan gongling*.[14] In early 2005, the MOLSS reported that 12 provinces and municipalities had closed all re-employment service centres managed by SOEs and former SOEs (MOLSS 2003).

The new deal: employment, global integration and capitalist labour relations

Up until China's entry into the WTO, Party history, memories of the Cultural Revolution and the violent end to the 1989 Democracy Movement had combined to give the reform process a somewhat temporary air. Indeed, many felt that 'crossing the river by feeling for the stones' didn't necessarily rule out stepping backwards to the safety of the original bank. However, by formally locking China into trading rules and facilitating further integration with the global economy, WTO membership considerably reduced the prospects of a policy volte-face. Further reassurance came early in the new century with two landmark speeches from President Jiang Zemin. In essence, the speeches recognized that membership of the country's ruling class and control of the nation's resources and wealth was no longer restricted to the upper echelons of the CPC and the army. Jiang's ideological staff developed the Theory of the Three Represents through which the CPC was deemed to represent all three advanced elements of production, including capital. The Party constitution was amended accordingly and capitalists were permitted to join the organization despite opposition from the Maoist old guard.

WTO membership came during the aftermath of the Asian financial crisis as restructuring again picked up momentum and foreign investment increased significantly. In 2002, China knocked the US from its pole position as the favoured destination for FDI (OECD 2003). The last years of the twentieth century saw an expansion of labour markets, the completion of the dismantling of the iron rice bowl, and the consolidation of the role of private and foreign ownership in the economy.

As I have already pointed out, these socio-economic developments were far from unregulated. If the chaos of the former USSR's transition was to be avoided, the state's withdrawal from direct management of industrial relations required the development of labour laws and regulations. Unlike the Russian ruling class, the Chinese Party leadership was not subject to the intense pressure of 'Chicago School' economics and was aware that constraints on the behaviour of profit-seeking employers and local governments eager to generate income from investment were required, even if they were sporadically and unevenly applied. Indeed, although capitalist globalization has a justified reputation for removing legal limitations on the behaviour of capitalists, the Chinese experience is somewhat more nuanced. Since the mid 1980, Chinese labour legislation has flourished and between 1979 and 1994 alone over 160 labour regulations and rules were passed (Yuan Shouqi 1994: 338 cited in Ngok Kinglun 2008: 49). Before we look in detail at the legal framework for industrial relations that continues to be developed, I will briefly summarize the considerable changes that reform had brought to China's employment structure and this will give us an idea of what the state needed to regulate.

In Figure 1.1 we can see the full extent of the changes. In 1978, 70.5 per cent of Chinese were employed in the primary sector, 17.3 per cent in the secondary and just 12.2 in the tertiary. By 2006, these statistics were 42.6 per cent, 25.2 per cent and 32.2 per cent respectively (China Labour Statistical Yearbook 2007). In terms of urban employment structure by sector over the period 1990 to 2003, the number of state sector employees dropped by 34.7 million to 68.8 million whereas those employed in the private sector rose from 6.7 million to 42.7 million representing 46.5 per cent of the newly employed urbanites (State Council Information Office 2004: 5). These figures do not include rural workers coming into the urban areas to work. As most of these people end up working in the private sector, the numbers actually working in private or foreign-invested industry are much larger.

Underpinning these transformations has been the reserve army of unemployed so familiar to capitalist economies. From both political and economic perspectives, management of the numbers was of crucial importance to the Party. On the one hand, capital required a pool of unemployed workers to maintain a downward pressure on wages. On the other hand, the state could not allow the reserve army numbers to climb too high and risk nationwide social unrest. We can see clearly here the importance of phased redundancy or *xiagang* policy and the *hukou* regulations in terms of managing the political perils that came with economic reform. Political considerations apart, the burdens of compiling reliable empirical data on the number of unemployed were not inconsiderable. Firstly, there was the inevitable confusion between formal unemployment, an entirely new concept to urban workers more familiar with the securities of the *danwei*, and those who were still in the process of phased redundancy – itself divided into up to eight different categories (Solinger 2001: 671–88).

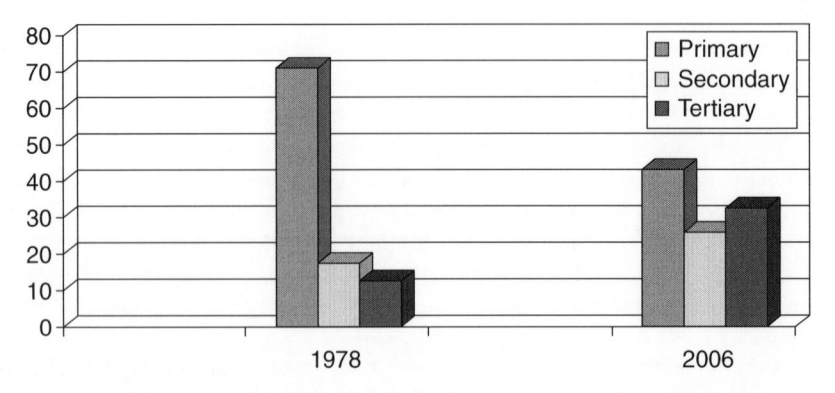

Figure 1.1 Comparison of employment structure, 1978 and 2006 in percentages
Source: CLSY, 2007.

Moreover, the informal sector was expanding rapidly, with all the usual grey areas. An ACFTU survey of re-employed former SOE workers found that

> 18.6 per cent were odd-job manual workers; 10 per cent did various sorts of hourly work (which usually refers to activities such as picking up others' children from school); 5.2 per cent had seasonal jobs; 60 per cent were retailers operating stalls; and a mere 6.8 per cent had obtained formal, contracted employment. A worrying 45 per cent among the stall keepers were discovered to be highly vulnerable, mobile peddlers selling in shifting sites without a licence.
> (Labour Insurance Bulletin 2000: 35 cited in Solinger 2001: 682)

In 2003, when registration as a *xiagang* worker was being phased out in favour of formal unemployment in urban areas, the official rate of unemployment was 4.3 per cent. In 2006, this had dropped to 4.1 per cent (China Labour Statistical Yearbook 2007: 172). In December 2008, the rate increased for the first time in five years to 4.2 per cent with a government projection of 4.6 per cent for 2009 (Tan Yingzi 2009). However, the true figure for unemployment is likely to be considerably higher as the *fan xiang* or return to the countryside movement has illustrated. As a result of the global financial crisis, 20 million migrants have temporarily returned to their farms (Branigan 2009). These people are not included in the official statistics for unemployment.

Managing capitalist conflict: the legal development of an industrial relations system

The State Council has described the regulation of China's emerging labour relations system as being based on 'autonomous consultation by both parties and regulated by the government according to the law' (State Council Information Office 2004: 16). The words are carefully chosen and the preference for 'autonomous' over 'independence' is not simply a matter of semantics. Nevertheless, the implicit subjectivity is a far cry from the command economy in which, according to Xu, the capitalist class was eliminated and the 'independent, free labourer was purged in favour of socialism' (Xu Xiaohong 2003: 15). Indeed, the need to regulate 'both parties' acknowledges the existence of separate interests. With the potential for conflict considerably expanded, the Party turned to 'governing the country by relying on laws' (*yifa zhiguo*) to 'complement the government's efforts at both political stability and economic reform' (Ying Zhu 2002: 161). Thus, law moved centre stage, a result of 'the paradigmatic shifts of China's labor policy in the reform era. Under the new labor policy paradigm, the role of law has been strengthened in governing labor relations and other labor-related affairs' (Ngok Kinglun 2008: 45).

Summarizing the situation in the early 1990s, Ngok identifies the return of capitalist labour relations and attendant worker unrest as the significant, if not overriding, factor in the formulation of a national labour law.

44 Industrial relations in China

> Both Chinese and overseas observers contended that the totally unregulated laissez-faire capitalist conditions of the early stages of capitalism were prevalent and that 'sweatshops' were revived in China. The plight of laborers was drummed into the national consciousness by media stories. Labor abuses, especially in the non-state sector, caused increasing militant actions of the workers and invited wide criticism from international human rights groups and labor groups. There was a widespread sense that the country had some serious labor problems that would endanger social stability. Facing these pressures, the state was forced to take some active measures to pacify disgruntled workers, and the Labor Law was seen as an important and urgent issue on the legislative agenda.
>
> (Ngok Kinglun 2008: 51)

The 1995 Labour Law was China's first national labour law. Although the law devotes considerable space to the individual labour rights of employees, its principal aim was to give legal sanction to 'two issues related to the role of the legal framework during this transition period': redefining the 'relationship between the government and enterprises' and to 'develop rules for enterprises with diversity of ownership to compete in the market' (Ying Zhu 2002: 163). Contracts were the key weapon.

Contracts

The individual labour contract became the starting point for the new employment relationship. Ngok argues that '[T]he most significant break with the old employment system was, undoubtedly, the introduction of labor contracts, and this fundamentally changed the relationship between workers and the state' (Ngok Kinglun 2008: 46).

Nichols *et al.*'s research on the role of contracts concurs with Ngok's view. One of their case studies involved a former mainland SOE that eventually reinvented itself as a fully foreign-owned enterprise following a brief spell as a joint venture. According to Wong, such transformations – and there were many – have been facilitated by WTO membership, the consequent 'SOE privatisation project' and the 'disintegration of China's protectionist policy' (Wong 2006: 80), while Nichols draws a direct link between China's legal enshrinement of contracted employment via the Labour Law (1995) and the unmaking ('dismantling') of China's traditional ('established') urban working class. Not that this process is unique to China. A hallmark of capitalist globalization has been the insecure irregular forms of employment 'accentuated by pressures of globalization, privatization, of production and social policy, new technologies and the competitive pressures on managers' (Nichols *et al.* 2004: 667).

If contracts in the era of globalization and Chinese economic reform were part of the process of dismantling the power and influence of China's established labour in the state sector, they were also the basis for the new relationship between employers and employed in the private sector. Of course, millions of migrant workers were not given the opportunity to sign contracts with their employers, and many of those that did had little choice but to sign ones that did not meet legal standards. However, the point remains valid: contracts and the concomitant commoditization of labour are now the legal basis of the relationship between labour and capital in China. The Labour Law (1995) devotes a whole chapter to employment contracts and of the 19 articles therein, all but three are related to individual contracts. Article 20 allows for three types of contract: fixed-term, permanent and flexible, all of which must contain clauses on terms, job description and duties, rights and protection, wages and salary, disciplinary procedures, termination and responsibility for violation. Since the law was passed, the overwhelming majority of contracts have been fixed-term and this fact has been crucial to China's emergence as a platform for exports via TNCs and global integration. Wong's research at the Tianjin branch of the Korean TNC Samsung found that China's emerging model dovetailed neatly with the

> 'Samsungisation' of labour relations [which] is taking place along typical Samsung HRM lines such as merit-based bonus [and] one year contracts based on three month appraisal tied to a yearly five to seven per cent dismissal rate. [This] serves to replace socialist-styled worker collectivism with individual and irregular labour relations.
> (Wong 2006: 87)

It certainly did in the white goods factory – euphemistically referred to as ChinaCo – Nichols and his team researched. In 1994, the year the NPC passed the Labour Law, 100 per cent of the company's workers were permanent workers. In 2002, this figure had dropped to under 35 per cent. About 60 per cent of the workforce was employed on fixed two-year contracts and the remaining five per cent on three-month contracts employed to cover seasonal fluctuations. Echoing Wong and many others, Nichols *et al.* remind us of both the extent of the transformation and the role of contracts in bringing it about.

> During the planned economy period, the managers of SOEs had little right to select workers and workers were allocated jobs from which they could not be fired. At ChinaCo, the new labour contract system made it possible for the number of workers to be cut by half during the joint venture period. But the proportionate change in the types of contract is no less striking and has generally drawn less attention from outside China.
> (Nichols *et al.* 2004: 673)

The promulgation of the Labour Law was followed by an extensive campaign to 'implement the provisions relating to labour contracts' (Ying Zhu 2002: 172). This did very little to persuade employers to move beyond superficially replicating minimum standards. The next 13 years saw large numbers of press articles, activist reports and labour protests that symbolized the failure of contracts to hold employers to account in the absence of a strong integrated national labour movement capable of operating in the new environment. As the horror stories piled up and unrest reached a new level, the state, under the new and more socially concerned leadership of Hu Jintao and Wen Jiabao, moved to strengthen the hand of unions and workers by introducing a Labour Contract Law (Ngok Kinglun 2008: 57). As with the original Labour Law, worker militancy was a major factor behind its formulation, the difference being that the original law was aimed at heading off unrest whereas the Labour Contract Law is an attempt to placate it. Following 2004, the capacity of workers to make their point was given an added weight by the advent of labour shortages in the Pearl River Delta and elsewhere as migrants organized strikes, occasionally blocked roads and, most frequently, voted with their feet. The challenge of labour unrest was again making its presence felt. A survey of 9,500 urbanites' attitudes to labour conflict (*lao-zi chongtu*) in 2002 found that 62 per cent of those asked agreed that 'labour conflict was increasingly serious'. The various grades of answers are given in Table 1.2.

Prior to its final draft, the 2008 Labour Contract Law (LCL) was subject to an extensive process of public consultation that facilitated employers, workers, TNCs, agents of foreign capital such as the US Chamber or Commerce or AmCham, as well as literally tens of thousands of NGOs and individuals to send in their views. The process sparked a national debate over the role of labour standards and their impact on employment and development. The so-called 'Beijing Faction' argued for a new law containing standards that fell into line with those set by the ILO and was led by the well-known labour scholar Professor Chang Kai. On the other hand, the 'Shanghai Faction', led by Professor Dong Baohua, put the case for lower standards that were more applicable to China's developing country status and therefore rendered the law more relevant to workers and employers. The new law was always going to be a compromise, yet the final version did give more workers more leeway to address some of the contract-related issues that the vaguer language of the original Labour Law had produced. For example, Li argues that contracts in China are based on the pro-employer model of 'stability on the basis of labour market mobility' i.e. fixed-term contracts rather than the pro-employee model of 'labour market mobility on the basis of stability' that would – in theory – have left more room for permanent employment (Li Kungang 2000: 6). Under the previous legal regime, the high degree of labour market mobility that

Table 1.2 Urban citizens' responses to the statement 'the problem of labour-capital conflicts is increasingly serious'

Response category	Individual responses	Percentage of total	Response category	Individual responses	Percentage of total
Completely agree	1,074	11.4	Partially disagree	1,474	15.5
Partially agree	4,811	50.6	Completely disagree	285	3.0
No opinion	1,856	19.5			
			Total	9,500	100.0

Source: Li Peilin *et al.* 2005: 182.

time-restricted contracts generally produce had made it very convenient for employers to resort to questionable and often illegal methods in order to retain workers in appalling conditions, delay wage payments or refuse work injury compensation. These included 'job deposits', deductions for a 'contract violation fund' (*weiyue jin*) and the substituting of labour supply contracts with labour dispatch companies for genuine employment contracts (Chang Kai 2005: 266–7).

It remains to be seen if the LCL can improve the situation for workers. While falling well short of levelling the playing field, the LCL does go some way towards reining in employer hegemony over contracts and as such drew fierce opposition from US investors (Brown 2006). Written contracts are now mandatory (Article 10) and labour stability is encouraged by the law's stipulation that employers are obliged to offer permanent employment to employees who have served two fixed-term contracts (Article 14). Severance pay for those workers whose contracts are not renewed is now a legal right of employees (Article 46), although this is subject to other conditions in the law being met. Equally important is that the LCL stipulates penalties for employer violation of these new rights and there are fifteen articles in the law that stipulate the conditions for employers' legal liabilities (Articles 80–95). For their part, some employers resorted to mass sackings in the run up to the promulgation of the law, weeding out those workers who were coming up for a third-term contract renewal and forcing those left over to sign new contracts that effectively cancelled out their employment history. This behaviour became so widespread that the ACFTU issued a nationwide notice instructing its branches to go after 'employing units' who were 'not only directly infringing the rights of workers and influencing harmonious labour relations but also producing a negative impact on socialist harmony' (ACFTU 2007c).

Collective contracts

The ACFTU began to push seriously for collective contracts in SOEs during the mid 1990s, but these efforts were undermined by command economy traditions and inexperience in bargaining (Clarke *et al.* 2004: 251). First, the economy still bore many of the hallmarks of a command structure and the notion of opposing interests that required bargaining to reconcile was still unacceptable to most ACFTU cadres who had not yet grasped the nature of the changes that lay ahead. Second, employer organizations were weak and largely established by the Party itself. Third, up until 1997, the restructuring of SOEs had proceeded with relative caution, especially after the trauma of 1989. Fourth, while three clauses on collective contracts were successfully inserted into the final draft of the 1995 labour law as a result of ACFTU lobbying, these hardly provided a sufficiently weighty counterbalance to an overwhelming individualistic law.

There is still no distinct law on collective contracts in China. Following an updating of the 'Regulations on Collective Contracts' undertaken jointly by the MOLSS, the ACFTU and the two national employers' organizations in January 2004 (MOLSS 2004), the ACFTU convened a national conference in September of the same year aimed at adding impetus to its work of increasing the number of workers covered by collective contracts signed via a process of collective consultation rather than bargaining. By the end of the year, the union was claiming that 628,819 enterprises and institutions had established a 'collective contract system' based on 'equal negotiation' (Chinese Trade Unions Statistics Yearbook 2005, 2006: 107). In its statistical yearbook for the following year, 2006, the ACFTU claimed that 529,749 enterprises were covered by regional (*quyu xing*) collective contracts and a further 111,736 enterprises covered by industrial (*hangye xing*) collective contracts (Chinese Trade Unions Statistics Yearbook 2006, 2007: 112). By the end of 2005, 413,706 enterprises had signed annual wage-only collective contracts for over 35.3 million workers (Chinese Trade Unions Statistics Yearbook 2006, 2007: 113). The relationship between these figures is not made clear. For example, it is not possible to ascertain from the statistics presented how many of the enterprises with wage-only collective contracts also had collective contracts covering non-wage related issues that are usually on a three-year basis. Previous research emphasizes that these figures should be treated with caution (Taylor *et al.* 2003: 191). In Chapter 4, I explain that the vast majority of these contracts were a result of top-down quota-driven targets producing agreements that at best met legal minimum standards and at worst undercut them! I believe these weaknesses give the case study in Chapter 4 that examines a pioneering bottom-up collective wage-bargaining process covering seasonal migrant workers added significance.

Labour dispute resolution

Throughout the latter half of the 1950s and for the following two decades, China did not have a formal labour dispute resolution system. Its absence was based on the ideological assumption that workers' ownership of enterprises excluded the possibility of antagonistic labour disputes that were inevitable in capitalist property relations. A labour arbitration system had been established in 1950 when the Party signalled that it would initially prioritize national reconstruction over the wider political project of establishing socialism, but it was abolished in 1957 following the near complete nationalization of industry. According to the CPC, the new property relations dictated that enterprise-level labour disputes 'ought to be resolved through various administrative and political means for settling internal differences' (Mo 2000: 21 cited in Shen Jie 2007: 108).

The return of labour-capital disputes in the reform era dictated that a formal dispute resolution system was again required. In 1993, the Regulations Governing Resolutions of Enterprise Labour Disputes were released. This legally binding document outlined a three-tier method of dispute resolution based on enterprise-level mediation, arbitration and finally the courts. Less than two years later, the system was given full legal status by the Labour Law (1995). It remains a hierarchical single-track system, referred to in China as the 'one mediation, one arbitration and two court cases' (*yi tiao yi cai liang sheng*). In practice, the system works as follows: subsequent to the outbreak of a dispute at an enterprise, the parties involved can apply for enterprise-level mediation. In large enterprises, this is delivered by a committee, but in smaller enterprises the job is generally the responsibility of the personnel manager who may well be union chair as well. If no agreement is reached, either party can apply for arbitration but this must be within 60 days of the date of the original dispute, a time limit that has been an important constraint on workers making use of the system. Once a case has been accepted, the appropriate level of the labour dispute arbitration committee (LDAC) organizes an arbitration tribunal to deal with specific disputes. The tribunal has up to three members depending on the complexity of the case. Finally, if either party is not satisfied with the LDAC tribunal decision, they have 15 days to apply for a court hearing and the opportunity for one appeal following the decision of the first instance.

Chinese workers have made use of this system despite its flaws. Past evidence suggests that they are likely to continue to do so in even greater numbers now that a specific Labour Mediation and Arbitration Law (LMAL) has come into force as of 1 May 2008. Incomplete statistics for 2008 demonstrate this is the case. The Ministry of Human Resources and Social Security – formerly the MOLSS – announced on 8 May 2009 that cases accepted by the LDACs increased by 98 per cent on 2007. Out of a total of 693,000 cases involving 1.2 million workers, 22,000 were collective disputes (Guangdong Labour Dispute and Arbitration Network 2009).

Arbitration is at the heart of China's labour dispute resolution process for two reasons. Firstly, enterprise-level unions are too weak to defend workers at the initial mediation stage, and secondly, courts are not allowed to accept cases that have not previously been through mediation, although there are local exceptions to this rule (Shen Jie 2007: 111–2) usually on the basis that the relevant LDAC is overwhelmed with work. The rather vague language and categorization of disputes has been slightly improved upon in the LMAL. Article 2 stipulates that LDACs may accept disputes arising from the confirmation of labour relations; contractual issues related to conclusion, performance, alteration or termination; dismissal or resignation; working hours and insurance; remuneration and injury compensation; and other labour disputes prescribed by laws and regulations (MOLSS 2008). Other problems that have been partially addressed by the new LMAL include the stipulation that arbitration decisions are legally binding, abolishing fees for arbitration, and extending the time limit from 60 days from the date of the original dispute to one year. The new law has also extended the scope of arbitrable matters to cover nearly all labour-related disputes, including disputes arising from determining whether an employee–employer relationship exists. This has been a major source of frustration for workers, despite a pro-worker Supreme Court ruling on the matter in 2001 that allowed LDACs to accept a case when there was no labour contract but sufficient evidence to prove a labour relationship existed (Huang Kun 2004: 279).

Nevertheless, more deep-rooted institutional obstacles remain, not least in the fact that although nominally tripartite and made up of representatives from the labour bureau, trade union and enterprise (Article 19), the state still wields largely unfettered influence over all these institutions. Despite this, LDACs and similar institutions of redress remain overburdened and under-resourced. The legal scholar He Weifang has been quoted as arguing that this has helped to render such institutions inefficient and unjust:

> originally meant to seek justice [but] have become institutions that dispense injustice. Institutions that were meant to resolve disputes have become institutions that create them and institutions that were meant to allay popular resentment have become institutions that stir it up.
> (He Weifang 2004 cited in Liu Shang 2004: 2–4)

In January 2007, 10 months before the LMAL was passed by the NPC in December, Renmin University's Institute of Labour Relations organized an 'International Conference on Labour Dispute Resolution' at which the keynote Chinese speaker outlined the problems of labour dispute resolution in China. In his speech, Professor Chang Kai argued that at the mediation level 'the systemic conflicts and shortcomings of the enterprise-level mediation committees has led to a decline in their effectiveness' and that the central position of arbitration in the resolution process was inappropriate in the current situation due to its 'structural vacuity (*jigou xuhua*), lack of authority and the unsuitable quality of arbitrators'. Moreover, the procedural rules governing the final court stage either failed to 'dovetail with, or were contradictory to, the rules of arbitration and lacked independence' (Chang Kai 2007: 32). The LMAL is a sign of progress, but there is still work to be done in the area of facilitating workers' use of the law to uphold their legal rights and interests.

Health and safety

The early years of this century also saw the introduction of important laws pertaining to industrial health and safety. China's Law on Safety in Production was introduced in 2001 and stipulated 14 basic systems and/or measures which, on paper, are relatively strict, but implementation is constrained by a weak labour inspectorate and poor trade union participation (Pringle and Frost 2003: 315). Article 16 stipulates that production units must abide by all the relevant laws, regulations and industry-specific laws prior to commencing production, construction, excavation, etc. The law also provides for individual responsibility covering all aspects of safety (Articles 17, 74 and 75) and that health and safety concerns must be systematically integrated into all aspects of production: planning, the construction of production units and spaces, as well as the production process itself (Article 24). Article 46 stipulates the rights and responsibilities of employees pertaining to occupational safety. They are built around six core rights (Pringle and Frost 2003: 311): to safety information and training on prevention; to safety equipment that conforms to national standards; to criticize and make suggestions; to refuse to carry out instructions from management that violate laws or regulations; to stop work in life-threatening situations; and to receive compensation following an accident at work.

The Law on the Prevention and Cure of Occupational Diseases (LPCOD) came into force on 1 May 2002 and stated the responsibilities of enterprises with regard to safe working conditions, industrial accident insurance, measures to prevent occupational disease and the provision of information to workers. Article 4 stipulates that

> The workers enjoy the right to occupational health protection. The employer shall create the working environment and conditions that conform to the national norms for occupational health and requirements for public health and take measures to ensure that the workers receive occupational health protection.
>
> (ALII 2010)

Article 30 further demonstrates the central role of contracts and the rights and responsibilities of both parties:

> When signing with the workers labor contracts (including contracts of employment), the employer shall truthfully inform the workers of potential occupational disease hazards, the consequences in the course of work, the measures for prevention of such diseases and the material benefits, and it shall have the same clearly put down in the contracts; it may not conceal the facts or deceive the workers.
>
> If, during the contracted period of time, a worker, because of change in work post or assignment, begins to engage in an operation with occupational disease hazards, which is not mentioned in the contact, the employer shall, in accordance with the provisions in the preceding paragraph, perform its obligation by informing the worker of the true situation and, through consultation with the worker, alter the related provisions in the original contract.
>
> If the employer violates the provisions in the preceding two paragraphs, the worker shall have the right to reject the assignment where occupational disease hazards exist, and the employer may not thus cancel or terminate labour contract with the worker.
>
> (ALII 2010)

Writing in 2003, Pringle and Frost find in these laws potential opportunities to improve China's record on occupational health and safety, but pinpointed the absence of adequate representation as a key constraint to improved implementation of labour legislation in general and OHS law in particular.

> The new laws and standards provide a legal framework that could, if utilized, force enterprises to comply with adequate standards. There is more than adequate information available ... The problems lie in the lack of confidence and experience among younger workers and managers. Workers are in general ignorant of the laws and the vast body of expertise on OHS, while younger managers often feel compelled to manage facilities more in line with profit than fairness.
>
> (Pringle and Frost 2003: 315)

To date, workplace inspections have not matched the levels of industrial development that economic reform has induced. There are more than 3,000 labour inspection agencies in China and around 40,000 inspectors (Cooney 2007: 607), but the inspectorates are dependent on local government for their financing and managed by the local labour bureaux. As such, they are not inclined to offend powerful local interests, and they have very limited powers of enforcement. Article 7 of the Regulations on the Inspection of Labour Guarantees (*laodong baozhang jiancha tiaoli*) obliges these agencies to solicit the views of trade unions (State Council 2004). The ACFTU has its own network of labour supervision and inspection committees at various levels. It claims that almost a quarter of all enterprises and organizations had 'labour protection supervision and examination committees', with 1.621 million labour protection inspectors in 2006, covering over 40 per cent of the workforce, while a third of higher-level trade union organizations also had 'labour protection supervision and examination organizations'. Overall, the trade unions at all levels participated in 2.301 million safety production inspections in 2006 (ACFTU 2007d). In practice, these committees have no power over working conditions unless they have the backing of government departments.

Thus, we can see the steady development of labour legislation since the introduction of a first national labour law in 1995. While the recent LCL and LMAL are clearly important additions to the legislative framework, they do not address the structural concerns that simultaneously underpin and undermine China's current labour relations system: weak and employer-dependent primary trade unions and powerful and Party-dependent higher trade unions. Indeed, the history of labour relations in general suggests that individual and essentially individualist labour legislation is intrinsically incapable of solving the collective antagonisms that come with capitalist labour relations and the evidence to date demonstrates that the socialist market paradigm is no different. How then do China's trade unions and the Trade Union Law fit into the post-WTO membership picture in what remains, according to the Constitution, a workers' republic?

Trade union law and practice in the new era

It is appropriate to recognize the direct link between law and trade union activity in the current era. The ACFTU's attachment to traditional custom and practice from the command economy has proved a powerful constraint on trade union activity in the transitional economy. The union has tied itself to a conservative interpretation of labour and trade union law and regulations that has hardly induced initiative and innovation in the new environment. One of the aims of this book is to demonstrate that, despite this background, there are examples of the union reacting to the changes in the industrial relations map, and in particular to the labour unrest that these changes have brought. However, in all of these examples the ACFTU always subordinated its protection of workers' rights and interests to its role as upholder of Party-state policies. These contradictory tasks are set out clearly in the latest version of the Trade Union Law. Article 4 stipulates that unions must 'take economic development as the central task' and 'observe and safeguard ... the leadership by the Communist Party of China' and its political canon, chiefly Marxist-Leninism, Mao Zedong Thought and Deng Xiaoping Theory (Trade Union Law 2001 Article 4). The first paragraph of the ACFTU Constitution reinforces Party leadership stating that Chinese trade unions are 'mass organizations of the Chinese working class under the leadership of the Communist Party of China and formed by the workers of their own free will' (ACFTU 2008a).

The constraints are not new. What is new is the economic environment and industrial relations system in which the union must operate. Not surprisingly, it has devoted considerable effort to influencing the laws that are shaping these developments and indeed, this has been one of its chief functions during the reform era. Over the past 20 years, the ACFTU has taken part in the debates and drafting processes of the Labour Law (1995), the Trade Union Law (1992), the Production Safety Law (2002), the Regulations on Industrial Injury Insurance (2004), the Provisions on Collective Contracts (2004) and the Provisional Method for the Collective Consultation on Wages (2000). These laws, their subsequent amendments and their local interpretations have formed a major part of the ACFTU's efforts to promote workers' rights and interests. This function reached a pinnacle in 2008 when three new laws were passed: the LCL, the Employment Law and the LMAL. The new laws put more emphasis on trade union representation of workers, as opposed to a mediating role between capital and labour, but at the same time make no concessions on Party leadership and upholding rapid economic development which, in practice, constrain the union from improving its representative capacity and credibility.

The revision of the Trade Union Law in 2001 nudged the union towards a more defined sense of its responsibilities. Article 2 added the clause that the union and all its organizations 'represent the interests of the workers and staff members and safeguard the legitimate rights and interests of the workers and staff members according to law'. In a somewhat vague reference to the problems thrown up by the ACFTU's parallel task of representing the 'overall interests of the entire Chinese people' (Article 6) the revised law states that while protecting these wider interests the 'basic duties and functions of trade unions are to safeguard the legitimate rights and interests of workers and staff members' even as they take heed of their wider role (Article 6). A third important addition was the strengthening of the union's role with regard to collective contracts. Article 6 stipulates that the union shall take part in consultation over collective contracts on an equal footing with employers, a clause which, as we shall see in Chapter 4, paved the way for stronger regulations on collective contracts in general.

Apart from its acceptance of Party leadership, Chang illustrates the special characteristics of the Chinese trade unions as they operate in an authoritarian environment. Constitutionally they are obliged to mobilize workers in supporting the reform process, take part in the system of democratic management, improve the quality and education of workers as well as establish 'workers' teams to construct [standards] of ideological, moral, cultural and disciplinary [behaviour]' (Chang Kai 2005: 187). In practice, these legal stipulations mean that in the new era much of the ACFTU's efforts remain tied to government initiatives. In response to the poverty and insecurity that came with restructuring, the government encouraged the ACFTU to establish poverty relief centres for the laid-off SOE workers as part of an attempt to limit unrest rather than negotiate better terms for redundancy or indeed launch a campaign to defend jobs. These centres are discussed in more detail in Chapter 2. Likewise, following the onset of labour shortages in exporting zones in South China and the confidence this gave workers to demand higher wages from employers, the Shenzhen government announced increases in the minimum wage in July 2005 and February 2006 (Xu Shi 2006). These increases were rooted in workers' own activity rather than any public union campaign.[15] The ACFTU also increased its charity work via the 'deliver warmth' programme (*song wennuan*), that concentrates on cash and material gifts made to the urban poor at Chinese New Year and on National Day holidays. According to one senior trade union researcher, in 2005 the annual budget for this activity reached an historical high of approximately 40 million yuan (Fu Lin, interview, Beijing, 12 February 2006). As the leadership is well aware, these activities are essentially outside the workplace. And despite calls issued from the centre for local trade unions to increase their efforts in the workplace, the tension between stability and economic development on the one hand and exacerbating already increasing unrest on the other remains a constraint. In this scenario, the union tends to react after an incident, i.e. a strike or more serious labour protest, rather than take the risk of provoking an incident by raising demands on employers even as it establishes (*zujian*) primary unions rather than organizes workers into them.

Conclusion

The ACFTU has played an important role in both the pre- and post-Cultural Revolution models of industrial relations. However, its legally designated role and the absence of freedom of association have encouraged a culture of extreme caution. This is hardly surprising given the turbulent history of the last 60 years. Moreover, under both the command and market economy paradigms, the post-1949 decades have been dominated by the Party's prioritization of reconstruction, development and employment over all else. The consequent constraints on union activity have been illustrated in this chapter.

The reform era has seen the Party – i.e. the state itself to all intents and purposes – gradually withdraw from direct management of labour relations. There were high hopes that the ACFTU had the capacity to fill this gap, but the situation has proved more complicated than perhaps Deng imagined when he argued that between them SWCs and the unions could mount an effective constraint on capital. This has not been the case. Indeed, during the early 1950s when reconstruction dictated an industrial relations policy of benefiting both labour and capital (*lao-zi liang li*), it was clear that the ACFTU was more adept at controlling workers than at constraining capital. The same contradiction has re-emerged in the present reform era.

Yet the organization remains far from the 'dinosaur' that some sections of the Chinese media occasionally caricature. Throughout its history, the ACFTU has been at the forefront of debates on labour policy, even though its position was often defined by political factionalism within the Party itself. The factor that has highlighted the role of the ACFTU more than any other has been labour unrest. This has taken different forms according to which economic model has been in the ascendancy and the concomitant risks of taking action. However, it has been particularly marked over the last decade as the labour movement in China has moved to the forefront of global industrial relations. In Chapter 2, we explore the history of labour unrest in the PRC and find a lively tradition which, in the new economic environment, is developing into a major social force. Indeed, if the liberation of the working class is to be the act of the working class, the process requires the liberation – or replacement – of its sole legal representative from the shackles of past practice.

2 Labour unrest in the state sector
The rise and demise of decent work with Chinese – and some Russian – characteristics

Chapter 1 summarized the development of industrial relations since 1949, paying special attention to the changes over the last three decades of economic reform. In the final section, I discussed the challenges these changes presented to the trade union and the necessity of transforming into a more representative organization of workers. In Chapters 2 and 3 I discuss the consequences of the union's slow progress to date. In this chapter, the focus is on the state sector where the ACFTU's room to manoeuvre has been entirely constrained by its relationship with the Party. In Chapter 3, I examine growing militancy in the private sector where, in the current conditions, the consequences with regard to union activity are more nuanced. Chapters 4, 5 and 6 investigate how the emerging 'space' has been filled.

The current chapter is organized along basically historical lines. Section 1 takes a tour of labour unrest up to the reform era, using the available literature as my chief source. In particular, I examine the first eight years following liberation and the relationship between labour unrest and the taming of the ACFTU as the unions submitted to their new role of controlling an expanding and, at times, disappointed and frustrated working class – especially its younger members. During this period, the CPC successfully implemented the total nationalization of industry and suppression of capitalist enterprise. By the end of the decade, labour-capital relations no longer existed in the traditional capitalist sense and industrial relations were subject to administrative governance under conditions Chang Kai has characterized as working people having 'the absolute right to work' (Chang Kai 2004: 5), as opposed to the negotiation or bargaining between labour and capital over the allocation of resources that generally distinguishes a market economy. However, the 'extermination' of private capital (Xu Xiaohong 2003: 15) did not preclude conflict on the shop floor, as I show in a brief examination of labour unrest in the command economy in this section.

In Section 2, I make use of primary and secondary sources to track state sector labour unrest in the reform era. The 15th Party Congress, held in the autumn of 1997, was a watershed moment in this narrative of defeat. Up until 1997, the state proceeded cautiously with the implementation of SOE reform and the emergence of autonomous workers' organizations during the 1989 protests suggests that it was right to do so. Indeed, following an historical pattern – as we shall see – the suppression of the protests was followed by politically inspired concessions to the traditional working class that were brought to an end by Deng's Southern Tour in Spring 1992, an event that put the reformers back in the ascendancy and set the Party on the road to the 15th Congress and its historic decision to continue, full steam ahead, with SOE restructuring. This unleashed a wave of resistance, the nature of which is discussed in full via a literature review and close examination of its peak period in the north-east in 2002. My primary sources include interviews with workers and trade union officers conducted during the peak period of protest from 1997 to 2002. I also make use of a wide variety of secondary sources, including local and national media, workers' pamphlets and interviews with workers' leaders conducted by a journalist colleague for a video project on which I collaborated.

Labour unrest in the command economy

Between 1949 and 1997, China experienced a see-saw of economic paradigms that reflected its post-liberation political history. For reasons of space and clarity, I have concentrated on four distinct periods: Post-liberation 'New Democracy' in which a spirit of reconstruction and compromise in the urban areas existed alongside the reform of property relations in the countryside; the First Five-Year Plan and nationalization of almost all urban industry; the Cultural Revolution and the ascendancy of what might be called Maoist economic fundamentalism; and finally the reform era up until the 15th Party Congress in 1997. I use the changing role of the ACFTU as an anchor during this stormy voyage.

As we saw in Chapter 1, writers such as Walder (1986) and You Ji (1998) focused on the capacity of the Party/state to control workers and close down the space to organize collectively. Others have stressed the existence of a voluntary 'social contract' between Party and class (Tang and Parish 2000). More recent studies, such as Sheehan's new history of Chinese workers (1998) and, to a lesser extent, Chan's translations of media reports on the struggles of mainly Chinese migrant workers under 'assault' from the forces of globalization (Chan 2001), have shed light on the considerable influence that the working class has been able to exercise over post-liberation industrial relations in all the various shifts in political policy and economic model. Sheehan's work demonstrated that the stereotype of a liberated working class being alternately pampered or frightened into passivity by Party largesse or authoritarianism is an undeserved caricature of a so-called labour aristocracy. Chan's newspaper translations allow English-language readers to explore – and hopefully reject – the stereotype of rural-to-urban migrant workers as low quality (*suzhi di*) 'little people' from the sticks, incapable of standing up for themselves.[1]

The early days: liberation and new democracy
'benefiting both labour and capital'

In the aftermath of victory over the Guomindang, the CPC found itself in the position of reconstructing a war-damaged economy while simultaneously reinventing China as a workers' republic – or at least as being on the road to one. The pre-liberation experiences of governance garnered from the Party's administration of 'liberated areas' in the north had been skewed towards rural policy, developed, moreover, during wartime (Selden 1995: 169–213). Now in power in peacetime, the CPC had to govern large cities in the name of a working class with militant traditions – both real and imagined. This presented an entirely new set of challenges and objectives.

In urban areas, the Party embarked on a policy of compromise and reassurance towards capital. The 'Common Programme' was adopted by the Chinese People's Political Consultative Conference (CPPCC) at its first session in September 1949. Described by Liu Shaoqi as a 'people's programme of revolutionary national construction' (*yi bu renmin geming jianguo gangling*) (Bo Yibo 1991: 28), the document was distinguished by the complete absence of the term 'socialism' and instead concentrated on re-establishing industrial production under the 'people's democratic dictatorship'. In June 1949, Mao explained who was in and who was out.

> Who are the people? At the present stage in China, they are the working class, the peasantry, the urban petty bourgeoisie and the national bourgeoisie. These classes, led by the working class and the Communist Party, unite to form their own state and elect their own government; they enforce their dictatorship over the running dogs of imperialism – the landlord class and bureaucrat-bourgeoisie, as well as the representatives of those classes, the Kuomintang reactionaries and their accomplices – suppress them, allow them only to behave themselves and not to be unruly in word or deed.
>
> (Mao Zedong 1949)

Promoting a spirit of cross-class alliance building, the Common Programme stated that the new government promote nation-building and prosperity by 'taking into account both public and private interests, of benefiting both labour and capital, of mutual aid between the city and the countryside, and circulation of goods between China and abroad' (CPPCC 1949: 43).

As we saw in the previous chapter, in terms of industrial relations, the policy that emerged from the programme became known as *lao-zi liang li* i.e. 'benefiting both labour and capital'. Xu dates this policy from 1949 until 1957 by which time the party had completed the 'socialist transformation of the means of production' (Bo Yibo 1991: 2), and maps three distinct phases: an initial period in which capital occupied a dominant position; a second period with labour in the ascendancy; and a third period in which capital, as an expression of concrete class interests and power, was entirely eliminated (Xu Xiaohong 2003: 15).

Capital rising – and falling

It is difficult to overestimate the seriousness of the economic situation of the republic's early years. The weakening of central authority by war and widespread warlordism had resulted in the wholesale neglect of vital elements of China's economy. Industry was paralysed by hyperinflation and there was widespread

Labour unrest in the state sector 59

chaos in the markets and trading (Harris 1978: 37; Xu Xiaohong 2003: 16). On the other hand, a sense of optimism came from unexpected quarters. The *Far Eastern Economic Review* (*FEER*) concluded in early January 1950 that 'private trade is doing well and profits are high' (*FEER* 12 January 1950 cited by Harris 1978: 42). Such sanguinity was more likely an expression of editorial relief at the conciliatory noises towards industrialists coming from the CPC leadership rather than a measured economic assessment. It was also a little quick off the mark. Between January and April 1950, 2945 factories across 14 major cities closed down; 1567 shut in Shanghai in the month of April 1950 alone, and a further 2948 in May. Between March and April of the same year, national unemployment increased by 'hundreds of thousands' and production in key sectors dropped dramatically in the first five months of 1950: cotton by 38 per cent, silks and satins by 47 per cent, tobacco by 59 per cent and paper by 31 per cent (Xu Xiaohong 2003: 16–17). Then, as now, creating jobs was a key issue for the Party and this meant '[W]e should introduce suitable readjustments in industry and commerce and in taxation to improve our relations with the national bourgeoisie rather than aggravate these relations' (Mao Zedong 1950). The strategy of allowing capital to gain the ascendancy on the industrial front was cranked up a gear. Thus, as the economy recovered '[T]he number of businessmen in eight major cities increased by twenty-seven per cent by the end of 1951, and the average rate of profit was a remarkable twenty-nine per cent in 1951 and thirty one per cent in 1953' (Statistical Work Bulletin 1956 cited by Gluckstein 1957: 198).

Capital's ascendancy did not go unchallenged. Many workers found that the benefits of national liberation did not match their expectations for the new order. Throughout the period 1949–1957, it appeared to some workers – particularly young workers and apprentices – that the benefits of liberation seemed to diminish in inverse proportion to the degree that the increasingly state-controlled media talked up the role of the working class in bringing the CPC to power and keeping it there.

Indeed, the role of the working class in China's revolutionary history remains a moot point. It has been argued that its distance from the revolutionary frontline, dating from the CPC's urban defeats by the Guomindang in 1927, was a key factor in the Party's labour policies once in power. Gluckstein, for example, argued that the 'urban working class did not play any role in Mao's rise to power' and this contributed to the prohibition of the right to strike and 'compulsory arbitration' introduced in the 1950 Regulations Governing the Procedures for the Settlement of Labour Disputes (Gluckstein 1957: 214). Four years later, as the Party entered the second stage of 'benefiting both labour and capital' and embarked on a programme of nationalization, it hardly endeared itself to workers with new laws on labour discipline. According to Harris the 'Outline Regulations for State-Owned Enterprises' (1954) were little more than a 'foreman's charter' (Harris 1978: 91) that concentrated on discipline and the determination of wages and conditions at the expense of worker participation in management.[2] On the other hand, Perry has contended that the skilled urban working class background of individual CPC labour leaders such as Li Lisan was an important factor in their securing the

60   Labour unrest in the state sector

lifetime employment policy for urban workers via *danwei* membership (Perry 1997: 13). Nearer to the argument proposed in this book is the aforementioned view that it was – and remains – working class militancy, actual and the threat thereof, that has been a consistent and dominant influence on the labour policies of the CPC in general and the ACFTU in particular.

Less problematic than determining the extent of the working class's participation in the revolutionary victory is the fact that workers were certainly quick to express their disappointment and opposition to the compromises deemed necessary during the first stage of the aforementioned benefiting both labour and capital policy. The Party, principally acting through the unions, expended considerable efforts to restrain the daily fact of class struggle in urban areas by simultaneously trying to persuade workers to temper their demands and expanding employment. Thus, the ACFTU was instructed to draft and ratify two temporary methods (*banfa*) – on collective contracts and labour relations – and a set of rules (*guiding*) on dispute resolution. In the private sector, the institutional manifestation of this regulatory regime was the Labour-Capital Consultative Conference (LCCC). LCCCs were established in factories and shops of more than 50 workers and were also permitted at industrial (*chanye*) and sectoral (*hangye*) level. They operated under guidelines (*zhishi*) issued by the Ministry of Labour in April 1950.[3] The chairing of these meetings rotated between the labour side – usually the trade union – and owner of the enterprise with both sides having power of veto. The result, according to the ACFTU chairman of the time, Li Lisan, was a 'genuinely equal, voluntary problem-solving' process of consultation over working conditions that included collective contracts, production bonuses and fines, factory rules, wages, working time, occupational safety, injury and disease, welfare and special conditions for women workers (Xu Xiaohong 2003: 20). We should note, however, that Li's qualifications to judge whether or not the LCCC was an institutional expression of industrial equality were somewhat marred by his simultaneously held position as Minister of Labour; at least they were until he was sacked from his union post following accusations of economism in 1951. In fact, it is difficult to ascertain how effective this institution was in advancing workers' rights, facilitating worker participation in management or indeed reassuring capitalists that their property and assets would remain safe for the foreseeable future. Harper holds that, at the end of the day, the LCCC was a 'potent instrument for use by the Party or union against the capitalists' (Harper 1971: 119) which may well have been the case by the mid 1950s as the institution approached the end of its shelf life.

In keeping with Mao's relaxed attitude towards capitalists, Liu Shaoqi and to a lesser extent Li Lisan made repeated calls to workers in the private sector to moderate their demands. First, workers needed to be educated that there were limits to the exercise of their new power and status. Somewhat disingenuously Li announced that, unlike the land reform process, factories could not and should not be divided up for workers to manage themselves – this would only lead to unemployment (Sheehan 1998: 16–17). In his Tianjin Speech in the late spring of 1949, Liu had argued for cautious post-liberation industrial policies.

Labour unrest in the state sector 61

> Some people argue 'if the capitalists don't open [or re-open] their factories then we [the workers] can open the factories ourselves.' Have there been cooperatively-managed factories opened up? Yes, many times, but not one has been successful. This is the reality and we have made this kind of mistake [too] many times in the past. Workers' cooperatives have not been well managed so we won't allow them.
>
> (Liu Shaoqi 1988: 352–3)

In the same speech, Liu argued that the problem in China was not that there were too many capitalists but rather that there were too few and that to harm capitalists would, in effect, harm the workers themselves by causing more unemployment and slowing down the development of the economy. It was perhaps no accident that Liu made these appeals in Tianjin which was liberated on 15 January 1949. Despite his words of caution, Tianjin's workers heralded liberation with

> street-level committees [that] had been set up by rank-and-file cadres in the aftermath of liberation with district-level governments based on them; in June 1949 the street-level committees were abolished and the district governments reduced to district offices of the municipal government set up by the Military Control Committee.
>
> (Maitan 1976: 21)

As was the case in other cities, workers and grassroots cadres often reacted to the new order with an enthusiasm that had the potential to manifest itself in new and militant institutions of power – as was the case in Tianjin – that were not always overly concerned with the intricacies of the national Party line at the time. Although the Party acted quickly to demonstrate its political supremacy over capital, it was clear that some union activists and cadres in the liberated areas were nevertheless taking the side of militant workers anyway. So much so that in January 1949 Mao issued a directive aimed at newly liberated cities that pointed out the danger of emulating 'agricultural socialism' in the cities, which led to the 'mistake of too strongly advocating the one-sided, temporary interests of the workers' (Mao Zedong 1949 cited by Maitan 1976: 21).

Turning to the unions, Harris has argued that in the new People's Republic, unlike the Soviet Union, 'there was no debate on the role of the trade unions' in the first years of CPC government (Harris 1978: 104). The labour unrest that distinguished the first two post-liberation years and the debates it prompted demonstrates that this was an oversimplification. In fact, differences of opinion over the role of trade unions emerged at both ends of the labour movement. At the top, ACFTU chair Li Lisan argued strongly that the policy of mutual benefit was not the same as mutual 'cooperation' between labour and capital and outlined three main differences. First, mutual cooperation was essentially a social democratic slogan that ignored the primacy of class struggle in the name of class cooperation. Second, labour-capital cooperation did not permit strikes while the policy of mutual benefit implicitly recognized that strikes were a way of preventing the long-term consolidation of pro-capital forces. Third, mutual benefit to both sides placed economic development over all other concerns, as opposed to labour-capital cooperation which, according to Li Lisan, aimed to ensure the future of the capitalist system by 'muddling the class consciousness of workers' (Li Lisan cited in Xu Xiaohong 2003: 17–18). Given his lack of confidence in workers' capacity to run factories, it is hardly surprising that Liu Shaoqi took a rather more nuanced view on the question of strikes and whether or not trade unions should organize them as a way to bring capitalists into line. In his 'Report on the Trade Union Question' he stated that strikes harmed capitalists and workers alike and, although they were not banned, the Party would not organize strikes and would go out of its way to ensure that they didn't happen.

> In cases where capitalists have mistreated workers there is a need to conduct appropriate [levels of] struggle and this struggle may take various forms. But we do not advocate strikes. All problems that arise can be solved without recourse to strike action.
> (Liu Shaoqi 1988: 398–9)

Such differences translated into frequent shifts of position among 'the newly-established official unions' from enthusiastic support for workers' demands to wholehearted backing of the Party against union autonomy or for the dismissal of workers' demands by enterprise management. At the other end of the labour movement, workers in both the state and private sectors were resorting to strike action anyway as they 'lost any chance of exerting influence through the formal channels of democratic management' (Sheehan 1998: 23) such as the LCCC and its more robust equivalent in the state sector, the WRC.

The Party's response to the rise in labour unrest was to purge the leadership of the ACFTU in order to stamp out the development of syndicalist tendencies and launch a series of campaigns – the Democratic Reform Movement, The Three-Anti and the Five-Anti movements – that aimed to put capital on the back foot, institutionalize worker participation in management and, in effect, prepare industry for full nationalization and the attendant industrial peace this would – hopefully – bring. These campaigns gave formal impetus to the labour movement even as they brought it firmly under state control via the ACFTU. At the 7th ACFTU Congress in 1953, union cadres at primary level were heavily criticized for economism, while some workers pointed to this Congress as the point where the ACFTU 'lost their guts' as it formally bowed to Party leadership (*Workers' Daily* 21 May 1957, cited in Sheehan 1998: 13).

Workers rising – and falling

The debate over the role of trade unions and their subsequent total incorporation into the state machinery cleared the path for the ACFTU to become an enthusiastic supporter and enterprise-level implementation agency for China's First Five-Year Plan. Launched in 1953, the Plan heralded a renewed emphasis on production and the further concentration of political power in the hands of the Party.

At the time, there was an underlying feeling of disappointment as the 'greatly stimulated class consciousness of the workers was prevented from developing into directly political forms but was channelled into the expansion of the trade unions' (Maitan 1976: 21). Indeed, disenchantment with the lack of political gains from the nationalization of hitherto private enterprise – the 'socialist transformation of the [private] means of production' no less – contributed to the strike wave of late 1956 to early 1957. On the other hand, the working class had made collective social and economic gains under the first four years of CPC rule and this progress continued under the new plan. By 1957, there were almost nine million more workers than in 1952, unemployment had decreased and 'wages were about 30 per cent higher' (Maitan 1976: 25). Yet, as the plan reached its largely successful conclusion, strikes broke out in late 1956 and rolled on through to spring of the following year as workers participated in the Hundred Flowers Movement, formally launched in May 1956 (Sheehan 1998: 47). The campaign was initially sluggish, with few responding to the Party's invitation to free speech. But by May the following year, even the *People's Daily* was publishing articles calling for the 'right of the people to freely express differences in opinions' (Maitan 1976: 39).

The eradication of capitalist class interests was a process that began with the Three- and Five-Anti movements and ended with full-scale nationalization during the first Plan which was deemed complete by 1957. Yet, labour unrest continued to influence state policy. The flush of success derived from nationalization was qualified by the news of a major uprising in Hungary and huge strikes in the Polish city of Poznan. These factors combined to alarm the authorities into permitting a more open atmosphere in China during 1956–57. In his famous speech of February 1957, 'On the correct handling of contradictions among the people' Mao argued that the period of 'the large-scale, turbulent class struggles of the masses characteristic of times of revolution have in the main come to an end' (Mao Zedong 1957) and social relations and the contradictions that they threw up were henceforth of a non-antagonistic nature. Mao's speech also acknowledged the 'possibility of mass unrest provoked by bureaucratism' (Maitan 1976: 39), even as striking workers in Shanghai were employing the slogan 'Let's create another Hungarian Incident' (Perry 1993: 11).

In fact, while intellectuals and social democrats initially displayed a reluctance to take up the Party's invitation to free debate and criticism in the early stages of the Hundred Flowers, workers showed much less reticence in airing their views. Indeed Gipouloux argues that Mao's 'On Contradictions' speech was in part a response to worker unrest (Gipouloux 1986), although others point to a rapidly deteriorating relationship between rural cadres and peasants following collectivization and 'movements away from the cooperatives' that had begun in 1955 (Maitan 1978: 30), and continued throughout 1956. While there are no publicly available completed statistics on strikes in this period, incomplete figures compiled by the ACFTU at the time give us a snapshot of the militancy unfurling.

> In the cities incidents of strikes and petitions occurred continuously. According to incomplete statistics from the ACFTU, in 1956 there were 29 strikes and

57 petitions amounting to 86 incidents in total. There were six in the first quarter, 19 in the second, 20 in the third and 41 in the fourth quarter ... that involved between tens, hundreds and even thousands of people. Between October 1956 and June 1957 in the city of Tianjin there were 110 incidents of workers' disturbances that directly or indirectly involved 3,683 people. In Guangdong province there were 136 strikes during 1956. Incomplete statistics for the period from September 1956 until March 1957 record more than 10,000 workers taking strike action.

(Li *et al.* 2005: 3)

While these figures represent only a small minority of workers in a rapidly expanding working class, the numbers are almost certainly conservative and represent no more than what an only recently chastened and purged ACFTU was prepared to admit to Party leaders. At the same time, the Party itself appeared to be upping the stakes. On 7 April 1957, the *People's Daily* formally blamed the strikes on 'bureaucratic methods'. This was followed by a 'sensational interview' given by the literary intellectual and senior Party member Chou Yang in which

he recognised the legitimacy of strikes and protest demonstrations and, declared that it was wrong forcibly to suppress such dissent and called for a redistribution of the national income so as to avoid marked inequalities.

(Maitan 1976: 39)

Given the national and international situation, the strike wave was politically significant and to a large extent represented disappointment at the results of nationalization, the new national wage structure, the authoritarian methods of many enterprise cadres and exhaustion resulting from the Plan's emphasis on developing heavy industry and ensuring continued rapid accumulation. Quoting Gipouloux (1986: 186), Sheehan found that the situation in 1957 reflected conditions in the previous year.

Looking at disputes in 1957, we find that '[w]ages, authoritarian assignments, working and living conditions were at the centre of all demands' with inequality between workers' and cadres' households a particular cause of friction and the picture is similar in 1956.

(Sheehan 1998: 55)

During the spring of 1957, as much as half of the workforce on the Guangzhou docks came out in an undeclared strike against a new shift system that reduced net monthly pay. More worrying still for the Party was that these complaints were beginning to take on a political character that ran the risk of going beyond the non-antagonistic contradictions formulated by Mao in February 1957. For example, in the capital itself

An embryonic form of workers' management grew up at the Peking Tram Company, where a workers' conference won the right to control management, set up plans for production and finance, elect the directors and his associates and decide on wage problems, social welfare etc.

(Maitan 1976: 39)

As the Hundred Flowers reached its zenith and working class militancy continued to grow, autonomous unions began to make an appearance, mostly restricted to a single enterprise, although there was 'some liaison and coordination between enterprises and districts' (Perry 1993: 11). These were quickly suppressed in the Anti-Rightist movement that followed the Hundred Flowers Movement. Setting a precedent for future working class activists, the workers who were sent to labour camps during the Anti-Rightist clampdown were labelled 'bad elements' rather than 'rightists', a political tag reserved for intellectuals.

The ACFTU responded to the strikes with a cautious attempt to carve out a more autonomous role resulting in a second purge of the leadership. In an attempt to prevent the unrest building up yet more steam, the Party employed a strategy that was to be replicated during the early years of the reform period: the Staff and Workers' Representative Congresses (SWRC). They were introduced in 1957 following six months of debate over their democratic character. Sheehan notes that despite the hullabaloo accompanying their arrival – an event given an international dimension following the events in Hungary earlier in the same year – workers largely ignored the congresses as relations between workers and cadres continued to deteriorate (Sheehan 1998: 75).

The cultural revolution

The first decade of CPC rule ended with a thoroughly domesticated trade union movement and a physically exhausted working class. The Great Leap Forward of 1958–9 saw the CPC exhorting workers to 'catch up with England' within 15 years, largely on the basis of willpower and mostly disastrous technical 'innovations' on the shop floor. Exhaustion turned to hunger in the cities and mass starvation in some rural areas as the most serious famine in human history descended on the countryside (Becker 1996). The mistakes of the Great Leap and the tragedy of Three Years of Bitterness were traumatic enough to facilitate a swing in the balance of power away from Mao towards Party 'technocrats' led by Liu Shaoqi (Karnow 1984: 132–4). This in turn opened up the space for Deng and Liu to prosecute policies that allowed limited free enterprise in the countryside and a relaxation in the relentless pace of production in industry.

By 1963, a recovery of sorts hove into view and Mao deemed the economy sufficiently buoyant to risk attempting a return to total power and the Maoists launched the Socialist Education Campaign of 1963–4. After this somewhat halfhearted attempt to radicalize literary and artistic work petered out, Mao garnered his forces and, in September 1965, embarked on his plan to 'storm the citadel' by launching the Great Proletarian Cultural Revolution, nothing less than an extraordinary and prolonged attack on the Party bureaucracy itself. As an arm of that bureaucracy, the following 10 years were to prove a disaster for the ACFTU.

Radical Red Guard organizations targeted the unions as evidence of the continuing existence of capitalist relations of production. In late 1966, Jiang Qing – Mao's wife – supported the formation of a new trade union, the All China Red Workers General Rebellion Corps that 'had taken over the Ministry of Labour and planned to dissolve the National Federation of Trade Unions' [ACFTU] (Karnow 1984: 264).

Trade union cadres were subjected to struggle campaigns conducted by contracted migrant workers and apprentices angry at their exclusion from the full benefits of the *danwei* system described in Chapter 1. As more and more workers took part in the Cultural Revolution, strikes spread through major cities and brought much of industry to a standstill. The strikes were inspired and partly led by the aforementioned young migrant workers from the countryside who employed Maoist rhetoric to 'camouflage a basically economic labour revolt' that demanded improved wages, housing and medical care (Karnow 1984: 265). Despite the material basis for the strikes, they were quickly politicized in the increasingly chaotic atmosphere. To a certain extent this was inevitable because wages, the intensity of labour and working conditions in general were all determined exclusively by the state. For their part, management was only too happy to oblige strikers' demands in order to deflect criticism, personal attacks or worse. The strikes spread from the ports to the railways and the mines, dramatically heightening the political tension as armed struggles broke out between 'conservative' and 'radical' Red Guard factions that both claimed to represent the proletariat.

Mao's initial support for the working class's participation in the Cultural Revolution suggests that he had miscalculated. Radical leaders, including Mao, quickly began to backtrack as panicky decrees from Beijing ordered workers to stay at their posts. Clearly, it was one thing for students to attack teachers and Party cadres, or for the trade unions, always a potential rival bureaucracy to the Party, to be brandished as relics of capitalism. However, it was another matter entirely when a mobilized working class armed with at least the rudiments of Marxist analysis took advantage of a violent faction fight within the Party to push for higher wages and better working conditions. Within weeks of issuing instructions to Red Guards to 'storm the positions' of Party power, Mao resorted to what ruling classes generally do when faced with social movements they deem out of their control: he called in the army and five days later, on 28 January 1967, decreed that the 'cultural revolution should be postponed for the time being' (Karnow 1984: 283). This by no means brought an immediate end to the struggles and indeed during the following 18 months China appeared on the edge of civil war on at least two occasions. However, Mao's confidence in the PLA to restore production and some sense of routine proved well placed, although a number of senior PLA leaders were sacrificed on the radicals' altars in the process. Order was restored, as we saw in Chapter 1, with the establishment of Revolutionary Committees. Formally, the committees represented a triple alliance between recalled Party officials – of whom many had previously been targets of radical factions and were taking great risks in resuming political responsibilities – Red Guard organizations – but only those approved by the army – and the PLA itself.

But it was the army that had the guns – or at least most of them – and as Zhou Enlai admitted in February 1967 'the country was under military control' (Karnow 1984: 297).

The first three years of the Cultural Revolution (1966–9) left the unintended legacy of significant numbers of workers and young people with direct experience of organizing as a result of their membership of Red Guard organizations. From mid 1966 onwards, local governments' solution to this dilemma was to send millions of university and high school youth down to the countryside to 'learn from the peasants'. This movement picked up pace once the call for order was established and its goal shifted away from encouraging political exchanges between urban youth and peasants to the more practical one of preventing organized groups of young people from stirring up trouble in urban areas while alleviating the growing problem of unemployment in the process. Perhaps somewhat ironically, some youngsters joined the army as a preferred option to 'learning from the peasants'.

However, this was hardly a measure that could be applied across the working class – especially not to skilled workers and technocrats – who were needed at the workbench and office. From 1970 to 1976, a hectoring, Gang of Four-driven emphasis on production and labour discipline, combined with the absence of significant wage rises, meant that the limited gains from the 1967 strikes were cancelled out. The resulting tensions were captured by the big-character poster written by four former Red Guard activists under the pseudonym of Li Yizhe that went up around Guangzhou during the autumn of 1974. The poster, entitled 'On socialist democracy and the legal system' pointed out that, despite the speechifying and violence of the Cultural Revolution, China remained a country of great inequality. The poster pointed to the lack of material incentives for workers, the pay freeze and the special privileges enjoyed by Party cadres as well as referring to the lack of democracy and legality in China.

As the Gang of Four lumbered from one political campaign to another, it faced increasing labour unrest. In Hangzhou in 1975, over 30,000 PLA troops were deployed to bring an end to a 'summer of unrest' (Sheehan 1998: 146). This was immediately followed by dissident activity in Nanjing that spread throughout China and culminated in the 'Tiananmen Incident of April Fifth', 1976. During the Chinese Qing Ming Festival – traditionally a day to remember the dead – up to half a million ordinary citizens travelled to Tiananmen Square to lay wreaths and poems in honour of Zhou Enlai whom many revered for saving China from descending into civil war during the Cultural Revolution. Correctly interpreting this outpouring of collective grief as direct criticism, the government removed the wreaths from the Square overnight, which led to violent and widespread unrest the day after, 5 April: the April Fifth Movement was born. It constituted a short 'spontaneous, bottom-up' expression of ongoing disdain against leftist dogma. The government's crackdown was correspondingly brutal as workers voiced dissenting opinions on the widespread existence of favouritism, and cadres' hypocrisy and inequality. Although the dissent was quelled relatively quickly, the end of 10 years of 'fundamentalist Maoism' was now in sight. Within four weeks of Mao's

68 *Labour unrest in the state sector*

death on 9 September 1976, the Gang of Four was under arrest. The 'ten years of chaos' was over.

Deng Xiaoping's long road back from manual work in the mid 1960s to 'paramount' leader in 1978 was closely followed by an outbreak of open debate in Beijing that was emulated in other cities. The Democracy Wall Movement developed around a wall near the centre of Beijing on which a myriad of 'big-character posters' were pasted. Their content discussed not only the Chinese political system, but also systems and events taking part in other parts of the world as well – especially Poland and the rise of the Solidarność trade union. In many ways, the movement took up where the April Fifth Movement had been suppressed, and indeed it was the reversal of the government's official verdict on the latter that sparked the flowering of posters, speeches and magazines that constituted such an important part of the Democracy Wall Movement sometimes referred to as the Beijing Spring. While the movement did not constitute a mass, spontaneous working class movement in the vein of April Fifth, it certainly provided workers with an opportunity to express their disappointments and grievances with the *danwei* system: wages falling behind inflation, the existence of a bureaucratic elite, and absence of effective democratic accountability. The journal *Sailing Ship*, based around the Taiyuan Iron and Steel works, was unequivocal about the need for better worker representation arguing that workers

> must begin to organize themselves, to rely on their own strength, and to elect their own representatives to speak for them, and if at any time their elected representatives do not represent them properly, they will be recalled and another election held. This sort of demand on the part of the broad popular masses is the social basis for China's democratic reform.
>
> (Sheehan 1998: 187)

The Democracy Wall Movement went beyond the parameters set for it by Deng Xiaoping and the party reformers, with whom it had a temporary collaboration. As we saw in the Introduction, the CPC tried to address the workers' grievances by stressing the democratic role of workers' congresses in the factories and playing up the role of a recently restored ACFTU. The latter certainly helped to restore the careers and status of union cadres but, as we shall see, it was not to save the working class from capitalism.

Labour unrest in the reforming economy

The early reform era: 1978–1997

The role of workers during the Cultural Revolution only served to reinforce the experience of the 1950s when two major strike waves had demonstrated the economic and political muscle of the working class and its capacity to influence state policies. As we saw in the Introduction, the government consequently proceeded with prudence in reforming China's industrial relations topography as it entered a period of sustained economic reform. Nevertheless, following pilots, industrial managers were given power over hire and fire in 1986 and the spectre of dismissal and joblessness returned as a topic of conversation in working class homes.

During the 1980s, there were scattered incidents of worker unrest in the SOEs. Generally speaking, however, the reluctance of enterprise directors to make use of their new-found autonomy in order to 'avoid unrest' (Liu Aiyu 2005: 86) combined with the Party's reluctance to commit to a dramatic rise in urban unemployment. Consequently, the destruction of the 'iron rice bowl' was not a one-off event but a simmering combination of regulatory change, foreign capital, competition from TVEs and the removal of ideological constraints on the accumulation of wealth as urbanites were encouraged to leave their state jobs and 'jump into the sea' (*xiahai*) of entrepreneurial activity. In short, the iron rice bowl's disappearance was a direct result of the return of capitalist labour relations rather than a deliberate state policy.

Alongside this transformation, economic tensions were building as the removal of price controls on the long-subsidized basics of urban living led to a rise in the cost of living. While workers had seen a considerable increase in their wages, this was partly cancelled out by inflation. Frustration, both with reform and with the consequences of reform, resulted in student demonstrations, principally in Shanghai, during the mid 1980s. In retrospect, although these demonstrations were significant, they were a dry run for the unprecedented wave of popular revolt that engulfed the cities in the spring of 1989. In April of that year, students began to gather in Beijing's Tiananmen Square to discuss politics and organize demonstrations to demand an end to corruption and the introduction of open government. The protesting students emerged on the streets from democracy salons held on the university campuses that dated back to the previous demonstrations of 1986–7. As the crowds on the Square increased in size, the students organized themselves into autonomous societies and associations, independent of the official student union.

The activity in the Square began to attract the attention of Beijing citizens, including one of the founder members of the Beijing Workers Autonomous Federation (BWAF) and a so-called 'black hand' of Beijing, Han Dongfang (Black and Munro 1993). Soon enough, Han and other workers were making speeches calling for an end to corruption and solidarity with the students. By the end of April, the BWAF was organized. According to founder members, the original core group was made up of mainly blue-collar workers from steel factories, the railways and the aviation industry, as well as shop assistants and casual workers. However, as Han later explained, most of the almost 20,000 plus workers who signed up to the BWAF did so as 'individual citizens' rather than workplace-based organizers. Still, the WAFs spread to other cities and there is little doubt that a sense of panic was enveloping Party leaders, some of whom, such as Zhao Ziyang, even appeared to jump ship and side with the students – though pointedly, not with the workers.

The BWAF initially concentrated its activity on signing up members and distributing leaflets critical of the official trade union. The organizers also set up a loudspeaker system and began broadcasting their opinions and demands. Both the

70   Labour unrest in the state sector

leaflets and broadcasts proved popular with Beijingers who had come to see what was going on. This popularity translated into huge demonstrations in support of the students and their demands for cleaner government and democratic accountability. But while they had a strong presence on demonstrations, the BWAF failed to make inroads where it really mattered: in Beijing's offices and factories. Internally, and always aware of the state's potential to move against them, the BWAF concentrated on short-term capacity-building such as consolidation, publicity, recruitment and development of resources and leadership skills. It also began to draft a constitution and develop a programme of demands that echoed workers' propaganda in previous episodes of labour unrest. BWAF leaflets offered critical assessments of cadre privilege, income gaps between workers and managers, lack of workplace democracy, poor safety standards and the deterioration in living standards. Implicit in all this was a recognition that workers were losing out in the reforms. Above all, there was the demand for legal status and the right to organize outside the ACFTU; not, they stressed, to replace the official union, but to allow workers a choice that would ultimately be of benefit to all concerned – including the ACFTU itself!

During its short existence, the BWAF looked outwards. Relations with the students were initially very weak, and throughout May its tents were restricted by student leaders to a far corner of the Square, despite the efforts of some worker organizers to forge links. The BWAF also had contacts with sympathetic sections within the ACFTU. Importantly, the organizers made it clear that they meant to build the union through constitutional means and, as an organization, neither opposed nor supported the rule of the CPC. However, as student numbers on the Square dwindled and the balance of forces began to shift back towards the authorities, the official position of the ACFTU towards the WAFs hardened and on 2 June 1989 the *Workers' Daily* called for the banning of the WAFs as illegal organizations. Two days later, troops fought their way into the Square, destroying BWAF tents in the process. In the repression that followed, hundreds of workers suspected of taking part in WAF organizations were imprisoned and the WAFs themselves disappeared.

Yet, in the aftermath of the violence, workers' activism continued to make its mark on policy. Some have argued that SOE workers succeeded in using ostensibly reinvigorated channels of democratic management and the temporary halt to SOE reform that followed the events of spring 1989 to further their collective interests. Hussain and Zhuang claimed to have found evidence of enterprise-level collective bargaining developing in the early 1990s and the Party's subsequent move to control this development by channelling the demands into revised regulations on collective consultation (Hussain and Zhuang 1998: 43–68). However, as I stated in Chapter 1, while wages did rise in the state sector, this was more likely a result of managers wishing to avoid attracting attention to their enterprises rather than overt labour unrest, especially given the restrictive political climate of the time. Nevertheless, the WAFs had deeply alarmed the Party and concessions were on the table for a short time.

Deng's Southern Tour revived the economic reform process and calmed post-Tiananmen anxieties about stability. Five years later, as negotiations to enter the

WTO gathered pace, the 15th Party Congress came to an historic decision on the fate of the country's SOEs that was to have an irreversible impact on the Chinese working class: 'holding on to the large and letting go of the small' (*fang xiao zhua da*) i.e. allowing smaller SOEs to go bankrupt or privatize but keeping medium and large SOEs under state control. In the event, it was a green light for many SOEs to shed huge numbers of workers regardless of their size. Not surprisingly, this decision, which was accompanied by further expansion of the private sector, heralded a new and dramatic wave of labour unrest that climaxed with troops stationed, but not deployed, on the outskirts of the north-eastern oil town of Daqing.

Prior to a discussion of these dramatic events, it would be timely to remind ourselves that the reintroduction of private capital and FDI as engines for economic growth and employment creation were already heralding profound changes in the demography of China's working class. Although new private- and joint-invested factories were at first restricted to four SEZs, these zones were expanded to a further 14 coastal cities in 1984. To begin with, relatively small numbers of peasants were permitted to apply for permission to leave the land temporarily and work in factories established in the various SEZs. Guangdong province was one of the main recipients of investment and its number one attraction for migrants and investors alike was a former fishing village that was being rapidly transformed into an export platform – Shenzhen. Zhejiang province in East China was no slower off the mark but differed from Guangdong in that it initially drew on home-grown entrepreneurial traditions and domestic investment rather than FDI to open up thousands of small- and medium-size enterprises (*Economist* 1995: 39–40). But no matter whether it was foreign or domestic capital that was attracting peasants into off-farm work, the net result was the same: the remaking, in struggle, of the Chinese working class. We will return to the struggles of private sector workers in Chapter 3.

Defending decent work and the demise of the state sector

Despite the demands raised by workers in the 1960s, 1970s and 1980s, Chinese urban workers' employment conditions compared favourably with those of other developing countries. The absence of freedom of association notwithstanding, the *danwei* system had awarded workers with most of the ILO's current benchmarks for 'decent work'. It is therefore worth briefly revisiting the *danwei* theme – discussed in detail in Chapter 1 – from a different perspective: its impact on workers' capacity to organize and defend it.

In recalling the *danwei* from a labour unrest perspective, it is possible to extract from the literature two basic interpretations that I have termed respectively 'the *danwei* as given' and 'the *danwei* as won'. Weighing in for the former, Walder viewed the *danwei* as a structure of complex, hierarchical but interdependent relationships of interests through which the Party was able to maintain control over the working class. He termed the organized dependency of workers and clientelist relationships between workers and *danwei* management that emerged from it 'communist neo-traditionalism' (Walder 1986). This arrangement enabled the Party to exercise a 'peaceful coercion' over the working class (You Ji 1998: 12). In fact, You Ji stiffens Walder's communist neo-traditionalist argument by reaching back to China's paternalistic, centralized past, describing the *danwei* as a 'tightly integrated mechanism of party/state control. Resembling China's traditional authoritarian state/family power structure, the system requires a high concentration of financial and remunerative power in the hands of the leaders' (You Ji 1998: 135).

We might easily conclude – as many capitalists have – from these studies that the Chinese working class had been reduced, in its last days, to a fading aristocracy rendered politically apathetic by, and economically dependent on, Party largesse. But such a formulation hardly stands up to the periodic expressions of militancy summarized above, and not surprisingly, there are alternative political interpretations of the *danwei* system. Championing 'the *danwei* as won' faction, Weil contends that the comparatively high standard of living enjoyed by urban workers in SOEs and, to a lesser extent collectively-owned enterprises (COE), was the fruit of socialist revolution through which workers *won* not just job security but access to health care, housing, pensions, education for their children and recreational opportunities (Weil 1996: 35). Moreover, workers already under assault from globalization made a political decision to defend these fruits of the revolution when economic reform threatened them (Philion 2007: 37–55). For some, this was a response that has put Chinese workers at the forefront of the international struggle against the neo-liberal offensive on the *danwei* and its traditional securities.

In an attempt to ameliorate the shock of restructuring and, no doubt, the potential fallout from unrest, the Party rolled out the *xiagang* policy, discussed in the previous chapter, on a national basis. Its essence was to retain laid-off workers on SOE books for up to three years, a policy that obviously carried the capacity to temper and defuse workers' resistance to restructuring as disputes retained a distinctly enterprise-based character. As I demonstrate later in this chapter, this dictated that most resistance took the form of demonstrations ranging from the violent – on one occasion I witnessed an SOE manager 'air-planed' through the streets by furious laid-off workers – to more sedentary sit-ins by pensioners in front of government buildings.[4] But no matter how radical or passive the forms of collective action taken, they rarely delayed or halted production itself and as a consequence the juggernaut of accumulation continued to build up steam. And although private capital was not yet driving the vehicle, it certainly had its hands on the map.

Reviewing unrest

The literature on labour unrest in the state sector during the 1990s, and especially during the period following the 15th Party Congress in 1997, demonstrates not only the cathartic nature of the transition but also the powerful legacy of the command economy. We should start by remembering a powerful constraint on interpreting this phase of labour history: the unavailability of comprehensive nationwide statistics on the number and form of workers' actions, especially with regard to strikes.[5] Without exception, scholars refer to the relatively rapid post-Congress build up of resistance to restructuring and mass lay-offs and point to official incomplete statistics, newspaper reports, academic papers and their own fieldwork as evidence. The absence of complete data renders it difficult to draw definitive conclusions. Yet, if nothing else, the paucity of reliable statistics adds value to the scholarly interpretations in the literature.

Writing in 2002, Blecher argued that resistance in the state sector, though widespread, had 'not yet produced significant strike waves and protest movements'. Somewhat despairingly, he asked 'why then has a class that was so well treated, mighty, confident and active in the recent past essentially rolled over, or better, allowed itself to be rolled over, in the past two decades?' (Blecher 2002: 286–7).

His fieldwork was concentrated in Tianjin and to be sure Blecher goes out of his way to remind readers that the city was not subject to the economic deprivation that emerged elsewhere as a consequence of SOE restructuring – although it does have a tradition of labour militancy dating back to the beginning of the twentieth century, examined in detail by Hershatter (1986). Blecher notes that the relative prosperity of the city partially explains his interviewees' apparent acceptance of the market and the absence of resistance to it.[6] Blecher argues that this represents acceptance of the state's dominant ideology, i.e. the market, and found that 'workers are more easily saturated with the state's discursive and symbolic messages than peasants' (Blecher 2002: 301). He develops his argument by reminding us of Burawoy's and Luckac's work in Hungary where transition from command economy and its shortages to the promised riches of the market atomized workers and encouraged individual rather than collective solutions.

On the other hand, Cai approaches the question from the opposite perspective. Instead of asking why workers have 'rolled over', he asks how workers in an authoritarian regime have been able to mount any form of collective resistance at all! Focusing exclusively on laid-off workers, Cai finds answers primarily in the Chinese tradition of petition and that 'the most important mechanism of mobilization, is not the issue itself, but the presence of organizers, or rather coordinators' (Cai Yongshun 2002: 327–44). He argues that China's tradition of petitioning higher officials dovetails neatly with the system of administrative government that the CPC has relied upon. This, in turn, is particularly suited to laid-off workers who need to attract the intervention of government officials as opposed to direct negotiations with an employer; the point being that laid-off workers are located beyond the workplace and that their struggles are chiefly about subsistence rather than wages and conditions. Thus, when engaged in protest, this group of former workers strives to attract the intervention of higher officials in order to expose the failings of those below them. Faced with a risk of exposure, local lower-level officials have two choices: to meet, at least temporarily, the livelihood demands of the protestors by reallocating money from elsewhere, or deploying riot police to disperse laid-off workers who have no other option but to gather in public places. There would be no point in the protestors setting up factory picket lines as most of their factories were already idle. While there are many examples of violence – we are hampered by the lack of data to construct an accurate picture across the nation – Cai argues that the general practice has been to disperse workers through peaceful means. He cites two interconnected reasons: first, protestors are keen to avoid giving the state a pretext for violence; and second, there are administrative constraints on local governments' use of force, a point I will return to later. Thus, he argues, space opens up for 'non-institutionalised action' by laid-off workers (Cai Yongshun 2002: 343).

Turning to the 'organisers, or rather, coordinators', Cai's research finds that such people act out of a combination of self-interest, community pressure and, occasionally, a sense of justice. These coordinators are essential to the dissemination of information and locating the physical spaces for the action. He found that out of 41 such coordinators, only nine were workers. Of the remainder, 12 were former enterprise leaders, nine were Party members and seven were current enterprise leaders (Cai Yongshun 2002: 335), results that cannot help but remind us of Clarke's work in transitional Russia – cited in Chapter 1 – in which he argued that there was a material basis for the common interest of the entire *trudovoi kollektiv* or collective workforce based on the economic negotiations over the 'plan' (Burawoy *et al.* 1993: 26) or in this case, the lack of it.

Cai's work on protests by laid-off workers also refers to the importance of both the sequence and size of events. Where lay-offs are phased or, to use Cai's word, 'sequenced', and in small- or medium-sized enterprises that do not accommodate their workers in large concentrated housing estates, there is less chance of protests having a significant impact. This is explained by the challenge of forging solidarity between those still holding on to their jobs and those laid off, rendering the task of would-be coordinators in organizing a cohesive response much more difficult. He predicted that restructuring larger SOEs with their concentration of housing and larger numbers of workers would be a more fraught process. As our discussion of widespread protests in 2002 in Daqing will demonstrate, this argument was borne out by events, although in the final analysis the state and enterprise leaders were able to combine the use of limited force with fostering divisions in the workforce to manage the event and effectively hold the line. On the other hand, bankruptcy, according to Cai, is more likely to produce coherent and longer-lasting protests as it tends to descend on the workforce simultaneously, producing material conditions for effective solidarity. He asserts that such actions are led, as often as not, by factory managers or senior technicians and engineers. Again, we are back with Clarke's common material interests (Clarke 1993: 27).

Chen's work on restructuring and privatization demonstrates how actually existing conditions combined with traditional Maoist attitudes in determining the strategy and tactics of SOE workers *if* they chose – and choose – to resist what Lee refers to as the 'whip of the market' (Lee Ching-kwan 1999: 44–71). Echoing Blecher, Chen concurs that 'the majority of workers have been quiescent, passive' but also awards significant weight to the resistance of SOE workers still inside the industrial system whose acts 'reflect the emerging economic conflict that define China's economic transition' (Chen Feng 2003a: 238). For Chen, the crucial difference between this group and Cai's laid-off workers, or Hurst's and O'Brien's 'contentious' pensioners (Hurst and O'Brien 2002: 346–60), is that their factories are still in business and as such hold out the possibility of job retention for workers under new property relations. But it is just these new relations and the *contracts* they require that fly in the face of iron rice bowl traditions. Chen's conclusions are so close to my own, and so well presented, it would be disingenuous not to quote them in full. He states:

> Many protests against restructuring, however, are motivated by what is called a 'suddenly imposed grievance' (Walsh 1981), as they often burst out immediately after a restructuring scheme, which usually entails collective layoffs, is made known to workers. Workers are fully aware of what their life will become if those measures are to be enforced. After all, the suffering caused by layoffs is already painfully visible in society and has been experienced and witnessed by too many people. Protesting workers are determined to prevent it from happening to them – or, at the very least, to ensure their basic well-being after restructuring has taken place. Thus, in this type of protest, strong subsistence anxiety translates into strong claims to firms' property and to a say in the restructuring process. Such claims derived from the old socialist precept of the nature of state property. SOE workers' protests, therefore, may be best viewed as either a refusal to enter new property relations disadvantageous to them or as an attempt at bargaining for some better treatment after restructuring.
>
> (Chen Feng 2003a: 242)

Chen's reference to Walsh's 'suddenly imposed grievance' echoes Cai's identification of the 'sequence' of events as being a major factor in the development and management of protests. Surveying the terrain of protest in China's reform-era industrial relations, Chen identifies three broad points of resistance: those laid off or unemployed and already outside the sphere of production; SOE workers still at the bench but facing major changes to their working conditions as a result of restructuring or privatization; and those in the private sector. He examines the differences and points of convergence and finds that workers resisting restructuring share similar problems with the mainly migrant workers in the capitalist private sector whose protests concentrate on pay and conditions but do not challenge property relations. This is not the case with state sector workers who bring post-liberation traditions and practices to their opposition to restructuring. These traditions are manifested in demands for inclusion in the workplace decision making, especially on matters that have a direct impact on their employment and, as such, 'may threaten their subsistence' (Chen Feng 2003a: 256). Anti-restructuring protests obviously cross over with the protests of laid-off workers, Chen's third category, but the parameters and demands of this category are impeded by the fact that such events take place 'after workers had been laid off for months, even years' (Chen Feng 2003a: 241).

Differentiating between privatization and 'restructuring without privatization', Chen also found that SOE workers battling privatization broadened the parameters still further as 'moral economy demands are increasingly permeated by "class consciousness." They are well organized, with claims framed in class language'

(Chen Feng 2006: 43). It is interesting to note that in 2003, when analysing data from protests against restructuring in the cities of Luoyang and Shanghai – that presumably did not involve privatization – Chen considered the absence of 'independent organizing, which is critical for the development of their class consciousness' (Chen Feng 2003a: 258) as a key issue. On the other hand, in the battles against privatization in a central Chinese city in 1998, 2000 and 2001, the presence of real live capitalists appeared to overcome legal and institutional restrictions on organizing *and class consciousness developed anyway* (Chen Feng 2006: 43). At the risk of overgeneralization, we can summarize these arguments by stating that in the absence of freedom of association *xiagang* did not produce any sense of confrontational class consciousness while privatization did.

Chen's distinguishing of protests between privatization and 'restructuring without privatization' is useful in understanding how workers at a factory in the city of Xianyang came to mount one of the longest strikes in the history of the PRC and certainly the longest in the struggle against restructuring, with or without privatization. In 2005, workers began a six-week strike against new working conditions imposed following a buy-out of the state-owned Xianyang Huarun Textiles Factory. As we have seen, the usual tactics of laid-off workers was to occupy public spaces and/or organize a demonstration outside government labour bureau offices for *xiagang* wages. But Huarun was still a working concern and this meant that the best way of securing the attention of both management and the city government was to strike and picket. Organizers from both the workforce and management quickly emerged and a 24-hour picket line was drawn up and successively blocked all three of the still-producing factory's gates – for six weeks!

The strike was sparked following the acquisition of Huarun Factory by the Hong Kong-based mainland conglomerate, China Resources. In autumn 2005, a restructuring plan was announced without prior consultation that included the mass dismissal of all workers and immediate rehiring of an unspecified number on inferior contracts that would not take into account seniority or pension contributions. Workers responded by walking off the job. Demands were quickly formulated: long-term contracts, the cancellation of a six-month 'probationary' work period, a central-government inspection team to review the terms of the factory's merger with China Resources and compensation for the loss of SOE employee status. The workers' 24-hour picket line at the factory gate prevented management from deploying scab labour. This action was complemented by the unauthorized establishment of a trade union, the election of representatives and the hiring of a Beijing-based lawyer to supervise the dispute through formal court proceedings. During the six weeks, 20 workers' representatives were detained following a railway blockade and stone-throwing incidents at the director's house. They were released, apparently without charge, in January 2005. A combination of a threatened deployment by the police – who had already used water cannon against the strikers but to no avail – winter weather and rumours of a management compromise brought the strike to an end with major concessions from the company that included the cancellation of a new 'probationary' period for rehired workers and the dropping of threats to cut wages (China Labour Bulletin 2005). Two years

Labour unrest in the state sector 77

after the strike was resolved, CLB director Han Dongfang noted the different material conditions of this dispute compared to many of the protests over restructuring that he had been involved in previously.

> The first thing to note was the degree of solidarity among the workers. They managed to stay together and were not divided by different types of *xiagang* or whatever. While management wanted to make cuts, the company still needed the majority of the workforce. This facilitated a strike by people in work rather than a protest by people without it.
> (Interview, Hong Kong, 12 March 2007)

There is no hard evidence available to suggest that these workers were imbued with the same class consciousness that was so prominent in the turn-of-century protests that Chen described in the central China city. But it is hard to imagine that six weeks of strike action could take place without some degree of class consciousness developing, accompanied by a departure from some of the traditions of the past. As Chen explains:

> Thus, it is natural for workers to use the moral rhetoric of the past as a point of reference to assess their present conditions and frame their claim. Strategic though it might be, workers' efforts to base their demands on old official norms has actually prevented them from redefining their interests in the market economy, and trapped their struggle into a direction that will not produce any significant positive outcome for them, as a return to the old system has become impossible.
> (Chen Feng 2006: 60)

It seems safe to conclude that the Xianyang strikers were not significantly constrained by tradition. The workers did not demand their old status as masters of the enterprise back, but rather that they were compensated for the loss of this status as stipulated by the regulations. It still remains to be seen if this strike was the dying gasps of a past era or the birth pangs of the new stage for the labour movement as it converges with the private sector. It is likely that the scholarship will turn to this question in the near future. In the meantime, I believe that SOE resistance to restructuring – as opposed to full privatization which is now the norm – and the policies that managed it, peaked with the great unrest of spring 2002. Here was an outburst of anger that appeared to simultaneously defy and confirm all the arguments in the literature.

Spring 2002: the iron rice bowl is broken

Protests against phased redundancy and its gradual progression into one-off severance pay (*mai duan gongling*) appeared to peak in the spring of 2002. Very large-scale and well-organized street protests by unemployed oil workers in Daqing, laid-off metal workers in Liaoyang and laid-off or retired coal miners in

78 *Labour unrest in the state sector*

Fushun emerged out of different conditions, but at more or less the same time. The course of these struggles attracted extensive attention from the international press and the trade union movement outside China.[7]

Daqing was – and to some extent still is – a politically significant and economically important city. Its name translates into English as 'big celebration', symbolizing the relief which the discovery of oil there in 1958 brought to a government that was on the verge of bankruptcy. In 2002, even with reserves in the oilfield running low, Daqing still met almost 30 per cent of China's oil requirements. The opening up of the field in the late 1950s occasioned a significant and still-remembered propaganda exercise as the commitment and sheer hard work of Daqing's first generation of oil workers were held up as examples of a superior socialist work ethic. Almost a quarter of a century into the reforms, Maoist icons such as Iron Man Wang and Lei Feng still carried huge symbolic weight among many of China's older workers, as the oilmen I talked to in Daqing were quick to point out.

> Look! [Pointing to the riot police jogging in formation around Iron Man Square] Do you know what they're doing? They are repressing the spirit of Daqing – the spirit of Old Wang. Those country boys have no idea what we went through to build this town and, for that matter, to build socialism.
>
> (Interview, Daqing, 28 March 2002)

When more than 50,000 of the city's oil workers took to the streets around Iron Man Square in protest against a comparatively generous one-off redundancy deal, the state faced the most significant challenge to the direction announced five years earlier at the 15th Party Congress. The Daqing protestors and the traditions they represented seemed to challenge not only SOE restructuring but, by extension, the legitimacy of the Party's entire reform programme. Thus far, the authorities had successfully managed the dislocated protests of workers by employing a carrot-and-stick policy. This involved targeting, and if necessary, imprisoning coordinators and organizers while persuading the mass of workers to return home with a small payout and the promise of more at a later date. However, conditions in Daqing were more serious. First, the Daqing workers had signed up to a one-off agreement based on seniority, known as *mai duan gongling*. This arrangement had become increasingly common as the *xiagang* or phased redundancy policy reached the end of its political shelf life. At the stroke of a pen, all connections with PetroChina were severed and by spring of 2002 the workers began to question the legal validity of the deal. Second, the relative affluence of former key energy sector workers and the brief appearance of an independent provisional trade union committee meant that the protestors were in a position to reject any carrots from the government and hold out for longer – more than six weeks. The Heilongjiang provincial government deemed the situation serious enough to deploy truckloads of troops to the outskirts of Daqing as both a precautionary and intimidating measure against the protesters.

A few hundred kilometres south, a four-year campaign against the corrupt bankrupting of the Liaoyang Ferroalloy Factory (LFF) in Liaoning province came to a head on 18 March when approximately 30,000 mainly laid-off workers from 20 of the city's SOEs marched in rare solidarity with 4,000 laid-off LFF workers.[8] In Fushun, sustained protests began in mid March 2002, when up to 10,000 laid-off workers, mainly from the coal mines, were joined by laid-off workers from cement, steel and petrochemical factories and blocked the railway line and the main road into Fushun over inadequate severance payments.

These disputes received widespread attention from the international trade union movement. International Trade Secretariats such as ICEM, which had previously maintained cordial relations with the ACFTU, issued a press release pledging support to the short-lived provisional union committee in Daqing (ICEM 2002). At a meeting of the ICFTU's China Working Party, one delegate expressed the view that 'after Daqing, everything is different' (Interview, Hong Kong, 15 March 2002). However, international support for the protests underestimated the state's capacity to handle this unrest without resorting to violence on a 1989-scale and also – unlike the CPC leadership – failed to grasp the fact that material conditions for more effective resistance, such as strikes and solidarity strikes, remained largely absent.

The state's response to the protests was to hold the line. Further politicization of the situation was avoided by refraining from a massed physical attack on the workers involved while simultaneously targeting their leaders with snatch squads and detentions. In this respect, the basic policy to 'seek progress while maintaining stability' was upheld (Hong Yung Lee 2000: 914–37).[9] Two years earlier, in 2000, regulations issued by the Ministry of Public Security had instructed local police forces not to treat workers' protests as a political threat but rather as a result of the rapid pace of political and economic change. An accompanying circular stressed that in the main such incidents were to be handled as crowd control issues and not political incidents (Ministry of Public Security 2000). Although there were dozens of temporary detentions, there were no reports of workers' representatives being arrested, formally charged and given prison sentences in Daqing.[10] Even though a provisional trade union committee representing the laid-off oil workers was said to have been established (ICEM 2002), there was still no Tiananmen-style attack on Iron Man Square as the security forces succeeded in driving the organizers deep underground rendering them ineffective as an organizing committee. The presence of troops on the outskirts of town and riot police in the Square itself was correctly deemed sufficiently intimidating. On the other hand, events in Liaoyang show the other side of this policy. Where workers' representatives successfully organized sustained cross-enterprise demonstrations or contact with groups outside China, they could expect arrest and prison sentences, as was the case with the Liaoyang Two – Yao Fuxin and Xiao Yunliang.

The Party's absolute priority was one of containment and avoiding actions that might result in solidarity protests beyond the immediate locality and even strikes. The potential for such a course of events to unfurl was briefly highlighted by the 'learn from Daqing' slogans employed by protesting laid-off oil workers from the Shengli oilfield in Shandong province later in the same year. Back in Daqing, government officials and PetroChina's directors went to great lengths to ensure that the protests did not spread to oil workers still in work, i.e. were not transformed into strike action, a situation that would have added fuel to a fire already 'permeated with class consciousness' (Chen Feng 2006: 42) albeit looking back towards tradition, and sustained by Cai's well-educated organizers (Cai Yongshun 2002: 327–44). The presence of demonstrators in Iron Man Square was embarrassing and nerve-racking for the government, but handled correctly it needn't impact on production and for the most part it did not prevent the rest of the city from carrying on with its business. Indeed, as the protestors' numbers gradually dwindled over the six weeks, local PetroChina officials grew in confidence. Towards the end of the movement, one labour activist reported that

> Right now the oil company is concentrating on public opinion and sowing discord among current and former employees. At the point of writing, the March bonus has not been issued and the company's explanation to all employees has been, 'this is a direct result of the demonstrations. Go ask the protesters'.
> (*Pioneer Monthly* 2002: 6)

Earlier on in the dispute, not paying the March bonus would have risked escalating the dispute, but by mid April the size of the gatherings in the Square had declined markedly and morale had dropped after nearly six weeks of tension. A shopkeeper on the edge of Iron Man Square told me that

> [I]t is more or less over now. It is hard to keep everyone together after all these weeks and some of the ordinary people (*laobaixing*) do not support them anyway. In my opinion, they should never have signed the redundancy deal in the first place.
> (Interview, Daqing, 28 March 2002)

The people taking part in these protests included Cai's laid-off workers, Hurst and O'Brien's pensioners and, albeit briefly, the still-employed workers facing an uncertain future who joined the LFF demonstration on 18 March. The scale and sustainability of the actions as well as their relative geographical proximity seemed to offer the prospect of a movement. But while it is not possible to draw definitive conclusions due to the constraints on fieldwork, the absence of strikes and the momentum that they necessarily produce was a key factor in the state's favour. Participants were, by and large, *already* laid off from the workplace itself. As we have discussed, production itself was rarely affected and as such enterprise leaders did not need to negotiate with their former employees, essentially reducing the protests to a matter of crowd control, albeit with significant political implications should they be badly managed. Apart from blocking roads and railway lines, a course of action that invariably drew forceful intervention and arrests from the People's Armed Police, the majority of state workers' actions did not, in the final analysis, have the capacity to directly impact on production itself simply because, as one veteran labour academic observed, there was, in most cases, 'no work to strike against' (*wu gong ke ba*!).

Perhaps ironically, the brief coming together of different categories of workers in Liaoyang, and the sheer size of the demonstrations in Daqing, actually illustrated the capacity of phased redundancies – *xiagang* – to achieve its aim of strangling a potential labour protest movement at birth between 1997 and 2002. The different categories of laid-off workers such as early retirees, internally laid-off workers, workers placed on extended leave, external laid-off workers and, towards the end of the first phase of restructuring, those offered one-off redundancy deals (*mai duan gongling*) tended to dramatically reduce a sense of cohesion among different groups of laid-off workers.[11] The 30,000-strong cross-enterprise demonstration in Liaoyang on 18 March 2002 was the exception rather than the rule. As Lee has noted, it was much more common for workers to confine their protests to their own specific group according to the nature of the grievance and status of those involved in divisions reinforced, if not created, by state policy: '[B]eneath the surface, variation in worker grievances is the common pattern of worker unrest organized around localized, bounded work units or their subgroups, whose boundaries are defined and fractured by state policies' (Lee Ching-kwan 2007: 120). The state's application of targeted repression and concession did nothing to break down these divisions within the working class.

The unions and restructuring

The role of the ACFTU in all this was marginal as far as workers were concerned. While it is notoriously difficult for trade unions to resist redundancies, the ACFTU at no point entertained an intention to resist them, at least not in public. And if unions are constrained by the objective realities of unemployment, the ACFTU was further handicapped by its subjective acceptance of Party leadership.

The most important slogan that emerged from the 15th Congress was '*caiyuan zeng xiao*' (shed jobs to increase efficiency). The response of the ACFTU to the job losses was naturally premised on its role of explaining Party policy, which deemed all except the very large SOEs inefficient and in dire need of downsizing or closing down altogether. As a consequence, the cities came under enormous pressure to provide employment opportunities. In 2002, the Ministry of Propaganda and the MOLSS released a joint document in which they estimated the period of the 10th Five-Year Plan (2001–2005) would see an average annual urban shortfall between jobs available (between seven and eight million) and job-seekers (between 22 and 23 million) of 14–15 million (CPPCC Propaganda Department and MOLSS 2002). Thus, the union found itself pincered by neo-liberal influenced policies on the one hand and state socialist models of trade unionism on the other. As we have seen, the ACFTU acquiescence to Party priorities has not always gone unchallenged, but opposing the mass lay-offs would have left the union politically isolated, barring the emergence of a sufficiently strong opposition from within the Party leadership. There was opposition from the Party old guard who wished to preserve the SOEs as bastions of Chinese socialism, but the reformers' victory at the 15th Congress along with China's entry into the WTO had reduced their voice to an echo of the past. The result was a catch-22 situation that the ACFTU was ill equipped to resolve beyond attempting to alleviate the impact of unemployment on both its traditional membership and its own officials – which is precisely what it did.

Between 1995 and 1999, ACFTU membership declined by 16 million, from 103 million to 87 million members (Jiang Hong 2002). As restructuring deepened, trade union branches were merged into enterprise-level Party cells and many full-time trade union officers were either laid off or had their union time cut as they were forced to take up non-union posts and/or work in the leftover Party cells on tasks unrelated to union business. Much of this new work was the complete opposite of their traditional task of promoting the welfare of their members. Meanwhile, at the national level, union policy was increasingly focused on membership drives in the private sector as it followed the shifting terrain of labour unrest and the potential competition it faced from NGOs that were springing up in the private sector where the ACFTU was basically absent. The work of NGOs was considerably boosted by the space opened up following the Hu-Wen leadership's promise to improve the lives of the peasantry and migrant workers and the media focus on migrant workers. All this was in stark contrast to the paucity of reports on the plight of SOE workers and the success stories of laid-off workers transforming themselves into chirpy market traders, child minders, dog walkers, noodle stall holders and a whole host of occupations that made up an expanding 80 million strong informal sector (*PLA Daily* 2004).

Up until 2003, the main thrust of ACFTU basic work was outside the actual workplace and focused on the establishment of support centres for 'workers communities in need' (*kunnan zhigong qunti*). These centres were called Workers Support Centres (*kunnan zhigong bangfu zhongxin*) and targeted laid-off or unemployed workers whose basic livelihood needs were not being met. According to the *Workers' Daily*, many of those who received assistance were facing severe difficulties in finding re-employment and were owed considerable amounts of money in unpaid wages and medical costs from bankrupted SOEs. Most of the Workers Support Centres (WSC) were established between 2002 and 2003 following the 9th Presidium Meeting (expanded) of the ACFTU 13th Congress in September 2002, that included a discussion on the experience of WSCs in the city of Tianjin (ACFTU researcher, interview, Beijing, 12 February 2006). The conference ended with a call to set up 200 such centres within three years, a call that was quickly upgraded to an opinion when the union released the 'ACFTU Opinion on the establishment of Workers Support Centres' in January 2003 (Beijing Federation of Trade Unions 2005).[12] By November 2005, the union had established WSCs in 10 provinces, 329 cities and more than 1,600 counties. By June 2005, city-level WSCs had issued just under 1.5 billion yuan to workers (Pan Yue 2005). In 2005, the *Workers' Daily* summed up the main tasks of the centres, some of which directly replaced the Re-employment Centres that SOEs were in theory meant to provide for laid-off workers, although in practice many of these centres were 'ghost towns'. First of all, the WSCs provided employment introductions and retraining and were an integral part of the union's 'three-year three one and a half million' (*san nian san ge yibai wushi wan*) employment project that aimed to provide training to 1.5 million laid-off or unemployed workers, employment introductions to another 1.5 million and re-employment to a further 1.5 million (Qiao Yu 2005). Second, the centres were to provide livelihood assistance, including medical costs and children's education costs. Third, was the provision of advice and direct assistance to workers who had found work and came to the centres petitioning the union for help following rights' violations. The response included sending teams to relevant work unit (*danwei*) or government departments to negotiate a satisfactory outcome. Finally, the WSCs were to provide legal assistance and/or advice to workers who were pursuing claims through legal channels.

The ACFTU's own statistics suggest that the WSCs had an impact, although as always caution is required when reviewing union statistics pertaining to the meeting of quotas. The *Workers' Daily* reported that by September 2004, the union at all levels had organized over 11.4 million job introductions, provided over two million training sessions to laid-off or unemployed workers and helped to find work for just over two million workers (Qiao Yu 2005). In 2004, the union issued over four billion yuan to over 3.5 million cases involving hardship, an increase of 36 per cent on 2003 (ACFTU Trade Union Rights Bluebook 2005). By the end of 2004, the ACFTU had set up 2,990 legal assistance services staffed by a total of 9,976 people, 766 of whom were qualified lawyers (ACFTU Trade Union Rights Bluebook 2005).

As the first half of this chapter has demonstrated, there is little doubt that if ACFTU cadres had played a more active role in defending their members' jobs and direct interests, they would have been slapped down. In the 1950s and perhaps even more strikingly in the 1989 Democracy Movement, during which the trade union made a large financial contribution to hunger-striking students in Tiananmen Square, trade union expressions of support for protests or alternatives to state policies led to severe reprimands or dismissals of ACFTU cadres and purges at the top. Likewise, as restructuring deepened, the union lost tens of thousands of enterprise cadres. There are incidents of union cadres being involved in protests but rarely in an officially sanctioned capacity. It should not surprise us that the organization concentrated on charity work *(song wennuan)* outside the workplace as opposed to organizing in it.

Unlike the growth of the private sector, the restructuring provided few opportunities for trade unions to reform past practices. While the Party has encouraged the unions to improve representation in the private sector, this was not an issue in the former public sector. Indeed, better representation of workers who the Party was officially encouraging to 'liberate [their] thinking' (*jiefang sixiang*), jump into the sea of society (*xia hai*) and basically swim for it, would have been an unsolicited and unwanted constraint on a central theme of the reform project. The resistance to restructuring at no point appeared strong enough to mount a coordinated challenge to ACFTU passivity and, by implication, restructuring itself. Indeed, the short-lived attempt to roll back economic reform by Party conservatives in the post-1989 climate (Naughton 1995: 275) demonstrated that there were no powerful elements within the CPC who might have exploited worker activism to push through a political change of direction.

In sum, the state's careful management ensured that it was in a position to sit out the protests during the period 1997–2002 and beyond. If laid-off workers had been more successful in making common cause either with each other, or, even more effectively, with workers still in work, there is little doubt that the politics of the situation would have been much more potent. As it was, policy and the absence of freedom of association were sufficient to prevent a movement from emerging out of multiple instances of localized resistance. The state's priority of rapid economic development was not seriously challenged at the national or even provincial level.

Positioning resistance to state sector restructuring

In general, the focus of collective labour actions against restructuring was not the workplace as such, but rather the social 'spaces' around it. As we have seen from the literature, workers were very often very angry about the potentially volcanic issues of corruption (Human Rights Watch 2002), pensions (Hurst and O'Brien 2002) and *xiagang* livelihood stipends (Solinger 2001), all against a backdrop of loss of status and declining living standards (Zou Zhongzheng and Qin Wei 2001). Demands almost always related to services previously delivered via the *danwei*: access to schools for workers' children, hospitals and medical care, housing and housing repair subsidies and heating allowances were demands that regularly featured on workers' home-made banners. One slogan – 'we want to eat' – in particular epitomized the sense of abandonment, although my own conversations with laid-off workers suggest that it was widely misunderstood outside China. While a dramatic drop in living standards was all too often the result of *xiagang*, especially for those households with two laid-off breadwinners, this slogan was generally misinterpreted by the Western media as a sign of pending starvation that simply was not the case. In fact, it was a reference to the 'iron rice bowl' and its livelihood-related subsidies that the *danwei* era had mostly provided.

The actions of these workers had an international significance. While some US unions were positioning all Chinese workers as helpless frontrunners in the 'race to the bottom', others have argued that SOE workers' resistance was widespread but constrained and dispersed (Chen Feng 2003a; Lee Ching-kwan 2007; Philion 2007; Clarke and Pringle 2009). Writing on the successful struggle to reverse a takeover of the Zhengzhou City Paper Mill by organizing around the factory's staff and workers' congress, Philion argues that the workers' leaders' policy of borrowing to reduce the mill's inherited debts was essentially a lost opportunity to develop a credible alternative to restructuring and privatization by deepening the direct participation of rank-and-file workers in the management of the reacquired mill – and presumably cancelling the debts. Such a strategy could, Philion argues, have been held up as an example to other SOE workers struggling to hold on to – or retrieve – SOE factory property in the face of institutional financial constraints (Philion 2007: 47). The mill workers had successfully used the staff and workers' congress to legitimize their protests – as they did in Daqing, Liaoyang and many other cases – and even regained ownership of the enterprise. The cost was high: four workers' representatives – the Zhengzhou Four – were imprisoned. Similar struggles against capital in the city led to battles with migrant workers hired to physically attack workers attempting to defend their jobs and way of life.

The struggles in Zhengzhou were framed in a Maoist egalitarian spirit directly inherited from the *danwei*. Although the course of events in the north-east was different, the same spirit infused the workers' handbills handed out in Iron Man Square and local neighbourhoods in Daqing in the spring of 2002 with titles such as 'Retrenched Workers Cherish the Memory of Chairman Mao' (*Pioneer Monthly* 2002: 17). In Liaoyang too, workers marched through the streets carrying pictures of Chairman Mao (Human Rights Watch 2002). And so we are back with Chen: 'strategic though it might be, workers' efforts to base their demands on old official norms has actually prevented them from redefining their interests in the market economy' (Chen Feng 2006: 60).

In this context, the state's refusal to refer to restructuring as 'privatization', even when this was clearly the case, had an impact on the resistance. Privatization was only one means employed to push through restructuring, alongside *gufenzhi* or 'shareholderization' whereby employees were 'offered' – sometimes on pain of dismissal – to buy shares in their SOE, mergers with foreign or domestic capital, downsizing, partial sell-offs and bankruptcy. All the same, there was a general perception among critics and supporters alike that SOE restructuring was part of a political programme to reorganize and even transfer property rights. In the public spaces and working class neighbourhoods where most demonstrations took place, this translated into the perception that restructuring provided an opportunity for enterprise leaders and government officials to enrich themselves by teaming up with or transforming themselves into capitalists and grabbing state assets that legally belonged to the state, if not the workers themselves. In this scenario the state could, and did, go after corrupt enterprise leaders – usually known to workers by name – not the more anonymous forces of private and international capital, even as they waited in the wings. In short, 'bad apples' were on the branches, but the overall health of the tree and its socialist roots remained sound.

Legitimizing the 'p' word would have reduced the Party's room to manoeuvre and hamper its crackdowns on especially venal examples of asset grabbing. Such apparently semantic concerns can easily acquire more concrete ramifications when it comes to the political framing of state force. Politically, there was the contradiction of prosecuting a privatization policy in what remains, constitutionally, a workers' state. The Party understood well that poor management of the mass layoffs carried the potential for the spark for local resistance to transform into a prairie fire. But should force become necessary, justifying the application of state violence on a coordinated national scale as necessary to transforming China into a strong and influential country would be far more digestible by public opinion and Party 'conservatives' than say, 'upholding lawful privatization'.

In my conversations with SOE workers during this era, the term 'privatization' (*siyouhua*) did occasionally come up, but it was rare for workers to make specific attacks on private capital as such. Even if they didn't always believe it, workers were nevertheless influenced by what they read in the state-run media and watched on the television, as well as by what enterprise directors told them, and privatization was not a word either the media or the bosses employed at the time. Blecher argued that Chinese workers were dazzled by the market, which was consequently able to impose its hegemony (Blecher 2003: 167). But it was probably more the case that, as a collective entity, the working class simply failed to grasp its consequences until it was too late. As a bitter laid-off worker clearly in need of hospital treatment told me, 'never in my wildest dreams did I think it would turn out like this' (interview, Wuhan, November 1998).

On the other hand, Chen argues that, unlike the struggles of pensioners and workers laid off from loss-making enterprises in which participants were easily bought off, workers who succeeded in identifying a capitalist target at the local level and framed their struggle accordingly were more likely to develop a 'them versus us' attitude (Chen Feng 2006). Thus, a more class conscious form of organization was likely to emerge in a struggle against the takeover of a *still profitable* SOE by private capital. In such a scenario, workers can make use of the state's avoidance of a formal privatization policy to 'poach the rulers' ideology and theater of legitimation' (Thompson 1991: 10 cited in Chen Feng 2006: 48). And in Zhengzhou they did just that – to varying degrees over four separate struggles.

Conclusion

It is the case that a recasting of the iron rice bowl would have required a social movement on the scale not seen since the CPC's administration of the liberated areas prior to the revolution. Our discussion above demonstrates that while resistance to restructuring was widespread, the constraints preventing these components from combining into a labour movement were simply too great. Moreover, there was the simple fact that the new economy was already up, running and moving towards the centre of the national and even international economy and that the old state sector was holding China back from the development path chosen by its leaders. Indeed, since the turn of the century, and especially since 2003, collective labour protests in the private- and foreign-owned sectors had been growing in effectiveness. Sustained high levels of FDI, a marked shortage of skilled workers, and the adoption of increasingly sophisticated tactics by migrant workers dictated that the focus of protest and of trade union responses to it had already shifted to the non-state sector.

3 From victims to subjects
The long march of migrant labour

In this chapter, I examine the gradual rise in the capacity of China's internal migrant workers to confront their capitalist employers and the underlying constraints and opportunities that have produced this situation. My sources include information derived from many conversations with migrant workers between 1999 and 2006; from interviews conducted with workers hospitalized as a result of occupational disease and injury; interviews with labour activists, labour lawyers and labour LNGO workers in Hong Kong and China between 2005 and 2007; and interviews with primary level trade union cadres. I also make use of interviews with workers in struggle, although I did not conduct all of them myself for obvious reasons.

We begin the chapter with the arrival of foreign and private capital and an examination of the constraints on the people working for it. I then focus on two major factors that constrained migrant workers from securing their rights in the factory system especially in the early years of reform – the *hukou* registration system and weak enterprise trade unions. We then move on to the factors that have contributed to improving workers' confidence. During the first years of the twenty-first century, we are – finally – able to identify at least some emerging factors that work to the advantage of migrant workers in general and skilled migrant workers in particular. These include labour shortages, an accumulated knowledge of the factory system, an improved legal environment, and the gradual acquisition of a collective bank of experience among migrant workers on how to squeeze concessions out of employers. A change in the labour market, dating approximately from 2003, provided conditions in which the economic strike has emerged as the weapon of choice for migrants seeking to win immediate improvements in working conditions. This narrative of struggle has been helped along by the acceptance of such phenomena as 'normal' by some leaders in trade union and party circles as both the ACFTU and the CPC have set great store on the creation of a formal system of labour dispute resolution. In the final section, I examine the relationship between workers' informal action and these procedures.

The core of my conclusion is as follows: the ongoing unrest demonstrates that the efforts by both the state and the ACFTU to direct labour unrest towards the juridical channels of dispute resolution discussed in Chapter 1 are insufficient – on their own – to bring industrial harmony, or at least a framework in which disputes can be properly addressed. The increase in strike activity has, in turn, led to significant pressure on the ACFTU from both above and below to be more active in representing its members at enterprise level. On the other hand, strict limits are set on how far the unions can go. The Party remains anxious that too many concessions to labour will exacerbate the situation and, in an echo of the arguments that raged during the 1950s, may lead to a powerful autonomous labour bureaucracy, independent trade unions – or even both! Thus, labour unrest emerges as the key factor behind the experiments in trade union reform discussed in Chapters 4, 5 and 6.

Facilitating capitalist super-exploitation

Indivisible from the destruction of decent work in the state sector has been the (re)construction of indecent work in the private sector. The establishment of a non-state labour regime has been premised on two major developments, one economic, the other social. Firstly, there has been the re-entry of private capital into the Chinese economy and the diverse forms of enterprise ownership that came with it, including private ownership, foreign ownership, joint-venture companies and township and village enterprises (TVE). Secondly, there has been a gradual but significant relaxation of the constraints on residential choice known as the *hukou* system. This has permitted large numbers of people to leave the countryside temporarily and seek work in off-farm employment both in the factories and in the construction and infrastructure projects that have smoothed their operation. The human migration that has ensued is possibly the largest rural–urban migration in human history. During the 1980s and early 1990s, over 150 million people found work either in special economic zones that concentrated on attracting foreign capital, or in TVEs nominally owned by the 'people' but primarily managed by local Party Committees and their appointees. As the economic reforms deepened, most TVEs morphed into private enterprises (see Chapter 1).

The provinces of Guangdong, Fujian and more recently Zhejiang have, to date, attracted the largest amounts of foreign, Hong Kong and Taiwanese capital. Located on the south and east coasts, they have chiefly produced for the export market. As with local private capital, foreign capital has also acquired a reputation as being highly exploitative and well connected with relevant government departments that have provided protection for employers facing labour protests. Nevertheless, throughout the 1990s and early part of the present century, the flow of rural migrants kept coming and the combined non-state sector has now overtaken the state sector in terms of numbers employed. According to ACFTU figures, at the end of 2006 there were over 101 million people employed in the non-state sector spanning various forms of private ownership compared to just under 73 million in the state- and collectively-owned sectors (ACFTU 2007a: 37).[1] While many migrants and would-be migrants target the eastern and southern coastal regions 'some migrants leave their homes to travel only a short distance to the nearest urban area' (Davin 1999: 1). Published in 2009, a survey of 68,000 households in 7,100 villages across 31 provinces conducted in 2008 revealed a total of over 235 million rural migrant workers – although 38 per cent of these were working in enterprises within their own home towns (*China Review* 2009). This left

140.4 million working outside their home towns. ILO researcher Li Shi uses National Bureau of Statistics figures to show that in 2006 132 million migrant workers were working and living outside their home towns for more than three months. Figure 3.1 demonstrates how the numbers of rural to urban migrants have continued to increase since 1989. Li Shi also reminds us that the total number of rural migrants is even larger than the number of rural migrant workers. Approximately 80 per cent of migrants stayed in cities with at least one member of their family and 20 per cent moved their whole immediate family. He states that in 2006, 'the total number of rural-urban migrants can be estimated at about 160 million' (Li Shi 2008: 5). Photograph 3.1 of migrant workers on the school run in Shaanxi province was taken by the author while interviewing miners from Sichuan who had established a small family-based community around a fairly remote shaft.

Rural poverty has been the main 'push' factor in this process and despite the generally appalling working conditions it has ensured that these coastal zones attracted a continuous supply of cheap labour. Indeed, it is the constant oversupply of labour that has acted as a major constraint on migrant workers' capacity to defend even their most basic legal rights and interests. On the other hand, migrant workers have not left the hardships they encountered entirely uncontested. For sure, the development of migrant worker self-activity and resistance to capital has been gradual, but from 'scattered' beginnings we are now in a situation in which large collective strikes have become a daily occurrence. Perhaps taking their cue from Silver's argument that democratic labour movements develop in the wash of mobile capital (2003: 41–75), some left-wing US trade unionists are now ambitiously asking '[C]an the Chinese Labor Movement Reverse the "Race to the Bottom?"' (Left Forum 2009).

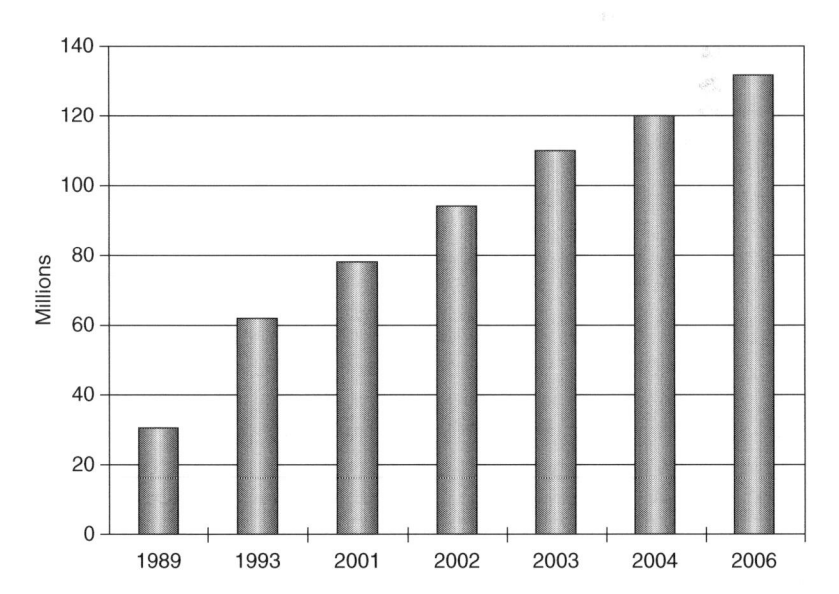

Figure 3.1 Rural–urban migrant workers, 1989–2006
Source: Li Shi, 2006.

Photograph 3.1 Migrant workers on the school run
Source: Tim Pringle 2005.

Constraints on private sector migrant workers

In her book charting migrant workers' conditions via translations from the Chinese media, Chan identifies three forms of workers' resistance in actions that she labels a 'struggle for social justice' rather than a social movement. These are 'spontaneous'[2] outbursts of collective violence, street protests that generally take the form of a march down to the local labour bureau and, finally, recourse to legal action (Chan 2001: 206). Despite one academic's recording of an 'unprecedented strike wave in FIEs concentrated in South China' (Jiang Kaiwen 1996: 139), Chan only provides two examples of strike action out of 23 case studies, and one of these involves SOE workers in Beijing. Although labour unrest was undoubtedly growing during the early 1990s, strikes were still regarded by all the actors – including the workers themselves – as unusual phenomena, an exceptional form of protest rather than the rule. By default, strikes require some form of organization if they are going to succeed and the material conditions on the ground were hardly conducive to such action. Local governments' determination to maintain an investor-friendly environment, restrictions on residence that allowed employers to replace striking workers with ease, inexperience with the factory system, and, above all, an overwhelming abundance of labour all combined to limit workers' confidence.[3]

> Outside the gates of every enterprise in our so-called Special Economic Zones, you can see small crowds of workers who are waiting to be hired even if the factory has no hiring policy at the time. When they do hire, this small crowd quickly turns into a crush of desperate migrant workers.
> (Han Deqiang, 4 November 2002)[4]

Announcing the 'ending of socialism in a developing, labor-surplus state' Solinger's inquiry into the 'floating population's' employment channels found an

From victims to subjects 91

'*extremely high level* of competition to fill low-skill niches in many of the trades we examined' (author's emphasis). Solinger shows first that access to the rural 'reserve army' was not limited to the factories, but also encompassed 'construction; marketing and services; cottage-style garment processing; manufacturing in factories; nursemaiding; begging and scrap collecting' (Solinger 1999: 4–5). And second, as my added italics emphasize, competition for jobs among migrants was intense and this in itself would have had a dampening impact on workers' opportunities to organize.

But the abundance of cheap labour was by no means the only constraint on migrant workers' challenging the status quo. There was, and is, the wider question of migrant worker rights. Labelling the managed migration from the countryside as a 'social structure of lost entitlements' (Liu Kaiming 2005: 7), the Institute of Contemporary Observation's (ICO) report on the protracted struggle of 188 migrant construction workers drew bleak conclusions. Noting the construction workers' tenacity in pursuing their claims across all three categories of contention listed by Chan, the ICO report argued that

> in the course of studying this case and the social, political and economic causes behind it, we found that the workers' loss of economic rights could find its source in the loss of their rights as citizens, their political rights as well as their social and cultural rights.
>
> (Liu Kaiming 2005: 21)

Accordingly, Liu found this grim state of affairs dictated that 'all their acts of protest were passive, economic-based and reactive' (Liu Kaiming 2005: 18). Given the nature of the playing field described by Liu and others, it need not surprise us that the results of ethnographic studies conducted in the 1990s by sociologists such as Lee Ching-kwan (1998) found an exhausted and sometimes cowed workforce 'whose job security was conditional on the good will of their employers, enterprise requirements and profit margins, and their own productivity' (Sargeson 1999: 3). While often angry at their lot, they were continually constrained from effectively confronting employers over poor working conditions by the discriminatory environment that governed their status as outsiders. Sargeson found that migrant workers looked to factors outside the workplace, such as the *hukou* system, to explain the exploitative conditions within it.

> With few exceptions, workers believe that the conditions which necessitate their waged employment and facilitate their exploitation are established outside the work place, by regional disparities, place and *guanxi* networks, the power of officials, and the unequal distribution of wealth and opportunities.
>
> (Sargeson 1999: 181)

Although protests were documented, Leung's conclusion that the protests of these workers in the early 1990s were 'scattered, spontaneous and unorganised' (Leung Wing-yuk 1995: 44) should not surprise us. Perhaps trawling for signs of hope, Sargeson tentatively points to an 'increasingly restive ACFTU', the organizational savvy of cast-off SOE workers and migrant workers as a potentially potent alliance. She suggests that '[I]f disaffected workers who have been shed from the state sector join together with the contract and temporary employees of non-state enterprises, China's proletariat may become extremely militant' (Sargeson 1999: 226). Nearly 10 years later this vision of convergence remains elusive.

Hukou zhidu: the system of residential registration

Without doubt the *hukou* system has been a major obstacle to the capacity of migrant workers to challenge employers. Originally a means of monitoring, managing and controlling the population that the CPC took over from the Guomindang, the system evolved according to economic and political priorities that privileged urban industry over rural agriculture. Wang explains that 'with food rations and numerous subsidies added later favouring urban residents, the PRC *hukou* system functioned in crucial ways in social stratification, resource allocation, capital formation, agriculture collectivization and the division of the urban from the rural' (Wang Fei-Ling 2005: 45).

The methodology was not subtle and involved nothing less than the forced exclusion of peasants from urban areas. In 1958, the Public Security Bureau (PSB) issued the 'Regulations on Household Registration in the People's Republic of China' that formally restricted peasants to their place of birth. Barring unlikely connections with powerful officials in urban areas, the only way for a peasant to supplement income derived from an agrarian commune system of remuneration based on work points was to be included in an organized transfer of labour from the rural areas to work on industrial or infrastructure projects (Harris 1978: 109–10).[5]

In contrast, the post-reform era has seen *hukou*'s function change from being an instrument of restriction – confining the peasantry to rural areas – to one of facilitating controlled migration to urban and semi-urban areas in order to provide a regulated oversupply of labour for the emerging private sector. Nevertheless, the right to urban residence remained – and for the most part, remains – temporary. This means that rural registration still excludes the majority of migrant workers from most of the welfare and insurance enjoyed by urban-registered citizens. On the other hand, the change in the method of delivery of hitherto urban privileges – from enterprise-based welfare to pay-as-you-earn insurance that relies on the large-scale pooling of insurance funds – has contributed to pressure to further relax and even abolish the system and the two-tier labour market it produces. There are currently in existence various pilot projects that further moderate *hukou* in order to keep pace with the changing labour market and the urbanization of large tracts of agricultural land. In 2005, 11 provinces announced plans to abolish administrative differences between town and country. In November of the same year, Ou Guangyang, deputy secretary of the Guangdong Provincial Party Committee, announced that the province would 'allow all farmers to register as urban residents in one or two years' (Zheng Caixiong *et al*. 2005). Since 2003–4 labour shortages and frequent human rights abuses have added stimulus to the anti-*hukou* lobby. In 2007, Cai Fang, the director of the Institute of Population and

Labor Economics of the Chinese Academy of Social Sciences (CASS), stated that 'obstacles in the labour market should be cleared' so that labour shortages did not contribute to inflationary pressure on prices (Cai Fang 2007). For 'prices' we can justifiably read 'wages'.

Conversely, there has been an opposing argument that rural registration and the access to land-use rights that come with it are an essential component of China's rural welfare policy. While the countryside's social safety net remains inadequate, land-use rights are an important factor in reducing conflict between farmers, officials and developers (Yu Jianrong 2007: 13), maintaining food security and avoiding large-scale landlessness on the scale of South America. This argument gained ground during the global recession of 2008–9 when up to 26 million migrant workers returned to the rural areas in the so-called *fan xiang* or migration back the countryside movement following widespread factory closures.

In the meantime, it is still the case that most migrant workers have to jump through administrative hoops in order to work legally outside their place of birth. These restrictions award both employers and local authorities a high degree of social control over migrant workers' lives, especially women, who have to prove that they have abided by family planning regulations (Pun Ngai 2005). The permits required include a 'Temporary Residence Permit' for anyone living away from their place of registration for more than a month. This is issued by the PSB and must be renewed annually. Also needed is a 'Migrant Employment Permit', which is actually two permits. The first is issued by the migrant's home labour recruitment agency and the second by the receiving locality's labour bureau. For women, a 'Planned Reproduction Certificate' is necessary. This must be obtained from a migrant's home-town agency responsible for planned reproduction. On arrival in the receiving locale, the certificate is approved by the local planned reproduction agency. Employers are not allowed to hire migrants without this certificate and none of the other relevant certificates required by migrant workers can be issued without it.

Employers have gained advantage from this system in two main ways. Firstly, going through such a rigorous process to work away from home obviously has a somewhat numbing effect on workers' willingness to risk collective action (Chan 2001: 9–10). For those that have taken the risk, vengeful employers and local authorities were able to ensure their dismissal and, sometimes, detention by the authorities (*People's Daily Online* 2008). Arranging replacement workers posed no particular difficulties for employers, at least not until the onset of serious labour shortages in 2004. In 2005, I stayed in a hostel (*zhaodaisuo*) that acted as the Shenzhen offices of the government of a mid-China city. It was also a shop and entertainment centre. The manager of this multifunctional and by no means uncommon establishment/agency was, as far as I could ascertain, a bona fide government official from the city in question. His job put him in a good position to appraise the labour market.

> One of our functions was to compile data on factories and ensure that migrants from our area are sent to the higher-paying factories that require

workers [i.e. before migrants from other regions get there – author]. Migrant workers hung round here using the phone and chatting if they couldn't find a job, but these days, they don't need us to help them find jobs any more. These days it has become easier for our people to find jobs with good wages and the workers have developed their own networks and *guanxi*. They know about vacancies before we do!

(Interview, Shenzhen, 11 October 2005)

The *hukou* system helped to keep wages down. In the Pearl River Delta (PRD), wages remained effectively static throughout the 1990s and in the early years of the present decade (Liu Kaiming 2005: 211–2). It also facilitated unfair practices by companies concerned about having to compensate workers for ill health due to use of unsafe chemicals in the production process. One tactic was to implement mass dismissals, immediately followed by hiring fairs. I spoke with one former worker who was recovering from benzene poisoning in a hospital who said he had been part of such a process.

It was a Taiwanese factory where I worked. The pay was slightly higher than others but we think now that this was meant to prevent workers from thinking seriously about their health. After the Spring Festival of 2004, they hung up a recruiting sign outside the factory. Three days later about 50 of us were dismissed 'due to the orders'. Since ending up in hospital I have tried to contact the factory. I received a letter saying that there were no contractual relations between us.

(Interview, 12 September 2005)

According to *hukou* regulations, a migrant worker has only a limited amount of time to find new employment when between jobs, a factor that has encouraged new hires not to pressure employers for contracts or to object to working for up to two months before receiving the first pay packet. Apart from facilitating a general environment of unfair and often illegal labour practices such as the extraction of job deposits, confiscation of ID cards and the use of wage arrears as an instrument of control over labour turnover (Greenfield and Pringle 2002), *hukou* has also enabled employers to scatter groups of workers who were able to mount a collective act of struggle. It has been especially effective in obstructing campaigns to win compensation for occupational disease or injury that are usually long and drawn out. The Asian TNC Gold Peak Limited, which has been the target of a five-year campaign to obtain adequate compensation for the ill-effects of cadmium, appears to have made use of the opportunities provided by the *hukou* system to avoid paying adequate compensation. One workers' representative who was formerly a line manager at Gold Peak's Huizhou Advanced Factory explained how the policy of sending migrant workers back to their home towns when they were out of a job – and their permits were no longer valid – had been a major obstacle to solidarity as they tried to present a united front to the company in between arbitration and court hearings.

Gold Peak initially gave us an option of either 3,000 or 8,000 yuan compensation depending on seniority and whether a worker was prepared to terminate their contract with the company. If you went for 8,000 yuan then it was a one-off payment. Some of us with excess but not poisonous levels of cadmium in our blood took the 8,000 not realizing that our cadmium count could go up as well as down. But once our contracts had been terminated, we either had to quickly get a new job or go home. Of course, Gold Peak wanted us to disperse and go home. But even when we didn't, word soon got round and as soon as prospective employers found out you were a former Gold Peak worker they would discriminate [i.e. not hire]. As a result many workers went home and keeping in touch with them has been a major problem for our struggle.

(Interview, Hong Kong, 14 December 2005)

It is interesting to note that the worker interviewed here was not personally subject to *hukou* constraints as she is a local of Huizhou, a point I will return to later. During a discussion with labour law experts and lawyers in Guangzhou, there was general consensus that *hukou* placed a heavy burden on migrant workers pursuing claims through arbitration or the courts.

Hukou works in favour of the employers. They know that a worker only has 60 days to get his or her case accepted by the arbitration committee and that if they can spin the process out by making false promises or even not turning up for the hearing, the pressure on the applicant to accept an inferior settlement grows with time. If there was no rule that forced these workers back, then our job [of assisting compensation cases] would be easier.

(Interview, Guangzhou, 12 June 2006)

While the new Labour Mediation and Arbitration Law (2008) has extended the time limit to one year, the continued, if weakened, impact of *hukou* will keep the ball in the employers' side of the court.

Weak enterprise-level unions

Union dependence on management at enterprise level has also acted as a severe constraint on unions' and workers' capacity to improve working conditions in the private sector. While the central leadership of the ACFTU has long recognized this problem, cautious attempts to initiate reform from above have been impeded by the dependence of primary trade unions on the local authorities, who have without exception prioritized rapid development over the rights and interests of temporary migrant workers. The situation is exacerbated by the limited leverage that higher trade union bodies have over their primary organizations, despite the fact that trade unions are still governed according to the principles of 'democratic centralism' – at least in theory. This limited leverage makes the higher-level trade unions reluctant to risk activating their enterprise-level unions for fear that they will lose control of such organizations, so they continue to endorse management control as the lesser of two evils. Indeed, as we shall see in Chapter 6, experiments with the direct election of enterprise-level trade union chairpersons and committees aimed at improving the credibility and independence of primary unions have been subject to this very caution.

The responses to a 2006 review of attitudes to trade union work from 60 enterprise-level union officials attending trade union classes in Guangdong province demonstrated the impotence felt by these officials in the face of their employers' control over union finances, appointments, and their own wages and career prospects. Consequently many expressed a preference for adopting a mediation role over representation when grievances arose. Supporting collective action was off the radar of most – but interestingly not all – of these part-time union officers. The exercise, followed up with interviews and group discussions, demonstrated a marked lack of enthusiasm for trade union work in general. Six of the respondents said they were directly elected, although two of these could not give any details of when or how this event had taken place. A further 11 were appointed by the general manager or CEO and 15 were in their posts as a result of negotiations between the next level of the union and the enterprise management.

Almost all said that their work for the company was more important than their union work, which took up time that could be better spent on personal advancement within the company. All the respondents pointed to the enterprise union's lack of financial independence. Enterprises are obliged to send two per cent of their wage bill to the higher-level trade union but negotiations over the logistics for this transaction did not involve the enterprise-level union. The latter's annual budget was largely, if not entirely, dependent on enterprise funds. In one follow-up interview, a respondent explained the budgetary constraints on union activity.

> The annual budget for union finances is first approved by the deputy general manager and then the manager himself. Final ratification is also required from the CEO. Expenditure items that fall within the budget are reimbursed by the [company] finance people and anything that falls outside the budget needs special approval or can be placed under another item of expenditure already in the budget.
>
> (Interview, Case Study Report, 2006)

Employer power and the local government's prioritization of an investor-friendly environment was a key factor in determining the lack of confidence expressed by the respondents in carrying out union representational activities on behalf of their members. For example, 20 respondents claimed that attempting collective wage negotiations would not be possible under the current management, and 17 said that it would be possible but only if, and when, conditions became appropriate; just two respondents claimed it was possible to attempt such work – but as yet had not done so; nine people couldn't answer the question clearly (*shuo bu qingchu*) and the remainder left the question blank. In focus groups, the participants pointed out that management would not accept the idea of negotiating with workers and that 'the boss was there to make money'. If workers didn't like the wages 'the boss can get someone else to do it'. The dominant view on collective wage negotiations was that such a process would 'make the employers feel threatened' and by implication harm the investment environment.

The relationships between the union and the workers and their rights were not close. In focus groups, the union representatives acknowledged that collective action could produce limited results in terms of wages, but the general view was that this should be balanced against the price paid by the organizers of such action. Many of those attending the discussions could not say for sure if the law gave workers the right to pressure enterprises for higher wages. However, when asked what position they would take in the event of a dispute with management, 20 people (42 per cent of those attending) said that they were aware that they should represent the workers but given the current situation, they would adopt a neutral position and pass on the demands of the workers to management. Only two people (four per cent) said they would stand by the workers in the event of a dispute and 25 people (52 per cent) said they would 'take an objective position and seek a fair resolution' to the dispute. Responding to a question on individual grievances, 22 out of 60 respondents said that workers would come to the union if they had a problem, but 38 per cent said that their members would not approach them if they had a problem.

Two main points emerged in the follow up interviews and discussions, both of which emphasize union dependency on the employers. Firstly, that for an individual part-time trade union cadre employed in a small- or medium-size enterprise, spending more time on union work rather than company work would certainly invite management censure. In short, it would put the individual's job on the line. The employers' power over hire and fire remained, in their view, virtually unchallenged by the presence of the union. Secondly, the inability of trade union officers at enterprise level to intervene on behalf of their members created an atmosphere of distrust between members and trade union officers. This was not helped by the fact that the union officers were overwhelmingly part of the management structure prone to take into account the interests of the whole enterprise rather than the more specific interests of their members.

Challenging capitalist super-exploitation

At least until the advent of global recession in the last weeks of 2008, migrant labour had progressed from being a largely passive victim of capitalist globalization to being a vital player in a scenario where Chinese labour relations have become the new contesting ground between international capital and labour that holds out the 'possibility of a new working class activism' (Chang Dae-oup and Wong 2005: 107–54). In the following section, I will discuss the rise in cases of unrest and examine the factors behind it: labour law and the rise of legal activism, labour shortages, home town associations and the role of skilled workers and supervisors.

Labour laws and legal activism

The impact of labour law on labour unrest in the private sector has been more ambiguous than *hukou*. On paper at least, the development of a body of laws and regulations designed to govern industrial relations – as opposed to administrative regulations that managed state-owned work units in which workers were deemed the 'masters' – has provided legal benchmarks against which workers can hold employers accountable. The evidence to date suggests that despite myriad restrictions ranging from the expenses involved in bringing an employer to court, to poor implementation of laws, workers' actions are influenced, if not guided, by the law and that this is a discernible trend. As new laws, such as the Labour Contract Law (LCL) and the Labour Mediation and Arbitration Law (LMAL), make it easier for workers to pursue claims against employers, the number of cases filed has increased (*Caijing* 2009). One Guangzhou-based ACFTU lawyer explained

> [T]here is an unmistakable connection between law and action in our labour relations system. It is probably quicker for workers to get a solution by going to the streets, but that by no means excludes using the law. And of course, the more comprehensive the law, the more likely workers are to use it. They are most likely to take action after trying to use the law and not making any progress.
>
> (Interview, Guangzhou, 18 June 2009)

This observation was backed up during conversations and interviews with LNGO staffers and labour activists between 2005 and 2008. Indeed, much of the contention that has marked Chinese industrial relations in the private sector during the reform era has been as much about the implementation of relatively high legal standards as about the absence of law itself. One reason is that the state and the ACFTU have responded to growing legal violations and unrest by drafting yet more laws. For example, while the unprecedented participatory *process* of formulating and passing the 2008 Labour Contract Law was an important departure from the traditionally opaque practice of law-making, it remains the case that had employers followed their contractual and legal obligations set out in spirit, if not the entire letter, of the original 1995 Labour Law and its subsequent modifications, the new law may not have been necessary at all! The same argument applies with regard to implementation. Had enterprise-level trade unions been strong enough, or at least sufficiently independent from the employers in the private sector to enforce existing labour laws and negotiate binding collective contracts, the LCL would not have been such a contentious issue. Another reason the LCL was deemed necessary by the ACFTU and the MOLSS lies in the practice of watering down national laws via local-level regulations ostensibly drafted to implement national law on the basis of local conditions, but in fact setting out reinterpretations that can neutralize the original intentions of the national law (Buhmann 2005: 74). Thus a dynamic tension emerges in which the central authorities raise the bar via new legal standards on contracts and labour dispute resolution procedures – such as the LMAL – and local governments bring it back down to what they deem a manageable height. This contradiction featured in the debates over the standards of the LCL. While employers were predictably vexed by the LCL, a less welcome argument broke out among labour advocates and academics, as we discussed in Chapter 1. To recap, the Shanghai Faction opposed raising standards to what they felt were unrealistically high levels. This would render China's companies out of sync with the principles of human resource management and their preference for performance-based appraisal. The Beijing Faction disputed the direct linking of labour standards with economic efficiency on the grounds that labour relations were also social relations.

Returning to the relationship between laws and labour protest and whether or not laws encourage workers to pursue their rights and interests, in the decade following the promulgation of the national Labour Law in 1995, migrant workers increasingly challenged employers in arbitration and then in the courts. This trend was facilitated by both the state's and ACFTU's allocation of considerable resources to the development of a functioning system of labour dispute resolution discussed in Chapter 1 and, as Gallagher makes clear, the inadequacy of enterprise-level mediation procedures to resolve grievances (Gallagher 2005a: 115). As much of this inadequacy was down to union weakness in the private sector, it is hardly surprising that the unions took the view that a functioning arbitration system was vital.

> Another key goal of the ACFTU is to make efforts to build a sound system for labour arbitration. Because labour-management relations have become so much more complicated in China, we are also seeing many more labour disputes than before. That makes the establishment of a labour arbitration system much more important.
>
> (Roberts 2005)

Indeed, arbitration and court cases have become important, if somewhat overwhelmed, institutions in the industrial relations system. Statistics released by the NPC show that between 1987 and the end of 2005, 1.72 million labour disputes went to arbitration, involving 5.32 million employees representing an average growth rate of 27 per cent per year (*China Daily* 2007). The figures in Table 3.1 illustrate the growth of cases registered with arbitration committees since the national labour law came into force in 1995.

In 2006, workers won 47 per cent of cases heard by arbitration committees, with employers winning just 12 per cent and the remainder partially won by both parties (China Labour Statistical Yearbook 2007: 516). Collective labour disputes are defined as those involving three or more people, and there were 13,977 registered collective labour disputes involving 348,714 workers in 2006. Non-collective cases involved 301,233 workers (China Labour Statistical Yearbook 2007: 517). Shen Jie's work on the available statistics is instructive. In 1995, China's courts handled 28,285 labour disputes but by 2004 that number had increased fourfold to 114,997. However, as Shen points out, official figures do not distinguish collective cases from individual cases or how many cases were filed by employers.

100   *From victims to subjects*

Table 3.1 Labour disputes registered for arbitration, 1996–2006

Year	Cases accepted
1996	48,121
1997	71,524
1998	93,649
1999	120,191
2000	135,206
2001	154,621
2002	184,116
2003	226,391
2004	260,471
2005	313,773
2006	317,162

Source: China Labour Statistical Yearbook, 2007: 515–516.

There appears to be a wide regional variation on the results of labour cases dealt with by the courts. Composite nationwide statistics on the results of labour-related court cases are not made public although Shen has been able to fill some of the gaps with figures released by the Supreme People's Court. Between 1995 and 2001, labourers won more than 62 per cent of cases filed in Shandong, 55 per cent in Guangdong and the same proportion in Heilongjiang. In some cities, worker victories were very high: 90 per cent in Ningbo and Zhejiang and Zhongshan in Guangdong (Shen Jie 2007: 130). On paper at least, for migrant workers with sufficient funds and time to take a case to arbitration and the courts, there is a good chance of winning. The combination of the LCL – making it harder for employers to lay workers off – and the LMAL – making it easier and cheaper for workers to pursue claims – and the global financial crisis are already having a dramatic impact on the statistics. For example in Dongguan, a key manufacturing town in the Pearl River Delta, the courts dealt with a total of 23,044 cases in 2008 – an increase of 159 per cent over 2007! When a journalist from the respected *Caijing* (*Finance and Economics*) magazine asked the Dongguan Labour Bureau for figures on arbitration, he was informed that at present these statistics were 'too sensitive' and remained secret (*baomi*). The last available statistics from the Shenzhen Labour Arbitration Court illustrated an increase in arbitrated cases in the first quarter of 2008 of 277 per cent with some arbitration committees in manufacturing areas of the city, such as Bao'an and Longgang, posting increases of 392 per cent and 360 per cent respectively! (Zhou Qiong 2009).

At present, the cursory breakdowns on the nature of labour disputes that go through the official resolution procedure render it difficult to gauge the capacity of the system to deal with collective cases. State intervention in serious large-scale disputes suggests there is a long way to go. Until the LMAL abolished the arbitration application fee, it was in the interest of LDACs to divide collective cases into individual cases. Such behaviour generated income and looked good on an arbitrator's curriculum vitae, as a Guangzhou-based labour lawyer explained:

> In the labour disputes arbitration procedure, a 'collective labour dispute' is defined as 'a dispute in which one party consists of three or more workers'. Chapter Seven of the Procedural Rules for Labour Disputes Arbitration Committees sets out the rules for dealing with collective labour disputes arbitration. There are two kinds of collective labour disputes. A dispute arising from the performance of a collective agreement is one thing, while a dispute with one party of numerous persons is another thing. In Guangdong I have not heard of a dispute arising from a collective agreement. These days, labour arbitration committees do accept collective disputes according to the rules but this was not always the case. In 1998, I filed a case to an arbitration committee representing 58 workers. But the committee insisted on the case being separated into 58 individual cases. That caused me and my clients a lot of hassle. The reason was never expressly stated. But one can guess that 58 cases means 58 filing fees rather than one, and when evaluating an arbitrator's performance, 58 cases looks better than one!
>
> (Interview, Guangzhou, 18 December 2008)

The state's emphasis on juridical channels of labour dispute resolution, which includes the aforementioned new law on arbitration that should alleviate the problem described above, relates to the growth of legal activism which in turn is fed by the ACFTU's cautious approach to getting involved in disputes. This legal activism is manifested in the emergence of so-called 'black lawyers' – unqualified paralegals – and legal advice centres run by labour LNGOs in the boom towns of Guangdong province. LNGOs concentrate on labour law education, worker training, providing assistance to workers chasing compensation for injury via legal means, health and health education services and the provision of educational leisure facilities such as libraries, film shows and parties. They often offer legal advice in labour disputes, but generally avoid strikes as they can lead to accusations of subversion or organizing alternative workers' associations from the authorities. At the same time, most LNGO activists are well aware of the importance of workers' self-activity for levelling the labour relations playing field.

> Our aim is to assist workers to uphold their legal rights. We cannot become involved in militant actions such as strikes as the authorities will simply close us down. This has been proved in practice. At the same time, we foster workers' self-reliance and this requires workers to have knowledge of the law and its boundaries so that they can negotiate with the bosses or even take them to court.
>
> (Interview, Hong Kong, 12 December 2005)

For other groups, the emphasis on labour rights and engagement with corporate social responsibility projects form part of an overall strategy that avoids collective action.

Of course, we think workers should have the right to strike and demonstrate, but this is a last resort. If only employers, workers, contractors and brands obey the law and international labour norms there will be no need to strike.

(Interview, Hong Kong, 3 January 2006)

Paralegal labour practitioners are known as 'black lawyers' (*hei lüshi*). Their networks emerged at the turn of the century as an alternative to employer-dependent enterprise unions and nervous LNGOs. They have become a well-established part of the landscape, and in November 2007 a Hong Kong-based activist/academic attached to a labour NGO familiar with such networks estimated that there were over 600 black lawyers in Shenzhen and Dongguan. Most black lawyers are former workers who have been injured and have acquired knowledge of the law via personal experience of suing employers for compensation. They provide legal advice and even represent workers in arbitration and court appearances under the system of 'civil agency' (*gongmin daili*).[6] One former worker set up his network by successfully helping workers to resign from a factory with all the wages owed to them by the employer and charged 100 yuan for each successful case. Some of the more successful black lawyers have moved towards formal registration as labour service centres and in doing so have elicited the attentions of the local authorities. In contrast with the more cautious approach of LNGOs, the reaction to unwanted interference and veiled threats has been more robust. In 2006, for example, one District Labour Bureau and the Department for Urban Administration (DUA) in Shenzhen confiscated documents and computers from a black lawyer's service centre on the grounds that it was an illegal operation. The response of the centre's owner was to gather his staff and march into the DUA director's office to demand a legal justification for his orders!

Black lawyer networks have also campaigned against the 'administrative dysfunction' (*xingzheng buzuowei*) as manifested, for example, by the Bao'An District Labour Bureau in Shenzhen. Since 1999, at least 600 cases had been brought against the bureau on the grounds that it did not perform its administrative duty to ensure workers obtain legal wages. Many of these cases were at least partially won. The networks have also lobbied delegates to the Shenzhen People's Congress to submit a proposal prohibiting or lowering the labour dispute arbitration fee of 500 yuan. The lobbying was backed by a 'ten thousand thousand signature' campaign in the streets of Bao'An. According to one 'black lawyer', the central government sent a research team to Guangdong to listen to the legal grounds underpinning the campaign and in December 2006 the Supreme Court issued a judicial explanation that restricted backdated overtime wage claims to two years. The explanation encouraged many workers to claim 'forced resignation' on the grounds of unpaid overtime, which in turn opened up the path for them to claim the maximum two years of underpaid overtime wages as specified by the Supreme Court. Another black lawyer reported in December 2007 that his company had received 120 such cases, most of which involved middle-level managers. In another incident, 606 workers resigned en masse (Interview, 18 November 2008).

Challenging capitalist super-exploitation: the 'normalization' of the economic strike

The rise of legal activism reflects growing rights awareness among migrant workers. However, it does not offer an adequate explanation for the scale of the growth of collective action by migrant workers. As experienced and second-generation migrant workers have accumulated a better understanding of the factory system and the laws that are meant to protect them from its worst excesses, there has been a concomitant shift in the occurrence and nature of their response to capitalist super-exploitation. And as labour unrest has climbed to an altogether higher level, workers' awareness of their collective strength has also grown. Strikes and picket lines have gradually replaced sit-ins and marches to government labour bureaux. There has been a 'normalization' of strikes and a recognition from the state that workers need representation at enterprise level if the situation is to be stabilized without resorting to blanket repression. Skilled migrant workers in particular have brought about a situation in which 'strikes are by far the quickest and most effective way for workers to improve pay in particular and working conditions in general' (Interview, 12 June 2007). Line supervisors' willingness to side with workers has also contributed. As Cao Menghua, a former employee turned activist from Gold Peak explains:

> That night we staged a general strike covering all the factory workshops. The workers in the milling shops and assembly workshops demanded the test results, while the others requested a health check-up. We were ready to fight for our rights. In the initial period of our struggle, workers were not well organized and only a few line supervisors supported us. But this time the line supervisors took part in planning and how to make the strike successful. They appointed different batches of workers to block places, and they arranged shifts to guarantee the blockage was maintained around the clock. The strike was efficiently organized, similar to the organization of production. The girl safeguarding the elevator told me: 'Hua, I have locked up the elevator, and no one can take it now. You can relax!' Women workers in the assembly department got very excited when they noticed the success of their action – earlier in May their strikes were unsuccessful. Some commented 'Hey, when line supervisors join us, it really makes a difference!'
>
> (Globalization Monitor 2009)

The growing success of strikes by workers able to command higher than average wages has also impacted on unskilled line workers reliant on the minimum wage. Following a wave of strikes in 2004 and 2005, the Shenzhen city authorities increased the minimum wage dramatically in July 2005 and July 2006, by one-third over the two years for those employed inside the SEZ, and 46 per cent for those employed outside the SEZ (Chan 2009: 60–77). These significant increases aroused the workers' expectations, so that when the city government failed to increase the minimum wage in July 2007 a new round of strikes erupted. In short, 'collective bargaining by riot' (Hobsbawm 1964: 6–7) has gradually emerged as the most efficient method for workers to defend their rights and interests. Many have developed a very good idea of what they can get away with and how far they can go, so that short sharp strikes and protests have become an extremely prompt and effective way of redressing their grievances.

These developments are giving weight to the argument that migrant workers in China are no longer simply passive victims. Whereas in the past a collective strike was, generally speaking, a last resort to be used only after other forms of redress had been exhausted, it is increasingly the case that workers take strike action as a more efficient alternative to formal and crowded dispute resolution procedures. In other words, they have become more militant. The lack of a clearly protected right to strike in China and related restrictions on the official reporting of strikes means that there are no clear figures either on the number of strikes or the number of working days lost through strike activity. Nevertheless, there is considerable evidence to suggest both that strikes are rising in number and frequency and that there is a corresponding trend away from repression towards concession on the part of the state (Clarke and Pringle 2009: 93). We can get an idea of their geographical distribution by looking at figures for arbitration and court cases. As we can see in Table 3.2, provinces and municipalities with high levels of FDI, Hong Kong and Taiwanese investment and private capital were topping the 'disputes league table' at least as far as we can judge by statistics for cases registered for arbitration. These figures suggest that industrial disputes and strikes are predominantly in the oldest zones where labour shortages are most obvious.

Migrant workers' capacity to organize collective disputes has been greatly enhanced by two factors: firstly, the impact of labour shortages and, secondly, the accumulation of experience in the factory system, especially among skilled workers. The Chinese media began running stories on labour shortages in Guangdong province following the Spring Festival in February 2004, when the annual return to work failed to meet employer demand in some areas (Barboza 2006; Yuji Miora 2007). These reports linked the shortages to low wages and poor working conditions as well as competition from other apparently better-regulated regions such as the Yangzi River Delta running inland from Shanghai. A report released at the

Table 3.2 Top six provinces for recorded labour disputes going to arbitration

Province	Cases accepted
Guangdong	54,855
Jiangsu	43,984
Shandong	23,625
Shanghai	24,172
Beijing	22,647
Zhejiang	21,036

Source: China Labour Statistical Yearbook, 2007: 517.

end of December 2004, pointed out that real wages in the PRD had risen just 68 yuan in 12 years (Wen Dajun Dale 2007: 30–5), and employers even began to worry that the flurry of press reports would encourage workers to demand better wages. An owner of a Shenzhen plastics factory, who I interviewed in Hong Kong in late 2005, illustrated how alarm bells were beginning to ring among employers used to dictating terms.

> We are short of workers and I cannot see any improvement in the situation in the foreseeable future. My father and I have raised wages but the newspaper reports have taken an anti-employer attitude and this is making workers more militant. I have prohibited workers from taking newspapers into their dormitories but this is not going to stop them getting angry. They can read them outside anyway. We haven't had to deal with strikes, but I can see it coming. They are happening all over the delta.
> (Interview, Hong Kong, 12 October 2005)

The shortages continued through 2006 and 2007 but were not confined to the PRD as initial reports seemed to suggest. I interviewed a personnel manager at a large chemical factory in Hangzhou in spring 2007. His company's recent policy of hiring migrant workers on basically the same terms as local workers had been dictated by labour shortages.

> We no longer formally distinguish between local workers and migrant workers. Of course, local workers do not generally make use of the dormitories but they can if they want to. Likewise, a number of the skilled or older migrant workers on our books rent or have even bought homes nearby. You can hear if you walk around this district that there are accents from all over China. In fact, this is the second generation of migrants and they are totally different from the first generation that did not stay long and had different goals. Just look at the clothes they wear these days, you cannot tell them apart from local people. But to be honest, our policy is ultimately determined by the need to retain skilled, experienced workers in a completely different labour market environment.
> (Interview, Hangzhou, 21 March 2007)

Mid-term demographic factors also appear to weigh in favour of workers as 'the number of fifteen-year olds steadily declines over the next fifteen years or so, this will translate into more bargaining power for those entering into the labour force in the future' (Dali L. Yang 2005).

The shift in the market has not been lost on migrant workers. Protests in the past had generally involved a march down to the local labour bureau with the aim of getting officials involved in order to bring pressure to bear on employers. The most common form of dispute was over wage arrears (Greenfield and Pringle 2002; Lee Ching-kwan 2007: 165). While arrears remain a major issue, especially in the construction sector, the spontaneous march to the labour office is being replaced by more sophisticated tactics directly targeting employers and usually led by skilled workers demanding higher wages.

> The skilled workers themselves also use the situation [labour shortages] to their own advantage by demanding higher wages, often for all the workers in a factory. If the bosses refuse, it is these workers who will call and lead a strike. In cases such as wage arrears, it is also the skilled workers who generally lead the other workers in demonstrations to the government offices with complaints against the factory managers. They also make sure the demonstrations are peaceful, often repeatedly whispering their demands.
>
> (Xu Xiaohong 2004: 286)

Strikes often involve street protests. These can be an indirect way of getting workers from other factories to join in a strike or a deliberate attempt to up the stakes and force government officials to pressure employers to settle. The militancy of recent strikes is captured by Chan's research in Shenzhen as he explained during an interview in 2008.

> Workers also prepared at least three amplifiers, several cameras and some fundraising boxes. They wrote 'for our common interests, please put in your money!' on the boxes. They were soon full of money. The cameras were used to take pictures when workers were beaten by policemen. More and more workers from other factories joined in. At 1:00 pm the protesters, whose number had reached as high as 7,000 to 8,000, arrived in the immigration control station.[7] More than ten fire engines and over 30 water cannon stood in front of the station. The police used the water tap to drive away the workers, while the workers lobbed stones and bricks at police. The police attempted, but failed to move in as the stones kept raining down. But later on, the police sent out plainclothes to mix into the protesters. They strongly attacked workers suddenly. After the workers in the front fell down, those standing behind screamed and others retreated. Some workers were arrested during the day, but they were soon released. Thirty workers were sent to hospital and treated well. Their medical expenses were all paid by the police. The head of the district police bureau came to visit them, and gave each patient, workers and policemen alike, 100 yuan.
>
> (Interview, Hong Kong, 18 November 2008)

Home town associations can be both a constraint on and a resource for workers and self-activity was crucial in transforming traditional native place organizations into more effective class-orientated groups.

> [A]lthough the native place boundary and its attached gangsters were usually exploited by management to divide and pacify workers, they could function in the interests of workers when their structural power was increased. In this case, the strike was a turning point.
>
> (Chan 2009: 60–77)

Informal strikes and formal dispute resolution

In presenting her 'protests against discrimination' analysis of migrant worker protests, Lee gives us a road map of labour action: 'These workers resort first to legal activism such as filing petitions and lawsuits for collective labor arbitration, mediation and litigation. *Only when this institutionalized channel fails* (which it often does) do they resort to public disruption' (Lee Ching-kwan 2007: 9, author's italics). Lee goes on to draw quite distinct protest strategies between migrant workers and traditional urban workers' 'protests of desperation' in which the former emphasize legal and bureaucratic channels and the latter street action (Lee Ching-kwan 2007: 9–11). In contrast, the evidence presented here demonstrates that Lee's analysis is at best out of date and at worst plain wrong. Especially since 2003 and the onset of labour shortages, migrant workers are as likely to take strike action and/or block the streets as they are to file for collective arbitration. To be sure, migrant workers do use official channels of dispute resolution and are encouraged to do so by the authorities, including the trade union, but this does not exclude other tactics. On the other hand, if Lee's road map takes us down the wrong route, we can chart a development in the protest strategies of migrant workers from protests to well-organized strikes – both of which may or may not have included formal resolution procedures – in which actual existing conditions are the deciding factor no matter which 'insurgent identity' the participants may – or indeed, may not – adopt.

Migrant workers' labour militancy presents us with three main issues: first, who is the target of worker activism; second, the relationship between militant action and legalistic appeals; and third, the efficacy of the dispute resolution system. Of course, the problem underpinning all these issues is how the ACFTU responds to labour unrest.

Do migrant workers in China target employers or the state when they engage in labour actions? Migrant workers' actions in the 1990s were generally directed at the local labour bureau (Chan 1998). However, during the last seven to eight years there appears to have been a gradual move away from targeting the state to confronting employers directly, with the aim of forcing them to negotiate. I believe this trend was first identified by experienced LNGO researchers and staffers. Parry Leung conducted a survey of newspaper reports on collective labour disputes in the PRD between 2002 and 2005. Leung's data shows that just short of a third of newspaper-reported collective actions by migrant workers took place at the manufacturing site and did not involve street protests. A majority of the 67 protests involved street-level actions, but these were a collective extension of strikes rather than discreet petitions. In comparison with Chan's newspaper translations, the survey reflects a growing militancy: 23 strikes combined with road blocks; 14 strikes and street demonstrations but without road blocks; 16 strikes with no street demonstration; nine demonstrations in or around the enterprise; two detentions of senior managers; one work-in; one hunger strike; and one suicide protest. Of course, in organizing strikes, the workers can be confident of attracting the attention of the state. This risks police intervention as well as that of the local labour bureau. But either way, by organizing collective strikes rather than directly petitioning the state, the workers are openly targeting production and the employer. In fact Leung's survey found that migrants went to protest at government offices in only 12 protests (Kessler 2009).

In April 2005, the IHLO office in Hong Kong – which featured a photograph of a dramatic factory gate picket line during 2005 and 2006 on its website's homepage – observed that the nature of disputes was changing as they were increasingly aimed at halting production to force bosses to concede rather than relying directly on government intervention. The weapon of choice was now the strike and the picket line. Until quite recently, the Hong Kong-based LNGO China Labour Bulletin was keen to emphasize that workers took militant action only as a last resort (China Labour Bulletin 2001). However, in answering questions from the floor of an ITUC/GUF conference convened in Hong Kong in 2008 to discuss the emerging labour movement, CLB director Han Dongfang argued that strikes 'have become the most effective method to improve wages and conditions' and that the wider trade union and NGO community should 'catch up with Chinese workers'. My interviews with Gold Peak workers suggest that strikes were an initially preferred – if somewhat panicky – instrument of protest, effectively disabled by a combination of company tactics and, as we have seen, by the constraints of *hukou*. The reaction of milling shop workers at Gold Peak's Huizhou PP factory to the news that fellow workers had tested positive for excess and poisonous levels of cadmium in their blood was to strike. They demanded that the company talk transparently about the dangers of cadmium and they urged government intervention in order to compel Gold Peak to accept their compensatory obligations. The company's response was to play down the effects of cadmium, offer limited compensation and set deadlines for agreement that effectively terminated the employment of the more militant workers. Clearly Gold Peak wished to avoid further strikes and channel the dispute into a drawn-out process of legal wrangling. On the other hand, events have since proved that the company certainly underestimated the workers' tenacity.

The second issue concerns the relationship between militant action and legalistic appeals. While acknowledging that the state has been anxious to channel disputes into formal juridical channels, Chan states simply that '[A]t a certain point, workers' docility becomes transformed into collective protest and violence' (Chan 2001: 16) but does not expand on the relationship between official procedures and protest. However, Lee found that the state's effort to build formal dispute resolution procedures did not necessarily discourage radicalization. They could have the opposite effect:

> Radicalisation of conflict may occur in any stage of the arbitration-litigation process. When workers with standing grievances find legal grounds for their case, they expect official attention. But bureaucratic red tape and political pressure from the big companies or state firms may affect whether workers may even lodge a complaint.
>
> (Lee Ching-kwan 2007: 188)

On the other hand, some experienced Hong Kong-based labour activists who have been monitoring labour disputes in the PRD for many years have found that arbitration and litigation tended to rule out more militant forms of action as they risk incurring the anger of the arbitration committee or the courts. One activist with over 10 years of experience working for LNGOs explained that

> Sure, legal recourse is sometimes preceded by a strike or petition. However, in recent times there has been a rise in strikes that aim to damage the company economically [until such time as] it raises wages or cancels fees and fines. This course of action rarely involves arbitration or the courts.
>
> (Interview, 17 January 2008)

Pertinent here is the efficacy of the dispute resolution system as an institution through which workers can pursue their rights and interests even when they run counter to local government priorities. I have already documented the fact that, unlike the neighbouring transitional economy of Vietnam, workers do make use of formal procedures. However, both the courts and the arbitration committees have been reluctant to deal effectively with collective labour protests. Although there are political and financial aspects to this issue, the root of the problem lies with the largely unrepresentative role of the trade union during arbitration.

Trade unions generally play a passive role in the dispute resolution procedure, acting as a mediator rather than as a worker representative. On occasion, trade unions have even appeared in arbitration hearings on behalf of the employer. In any serious collective dispute, the trade union is very unlikely to support the worker against the management, and there have been plenty of cases of victimization of enterprise trade union leaders who have been rash enough to do so (Chen Feng 2003b: 1017). Thus, union avoidance of disputes and its strategy of restricting its representation of workers to 'cases where the violations are so bad that we will definitely win in court', as one lawyer in Guangzhou put it in 2006, is a major constraint on effective dispute resolution. In the absence of trade union representation, LNGOs and 'black lawyers' have become very active in offering legal support to workers in dispute. The ACFTU has begun to sponsor the establishment of legal advice centres for workers on an experimental basis and the contested establishment of such a trade union centre is the focus of my case study in Chapter 4. In a significant development in late 2007, the Shenzhen Federation of Trade Unions (SFTU) even approached labour NGOs and black lawyers with a view to collaboration, on condition that the labour NGOs severed any links with foreign sponsors.

Conclusion: the primacy of trade unions in 'actually existing conditions'

On the hitherto sensitive question of strikes, the deputy chair of the SFTU said in a speech to the People's Congress that regulations on the conduct of strikes need to be drawn up and that society should not be oversensitive about their existence. Strikes, he argued, 'are inevitable in the market economy and perfectly acceptable in today's society. Shenzhen needs to discard its oversensitive approach to strikes as this attitude has become an ideological millstone round our necks' (Wang Tongxin 2008).

While it is hard to avoid recalling senior Party official Chou Yang's somewhat ill-conceived public acceptance of strikes in the spring of 1957 (see Chapter 2), the evolving nature of global capitalism itself would appear to rule out history repeating itself. Perhaps more than ever, the behaviour of workers in the reform era is central to the future development, pace and direction of trade union reform. Indeed, the latter is now the key question for the future of China's industrial relations and the wider social harmony project. On the one hand, it has highlighted the potential role of the trade unions in developing institutionalized channels of conflict resolution; on the other hand, it has inhibited the trade unions from actively engaging with workers' grievances for fear of intensifying conflict. The development of sophisticated industrial militancy, especially in the private sector, has led to increased social and political pressure on the ACFTU to anticipate, and at times represent, workers' grievances.

The source of political pressure resulting from worker protest in the private sector is the CPC, which is keen to avoid too many instances of collective protest. The Party appears to have accepted that labour disputes are an inevitable consequence of private enterprise. Taking the view that the juridical resolution of disputes will discourage workers from taking more militant action, the ACFTU is therefore required to channel this unrest into constitutional, juridical and/or bureaucratic forms of dispute resolution, a strategy that to date has been hampered by union inexperience in responding to apolitical shop-floor militancy, a lack of capacity in bargaining skills and a corresponding fear that mismanaging its intervention may render matters even more tense.

On the other hand, the union has been successful, on paper, in rebuilding its membership base that was devastated during the years of SOE restructuring. Efforts to recruit private sector workers had been sluggish and inevitably constrained by the fact that up until its 14th Congress in 2003 migrant workers from the countryside were not recognized as part of the working class. In January 2001, the ACFTU launched a branch-building campaign that targeted *all* workers under the slogan: 'Trade union organizations (branches) must be established wherever there are staff and workers' (*nar li you zhigong, nar li jiu bixu jianli gonghui zuzhi*). The wording is important and gives us more semantic insights into the habitual mores of the ACFTU even at a time of crisis. The term 'staff and workers' is preferred over the term 'workers' and its implications of confrontational class consciousness. More important, however, is that the slogan does not call on cadres to go forth and 'organize' (*zuzhi*) staff and workers, but rather that trade union branches should be set up (*jianli*) wherever staff and workers are to be found i.e. the private sector. Thus, despite the acknowledgement of migrants as workers, traditional methods of establishing unions via the trade union's status as a government organization to secure employer agreement rather than directly approaching workers remained the dominant method of expanding membership. For many new recruits, the first sign that they had joined the union arrived with a deduction for union dues on their pay slip. Not that this quota-driven approach to expansion didn't produce spectacular statistics. By the end of 2004, the union had over a million primary level organizations and 137 million members, of whom 35 million were newly recruited migrant workers (Wang Jiaoping 2005). In a sign of further relaxation of *hukou* restrictions, existing union members working away from home were permitted to transfer their membership to their place of work rather than their place of residence.

A well-publicized exception to traditional practice was the ACFTU's tussle with Wal-Mart. The fiercely anti-union multinational's resistance to the setting up of trade union branches persuaded the ACFTU to adopt an organizing approach, recruiting individual employees to the union outside the workplace to provide the basis of a union branch. Nevertheless, even in this case the ACFTU has been hesitant about moving beyond its traditional model. Although the Wal-Mart case has been widely proclaimed as a breakthrough in the ACFTU's organizing strategy, after the first union branches were established Wal-Mart signed a recognition agreement with the ACFTU under which new branches would be established in the traditional way, in collaboration with management, although the preparatory committees would include employee representatives and the agreement provided for the election of the trade union committee. Asked why Wal-Mart had agreed to allow unions, a Wal-Mart spokesman reportedly said '[T]he union in China is fundamentally different from unions in the West ... The union has made it clear that its goal is to work with employers, not promote confrontation' (*China Daily* 2006). It remains to be seen how effective Wal-Mart's workplace trade unions will prove to be.

The combination of striking skilled workers and Party pressure on the union was apparent in a strike by 220 gantry and tower crane operators at the Yantian International Container Terminals Limited (YICT). YICT is a joint venture established by Hutchison Port Holdings and Shenzhen Yantian Port Group in 1994 and is responsible for port services at Shenzhen's Yantian port, now one of the busiest harbours in the world. Much better paid than Shenzhen's factory workers, the crane operators were nevertheless fed up with management arrogance and sleight-of-hand deductions from their pay packets. They were also angry at the absence of a trade union, calling the company-sponsored Staff Association a 'white collar club'. Following successful strikes by workers at nearby ports that had a powerful impact on the YICT crane operators, they struck for improved wages, reduced working time and the organization of a trade union in April 2007. The reaction from the Shenzhen government and the SFTU was immediate. A high-level delegation that included a deputy chair of the SFTU descended on the port in the early hours of the morning. It made rapid progress and by breakfast time the group had established contact with management; assured the strikers that a union would be established on the basis of Chinese law; promised that the SFTU would assist in the selection of worker representatives; and assured strikers that it would compel management to come to the negotiating table, a promise it was able to make due to the backing of the Shenzhen government and Party Committee.

It is interesting to note that, while the city-level union and indeed government intervention in such strikes has traditionally been limited to a fire-fighting role, the nature of the workers' demands at the Yantian port terminal dictated a more rigorous response. The SFTU's intervention was based on three premises: ensuring that the dispute did not spread and that a return to work took place as soon as possible; finding common ground between the two sides and supervising subsequent negotiations; and, most important of all, ensuring that the dispute was placed firmly within the parameters of the Chinese labour relations and trade union system in order to avoid any chance of a 'second trade union' being set up outside the control of the ACFTU. As a result, all the workers' financial demands were basically met even as their aspirations for an independently elected union committee were effectively squashed by management bad faith and the SFTU's unwillingness to challenge the company over election procedures. Negotiations ended with a three per cent pay rise, half an hour off the working day plus significant bonuses for working at height.

In March 2010, further evidence of migrant workers' capacity to exert pressure both on employers and the ACFTU emerged in dramatic fashion when up to 1800 migrant workers organized a series of strikes at a Honda-owned parts factory in Foshan, Guangdong province. Many of the strikers were recent school leavers or even school students on work experience schemes that Honda had taken advantage of in order to avoid the upward pressure on wages as the economy recovered from the 2008–9 global recession and labour shortages again made their presence felt. The demands on Honda included an across-the-board wage rise of 800 yuan and the reorganization of trade union representation in the factory via democratic elections. After some prevarication, Honda's senior management in Guangdong arrived to negotiate with worker representatives, no doubt spurred on by the inability of at least four other Honda car plants in China to continue production due to a shortage of parts. Most of the strikers' demands were met and post-strike organization in the factory remained strong enough for workers to issue an open letter of thanks to supporters worldwide. Importantly, the letter drew attention to the conditions of delivery drivers at the plant who were not directly employed by Honda. These events sparked a nationwide strike wave that brought wage rises of up to 30 per cent to participating factories and similar increases in minimum wage levels.

The Honda strikes came at the same time as a spate of ten suicides among young workers at the massive Foxconn plant in nearby Shenzhen. In the first six months of 2010, ten workers jumped to their deaths giving rise to widespread public sympathy over the plight of migrant workers – especially those employed in foreign enterprises. The tragedies also brought calls from China's leaders such as Hu Jintao for society to take better care of migrant workers.

The Honda strikes produced a woeful response from the local trade union which dispatched officials to the site – wearing yellow hats! – in an attempt to persuade picketing workers to return to work. The incident ended in a brawl between angry strikers and union officials. Apart from forcing the local township union to publish a public – if somewhat grudging – apology to the workers, the images in the media of yellow-hatted trade union officials brawling with disciplined young workers pursuing their legal rights against a Japanese multinational has increased pressure on the ACFTU to reform. The local union's behaviour has apparently induced damning criticism from senior ACFTU figures in Guangdong. Further evidence of the link between militancy and reform was provided by the chairman of the Standing Committee of the Guangdong National People's Congress. Commenting on the draft of the 'Regulations on the Democratic Management of Enterprises'[8] currently being debated Ou Guangyuan stated that '[T]hese regulations have been substantially revised based on discussions with all interested parties in the wake of the problems manifest at Foxconn and Honda' (China Labour Bulletin 2010).

The pressure on trade unions to stabilize labour relations is heaviest in areas where private and foreign capital has made the most significant inroads – chiefly southern and eastern provinces such as Guangdong, Zhejiang, Jiangsu and Fujian. Although pilot projects have been conducted in Fujian – union elections in a Nike factory, for example, Guangdong and Zhejiang have been the main locations for union innovation. In the following three chapters, I use case studies to examine critically three examples of union innovation at local level and their implications for overall progress in China's industrial relations system.

4 Experimental pragmatism I

Collective consultation in Xinhe town

'Segui il tuo corso, e lascia dir le genti' (Follow your own course, and let people talk).[1] Despite a dramatically altered industrial relations landscape, the continued traditional practices of Chinese trade unions at the local level have been a major obstacle to reform at the national level. Consequently, the transformation into a more responsive and representative organization of the working class is as dependent on local innovation, followed by the integration of successful projects into national trade union policy, as it is on Party edicts. In the main, the absence of a 'second trade union' (*di'erge gonghui*) tends to lull the ACFTU into taking a passive approach to reform and this adds to the significance of dynamic local initiatives if, and when, they occur. Understanding these initiatives is important for three reasons. First, Chinese governance generally operates on a pilot study basis and the results of any given pilot are analysed at the centre prior to being applied provincially, nationally, put on hold or rejected.[2] For example, China's national social security reforms were partly based on a large-scale pilot reform in Liaoning province. Second, China's authoritarian political system is neither monolithic nor seamless, and the unavoidable fractures leave room for local initiatives that are not entirely dictated by the restrictions and concerns of the central government in Beijing. On the negative side, this can facilitate local protectionism that has generally been a conservative force in Chinese politics. But on the positive side, it can provide the space for workers and union officials to pursue initiatives that might not be immediately acceptable closer to the centres of power. As the Chinese saying goes, 'heaven is high and the emperor is far away'. Third, China provides us with an example of combined and uneven development. Speaking of nation states, Marx argued that under a globally expanding capitalism 'the country that is more developed industrially only shows, to the less developed, the image of its own future' (Marx 1867: 1). The same applies to uneven development in China. For example, almost 90 per cent of the population of Guangdong province derives its primary income from non-agricultural activity; and yet a fifth of China's peasantry still lacks access to electricity. We should not be surprised, then, when traditionally minded ACFTU officials in less-developed and less-open Guangxi province cast a chary eye at the SFTU's recent groundbreaking – if somewhat double-edged – proposal to join forces with paralegal lawyers and LNGOs in the city.[3] But as the market economy develops in Guangxi, trailblazers in the SFTU could, if they knew their Marx, justifiably shoot back at their Guangxi counterparts that 'it is of you that the story is told' (Marx 1867: 1).

Party pressure on the trade unions to improve their representation of workers emerged in the late 1990s as SOE restructuring deepened and the private sector continued to acquire an international reputation for appalling working conditions that were partly responsible for growing labour protests from migrant workers. As the fourth most senior politician in China and chair of the ACFTU, Wei Jianxing was ideally placed to give voice to the Party's concerns.[4] In a speech to senior trade union cadres in 2000 he made these concerns crystal clear.

> The problems at the moment are: on the one hand, following the structural adjustments and the restructuring of SOEs and COEs, a considerable number of trade union organisations [and branches] have collapsed and their members washed away. On the other hand, the organisation of trade unions in newly-established enterprises has simply not happened. At the end of 1999, national trade union membership had dropped to 87 million, leaving more than 100 million workers unorganised. When there is not even a trade union, what is the point of talking about unions upholding the legal rights of workers? Or being a transmission belt between the party and the masses? Or an important social pillar of state power?
>
> (Wei Jianxing 2000)

The CPC's anxiety was, in large part, rooted in the fear that passive trade unions would be unable 'to prevent people from initiating self-organized and self-controlled actions that challenge the *status quo*' (Wang Kan 2008: 203). Thus, while the absence of competition from independent trade unions is hardly constructive to developing an internal dynamic driving ACFTU reform, there are times when the Party steps in to fill the void and encourage innovation. For example, the chair of the Shandong Federation of Trade Unions (and a member of the Provincial Party Committee's Standing Committee), Bai Xumin, has exhorted union cadres to work hard and 'blaze new trails in the fields of trade union theory and work' (Bai Xumin 2007). Of course, this can work in the reverse direction, as the ACFTU rediscovered following its decision to make a substantial financial contribution to the hunger-striking students of Tiananmen Square during the 1989 Democracy Movement. The gesture led to a comprehensive leadership purge.

On the other hand, Party pressure on the unions to reform is qualified by its anxiety that increased representation will lead to even higher levels of labour militancy. As a consequence, the framing, presentation and 'spin' of reform is particularly important and trade union innovation in the 'the new era of trade union work' (Wang Lianxiang 2005: 280) is often presented as having produced a win–win (*shuangying*) result or situation. The Wenling City Federation of Trade Unions (WFTU) used the phrase to describe the wage consultation project discussed in this chapter and has adopted a somewhat self-congratulatory tone ever since. The union stated that 'following several years of conscientious explorations and pilot practices, [the union] achieved the success we had anticipated. The enterprises were satisfied and the workers were delighted. It is a win–win situation' (Wenling City Federation of Trade Unions 2006). In fact, rather than anticipating success, the WFTU leaders must have had a pleasant surprise, as the innovative practices I discuss were specific to local conditions on the ground.

Given that labour militancy is now the major underlying reason for trade union reform, its political aim is to neutralize antagonistic capital-labour relations and produce the less exploitative environment originally envisaged by the post-1978 leadership. On the other hand, the consequence of the CPC's embrace of globalization has been to cast aside Deng Xiaoping's insurance policy against contradictions between 'socialism and the market economy'. Back in 1985, it seemed feasible enough that 'the public sector of the economy is always predominant' and by fostering economic growth 'we seek common prosperity, always trying to avoid polarisation' (Deng Xiaoping 1985). The disappearance of these socialist market benchmarks has rendered the ACFTU's task yet more complex and urgent.

In this chapter, I demonstrate how localized class struggle encouraged local actors to move beyond the constraints of enterprise-based collective consultations – the original location of the goalposts – to a sector-wide agreement involving 116 enterprises and over 12,000 workers. In the following chapter, I examine the protracted, contentious and eventually successful struggle to establish a workers' legal rights centre under the management of the local city-level trade union. I have tried to capture the essence of these two examples of union innovation by referring to them as manifestations of 'experimental pragmatism'. More formal national trade union reforms – also based on pilot projects – such as the application of enterprise-level trade union elections (see Chapter 6) have been positioned as attempts to democratize either the union or, indeed, China itself (Howell 2008: 845–63). In contrast, the following examples are presented as local responses drawing on local resources, including individual initiatives to meet the challenges of labour violations and strikes that arose from the rapid expansion of capitalist relations of production in small-scale enterprises; in short, innovation that travelled up the transmission belt rather than orders coming down it.

I have divided this chapter on collective consultation in the town of Xinhe, Zhejiang province into four sections. The first section summarizes the development of collective dialogue in industrial relations in China and highlights the major issues. The second briefly describes the economic and political backdrop against which the experiment in sector-level consultation took place. The third section narrates the process of collective consultation itself, and the final section analyses the events in the context of the research question: How can a local trade union act in defence of the interests and rights of its members and potential members? In other words, is bottom-up reform possible?

Methodology

This chapter is based on collaborative fieldwork in Wenling City and Xinhe town carried out in 2006 by experienced local labour researchers with excellent access to the various actors involved. The conclusion of a collective wage table covering over 100 small enterprises in one town had originally been the subject of a short paper written by labour researcher and lecturer Professor Xu Xiaohong and presented at a seminar I attended in 2004. Given the difficulties of the environment, the achievement interested me and gave rise to further discussions with a number of colleagues working in China. While the agreement did not constitute a fully participatory process of bargaining, it appeared to be sustainable and certainly warranted further inquiry, not least because it represented an innovative response to sophisticated labour militancy. After further background reading on the subject, I asked my mainland colleague who had written the original paper if further research was possible. He agreed and a research plan was put in place with the main interviews conducted in May 2006. We discussed the data and prepared follow-up interview questions that took place in September 2006. A full case study report was completed and this was subsequently the subject of discussion at further meetings as well as during my trips to Zhejiang on related fieldwork.

The development of collective consultation in the reform era

Context

Collective dialogue in China is informed by both the legacy of the command economy and the apparent durability of the transitional period. Officially, the current status of the transition is not contested. However, the Party's theoretical interpretations of actual existing social and economic relations are driven as much by political expediency as by intellectual rigour. On the one hand, China's revised Constitution still clings to socialist rhetoric even as the CPC has admitted capitalists into its ranks and private property has been awarded the same status as national assets. On the other hand, although the state still retains a directive role in the economy, there has been an explosion of capitalist social relations over the past 20 years and the state sector has been shrinking fast in relative and, in some sectors, even in absolute size (see Chapter 1). In the field of collective dialogue, the return of the openly separate interests of labour and capital in the workplace has been treated with great caution by the Party and the trade union has hardly been left to its own devices. As we saw in Chapter 1, during the command economy era, a triumvirate of committees known as the *lao san hui* administered labour relations in SOEs. The triumvirate was made up of the Party Committee, the Trade Union Committee and the Standing Committee of the Staff and Workers' Congress, with the Party Committee having ultimate authority. While such clear manifestations of Party power are no longer visible on the shop or office floor, it remains virtually impossible to have a discussion about labour relations in the PRD without reference to the CPC and its authority. Against this background, the complexities of inherited practices and the durability of the transitional period influence activity in three aspects of activity related to the development of collective solutions to industrial conflict: conceptually, legally and in practical application.

Conceptualizing consultation

Conceptually, 'labour relations' (*laodong guanxi*) is a politically correct term designed to fit the mixed realities of a socialist market economy. The term allows for the co-existence of public and private capital and replaced the more problematic 'labour-capital relations' (*lao-zi guanxi*) initially adopted following the introduction of economic reforms and consequent restoration of an industrial relations system (Warner and Zhu 2000: 24). For the Party-state, the term 'labour-capital relations' implied that the transition period was a return to capitalism or, at the very least, a conceptual step in that direction. In keeping with this reasoning is the use of the term 'collective consultation' (*jiti xieshang*) as opposed to 'collective bargaining' (*jiti tanpan*). Consultation implicitly suggests that a 'win–win' agreement between employer and employees can be achieved without serious contention, work stoppages, strikes and the like. There is no need, therefore, for the more aggressive 'bargaining' often perceived as a characteristic of 'Western-style' trade unions. As one county-level trade union cadre illustrated:

> Our role is to explain to employers that trade unions in general and collective consultation in particular are in their interests. If an employer is especially nervous of trade unions – such as some of the Korean investors in Guangdong – we patiently explain that we are not like western trade unions or trade unions in their home country and certainly do not organize strikes or that kind of thing.
>
> (Union official, interview, Pingshan, 10 October 2005)

Yet, there is clearly an underlying suspicion within trade union circles, labour academia and the pro-reform sections of the media that 'bargaining' might be a more appropriate conceptual approach and there has been a marked increase in press reports employing the term 'collective bargaining'. At the policy development level, Liu Yufang draws a direct link between the use of the terms bargaining, legal development and China's integration into the world market.

> The key point is that collective contracts are concluded via collective bargaining. Following WTO entry, China must not only accept and meet international norms on enterprise regulations and trade rules; we must also gradually bring our labour laws up to the level of international labour standards. In the global economy, collective contracts are a principal legal system for labour relations universally adopted by countries with market economies and moreover are a basic right recognised by the ILO. As a WTO member, the status of collective contracts will shift from voluntary to compulsory, an obligation clearly stated in the revised Trade Union Law.
>
> (Liu Yufang 2002: 23)

Whether the process is called bargaining or consultation, there is always the danger of attaching too much importance to words alone. Perhaps the main point is that the ACFTU is beginning to accept that 'to bargain and negotiate requires not only recognition that the interests of workers and managers can be opposed, but also willingness, courage and skills to confront. To bring about such a change in behaviour demands therefore fundamental changes in the pattern of incentives to trade union leaders' (Howell 2003: 105).

Legal development

Legally, the development of collective consultation has followed a gradual step-by-step approach to expanding the role of collective dialogue. A key issue arising out of legal constraints and ambiguities has been representation. Article 6 of China's Trade Union Law (2001) stipulates that '[W]hile protecting the *overall interests of the entire Chinese people*, trade unions shall represent and safeguard the legitimate rights and interests of workers and staff members, the unions must represent the interests of the workforce'. We can see that union representation is placed in a context so broad that it is even possible for a trade union chairperson to represent the 'overall interests of the entire Chinese people' by negotiating a pay cut. I spoke with one trade union official in a Guangzhou enterprise department store who did just that and was proud of her efforts as it 'saved jobs and gave a better deal to our customers' (enterprise-level union official, interview, Guangzhou, 21 October 2002).

The union cannot afford to be completely single-minded in its pursuit of members' interests at enterprise level as this would throw it open to accusations of economism, i.e. exclusively representing workers' rights and interests at the enterprise level at the expense of the collective development of, say, a particular township. This constraint is particularly serious in the light of the Chinese model of enterprise-based trade unionism. In the meantime, the debate over whether the ACFTU is – or should be – 'a multi-purposed institution to promote China's economic development and social stability' (Brown 2006: 65) frequently leads to condemnation from potential members in the private sector. As a former employee of Gold Peak's Huizhou Advanced Factory plant struggling for compensation following occupational poisoning explained, the union was 'useless at representing workers' interests at our workplace in Huizhou. They won't go after the employer for compensation as they want to protect Gold Peak and the local economy' (former Gold Peak employee, interview, Hong Kong, 14 December 2005). Indeed, it is not unusual to find collective consultations in which the trade union negotiator is a senior manager in the enterprise. In theory, there is no reason why a senior manager cannot negotiate a collective contract that union members find acceptable. In practice, however, it need hardly surprise us that this has not been the case and most collective contracts have been little more – and sometimes a little less – than a duplication of minimum legal standards that reflect a passive approach to negotiations by the trade unions. This passivity contrasts with the alacrity that senior unions can display in reporting back up the hierarchy the number of collective contracts completed on their patch as an indicator of their performance. There are cases of the local MOLSS, as the authority that approves the legal status of a completed collective contract, rejecting the document on the grounds of the enterprise union 'negotiating' standards that undercut the legal minimum (Taylor et al. 2003: 185). And, of course, there are long-term problems that arise from the coagulation of opposing interests. As Clarke has put it:

> The identification of the trade union with management has important implications for the development of industrial relations and the responsibility of the trade union to represent the rights and interests of its members in the enterprise because it means that differences between the employer and the employees are reconciled within the trade union apparatus, rather than through negotiation between employer and employee on the basis of the trade union representation of the rights and interests of its members.
>
> (Clarke et al. 2004: 241)

China's national Labour Law has just three articles devoted to collective consultation and contracts.[5] They include stipulations that a signed draft contract must be put to the local labour bureau for approval and that the contract is effective within 15 days if there are no objections. Standards set in a collective contract also serve as a minimum for those stipulated in individual contracts. With regard to the issues of interests and representation, Article 33 is most relevant:

> The staff and workers of an enterprise as one party may conclude a collective contract with the enterprise on matters relating to labour remuneration, working hours, rest and vacations, occupational safety and health, and insurance and welfare. The draft collective contract shall be submitted to the congress of the staff and workers or to all the staff and workers for discussion and adoption.
>
> (ACFTU 2000)

What is interesting here is that, in the absence of trade unions, the law allows for collective contracts to be 'concluded by representatives elected by the staff and workers of the enterprise' but there are, as far as I have been able to ascertain, no public examples of such a course of action.

More detailed procedures for collective consultation were originally mapped out in the Regulations on Collective Contracts (henceforth 'Regulations') issued by the Department of Labour that came into force in January 1995.[6] The Regulations were updated and expanded in 2004 by the MOLSS and included some important changes that may, in the future, impact on practice or perhaps prepare the way for progress at a later date. Some researchers have identified reasons for optimism in the aforementioned trend away from consultation towards bargaining, or at least improved representation. For example, Brown highlights Article 24 in the new Regulations. This stipulates that, 'negotiation representatives of the employing unit and those of the staff shall not act as each others' representatives' and suggests that this may at least temper the trend identified by Clarke and others with regard to trade union identification with management interests (Brown 2006: 39). The

MOLSS issued the Trial Method on Collective Wage Negotiation at the end of 2000, five years after the Regulations were promulgated. The WFTU referred to the Trial Method, also known as Document Nine, in articles posted on trade union websites and discussion boards in which it positioned the regulatory and legal environment as a component of the Xinhe collective consultation project discussed below (Wenling City Federation of Trade Unions 2006). In spirit and content, Document Nine does not differ from the Regulations, and its trial implementation appears to have been motivated by the need for annual wage negotiations as opposed to three-year collective contracts. The main reason for the legal separation of collective wage agreements from collective contracts has been that wage agreements have generally been restricted to the size of the total wage bill and rarely included wage rates for specific posts or occupations (Clarke *et al*. 2004: 247). The increased detail with regard to wages included in the expanded 2004 Regulations may well render Document Nine superfluous over time. For example, Article 9 covers all aspects of wages: wage levels, system of wage distribution, wage standards and wage adjustments. This may give employers the impetus to lock wages down for up to three years.

Since 2008, the Standing Committee of the Guangdong People's Congress has been debating drafts of the 'Regulations on the Democratic Management of Enterprises'. Up until August 2010, the draft included a provision for the union to organize the democratic election of workers representatives to engage in negotiations with management over wage levels if one fifth – later changed to half – of the workers requested it. The regulations also oblige management to take part in such negotiations. However, strong lobbying by Hong Kong business organizations whose members employ millions of workers in the province persuaded the Standing Committee of the Guangdong People's Congress to postpone further debate of the draft. Barring an outbreak of industrial peace, it is likely that the arguments over the draft regulations will resurface in the near future.

Practical application

At the practical level, the twin factors of union dependence on management and the absence of alternative trade unions render a genuinely accountable dialogue on working conditions an extremely unlikely occurrence. As a consequence, collective consultations are generally organized to meet top-down quotas that allow the ACFTU to post spectacular statistics on paper that do not, generally speaking, reflect an improvement in pay and conditions on the ground. Neither are they participatory. As Liu points out, '[I]n many enterprises the equal consultation [between workers and employer] is a mere formality and genuine negotiations over labour relations do not exist' (Liu Yufang 2002: 24). This mechanical approach epitomizes one of the central issues facing the ACFTU and gives rise to criticism that many aspects of its work at enterprise level are plagued by a formalistic approach (Clarke *et al*. 2004: 240). Formalism inevitably promotes the duplication of legal minimum standards or minimum model agreements provided by the MOLSS. If adhered to in practice, this may well constitute a significant improvement in

122 *Collective consultation in Xinhe town*

pay and conditions, especially in the private sector. Much more common, however, is for this somewhat superficial duplication of minimum standards in collective contracts to act as a significant obstacle to the pursuit of more tangible and enforceable collective interests. In this scenario, the meeting of top-down quotas reigns supreme. At the end of 2002, 16 provinces had set up collective contract systems. Approximately 308,600 individual enterprises with a total of 62 million workers had signed collective contracts. At industrial (branch) level, there were 18,000 collective contracts in 218,000 in enterprises covering over 112 million workers. There were also a further 65,300 cross-sector geographically based collective contracts in 743,000 enterprises that covered 21 million workers (Taylor and Li Qi 2003: 701–15).[7] By the end of 2006, a total of 862,000 collective contracts had been signed covering 1.538 million enterprises, 112.5 million workers or 59 per cent of all enterprise workers in China. The number of regional collective contracts signed across the country reached 66,000, with 753,000 enterprises and 29.6 million workers involved. Industry-specific collective contracts reached 19,000, with 172,000 enterprises and 12.9 million workers covered (ACFTU 2007b).

My interviews and conversations about contracts and working conditions with workers in China suggest that most of the workers covered by these contracts would have little or no idea of their contents or even existence. As Taylor *et al.* argue, the figures merely reflect a formalistic implementation of the ACFTU's policy direction on collective consultation developed during the mid to late 1990s.

> From the beginning of the second phase [of implementing collective contracts] the ACFTU headquarters instituted a mechanistic quota system setting out targets for the number of contract signings per year, which are then allocated to provinces and industries and so on down the chain of command ... The fact that in 1996, the implementation of the collective contract system could increase by more than 200 per cent should be attributed to the way the planned quota system is introduced.
>
> (Taylor *et al.* 2003: 190)

Some observers have suggested that there was an outbreak of a more participatory, even confrontational collective 'wage bargaining' in SOEs in the early 1990s following the decentralization of wage controls (Hussain and Zhuang 1998: 50). However, as we saw in Chapter 2, it is more likely that this was a result of managers heading off dissatisfaction among SOE workers faced with disappearing certainties rather than trade union activism.

To sum up, the development of collective consultation during the reform era has been characterized by the continued legacy of the command economy and the continued perceived integration of interests in the workplace. Consultation has been promoted as a Chinese alternative to bargaining and the trade union has concentrated on responding to the Party-state's anxiety to regulate industrial relations at enterprise level rather than bargain for class-based interests at a sectoral or even industrial (branch) level. Moreover, the trade union rarely goes beyond legally defined minimum standards in the name of furthering collective interests. Finally, there is minimum worker participation even in the state sector where the legacy of the past at least allows for a trade union presence, if not the exercise of trade union power. In the private sector, unions are weak or non-existent. I now turn to an attempt to trailblaze through these constraints – or at least some of them – at the local level. The Xinhe case study described below involves a collective consultation exercise at sector level that covered mostly small-scale private enterprises in which labour relations were tense and competitive, labour turnover was high, and in which almost all employees were internal migrant workers accustomed to voting with their feet. Using collective consultation to overcome these problems required the town trade union to experiment with a sector-level consultation process and agreement that has since been accredited by the national leadership, as evidenced by positive articles reporting the agreement in the official labour media (*Workers' Daily* 2003).

Xinhe: woollen sweater town

Beginning in 1995, the once quiet Changyu area – now incorporated into Xinhe town – has gradually transformed into the location of the pillar (*zhongdian*) industry of Xinhe town. The kilometre-long main street is lined on both sides with 110 woollen sweater factories employing more than 10,000 people. From August to December every year, the street hums with the sound of knitting machines producing sweaters with a collective value of over one billion yuan (Yu Li 2004). In 2003, the woollen sweater sector in Xinhe town was exporting much of this one billion yuan's worth of sweaters to America and Japan.[8] The town's total of approximately 12,000 woollen sweater workers were employed in 116 private enterprises most of which were owned by local people: former farmers, officials turned entrepreneurs and former COE workers. Until 2001, most of the workers were locals, but this demographic underwent a rapid change and by 2003 approximately 10,000 of the workers were migrants, mainly from Sichuan, Anhui and Hunan provinces. Over 90 per cent were female. Figure 4.1 shows the workforce according to size of enterprise and illustrates that three enterprises employed over 400 workers but the majority of the approximately 12,000 workers were spread across enterprises with between 10 and 200 workers (Case Study Report 2006). The labour turnover and instability that originally acted as a catalyst for the consultation process also made it very difficult to collate more accurate information on enterprise size by number of employees.

Trade union organization in Xinhe presented a familiar pattern for semi-urban areas characterized by small-scale private factory production. Just 30 of the 116 enterprises had primary level trade unions. Five village-level trade union federations (*cun lianhe gonghui* hereinafter VTUF) covered 16 villages. Enterprises in these villages had established trade union small groups (*xiaozu*) but these were not operational (Case Study Report 2006).[9] The VTUFs were dominated by village leaders and/or party secretaries and most of the workers were unaware that they were 'members'. Two out of the five union chairpersons owned factories

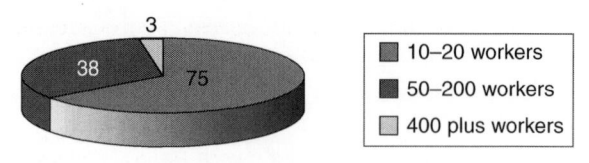

Figure 4.1 Number of enterprises by workers employed in Xinhe
Source: Case Study Report, 2006.

- 10–20 workers: 75
- 50–200 workers: 38
- 400 plus workers: 3

'organized' by the VTUF they chaired. The VTUFs were not in a position to carry out their trade union duties and there were clear conflicts of interests even by the consensus-seeking norms of the socialist market economy.

Xinhe's busiest season ran from August to October when orders were placed for the winter weather. The slack season – when many workers were stood down or simply cleared out of their own accord – was between March and May. Although labour-intensive, production also required skilled and experienced workers, such as horizontal cross stitchers, who commanded considerably higher rates of pay and were able to use their skills to organize actions in pursuit of wage hikes or payment of wage arrears. Wages were generally calculated on a piece-rate basis and usually paid quarterly rather than monthly, a practice that violated Article 50 of the Labour Law and caused considerable anger among workers. Employers deliberately used wage arrears as one of a variety of tactics to stop skilled workers from being lured away by higher pay. Others included illegal job deposits and keeping workers' ID cards. During the autumn busy season, labour relations in the smaller enterprises became extremely tense. Employers raised skilled workers' wages in an attempt to avoid the latter cherry-picking jobs and competition for experienced staff was fierce and at times had a disruptive impact on the production of woollen sweaters in the town. Skilled workers took advantage of their position in the labour market to demand still higher wages. Competition between employers for these workers was so strong that a voluntary cap on wages at 3,500 yuan a month unilaterally imposed by the Wenling City Woollen Manufacturers Association failed. Worker militancy was invariably led by the skilled workers.

> As soon as the busy season got going the skilled workers would start agitating in the workshops for across the board pay rises. A strike would start if the boss didn't agree. They would march to the township government offices using the already accumulated wage arrears to legitimate their actions. The main demand was for the government to intervene and sort out the wage arrears so that they could 'go home'. This threat was aimed at getting the government involved. The marches were well organized and very peaceful. There was no shouting or scuffles, just a procession to the government buildings and then repeated whispering of slogans designed to attract government intervention: 'We want our wages. We are not going to work here any more. We are going home. We want our wages and then we are going home.' The organizers were

keen to avoid conflict with the police and concentrated on securing government intervention.

(Case Study Report 2006)

By autumn 2002, local employers in Xinhe found themselves having to deal with migrant workers capable of taking advantage of the labour market to protect their own interests. Previously, most employees had been local.

> Some of the people we interviewed recalled that the labour disputes in the woollen sweater industry began to attract attention in 2001. Previously, most employees had been local people and the conflicts that arose were not so obvious. As more and more workers from outside arrived, they brought with them their experience gained from working in other places and they were much more skilled in looking after themselves. The number of disputes started rising and there were lots of strikes and petitions.
> (Interview, Case Study Report, 2006)

At the start of the 2003 busy season, there were five such strikes, involving 30 to 100 people with the longest lasting for six days. The organizers of these strikes were

> [A]ll skilled migrant workers from outside who had years of experience working in other areas. They were educated, knowledgeable about their work, had considerable organizing skills and were good negotiators as well as agitators. As soon as the busy season arrived, these workers began stirring up trouble, the employers got scared and the government became agitated.
> (Interview, labour researcher, Hangzhou, 20 March 2007)

Migrant workers in Xinhe were employing tactics that went beyond the general lessons learned in the 1990s by Chinese workers in both the state and private sectors. Lessons drawn from that era were summed up in the catchphrase 'small protest, small solution; big protest, big solution' that became popular among migrant workers at the time. A worker interviewed by Kessler noted the increasingly confrontational tactics employed by migrant workers in the PRD.

> The entire workforce of 400 people went to walk in the streets. We blocked traffic and raised hell. It was not till then that people paid attention to us and workers received their wages. It's worth feeling gratified that the appropriate government offices are already paying more attention to the question of withheld wages. It's not like before when the government fully ignored the grievances workers filed.
> (Kessler 2009)

In contrast, the presence of skilled workers with the organizing capacity to take advantage of the situation and – as far as I have been able to ascertain – avoid arrest was a crucial factor that led to the Xinhe experiment.

126 *Collective consultation in Xinhe town*

In the spring of 2003, the leader of the Xinhe Woollen Sweater Manufacturers Association (XWSMA), who also owned one of the three larger enterprises, and the newly appointed chairperson of the Xinhe Federation of Trade Unions (XFTU) met to discuss the worsening situation and how to avoid another strike wave in the approaching busy season. The result of the meeting between the XFTU and XWSMA was a decision to launch a sector-wide collective consultation on wages. The setting up of a sector-level trade union that would absorb the defunct VTUFs and cover workers across the smaller factories was also announced – the Xinhe Woollen Sweater Sector Trade Union (hereinafter XWSTU). The XFTU took the lead in the first consultation in 2003 and the new union was formally registered immediately after the consultation process was completed and took the lead in negotiations the following year.

Consultation

On 13 June 2003, the XFTU convened a consultative meeting to discuss piece-rates for the woollen sweater sector. Chaired by Fu Nanbao, the XFTU chair, participants included officials from the nearby Wenling City MOLSS, the WFTU, eight factory owners from the XWSMA, mostly from the larger factories, and 13 workers' representatives from various woollen sweater manufacturers, all of whom had been recommended by their employers. The XWSMA put forward rates for 59 work processes in five separate areas of work. Workers' representatives gave their reaction to these rates and discussion followed. The 13 workers' representatives then put forward alternative (higher) rates for the 59 processes and these were compiled by the XFTU into an aggregate table with individual suggestions for each process recorded anonymously. The table was handed to the XWSMA by the XFTU. The XWSMA organized a meeting of 113 enterprises to discuss the table and, following extensive discussion, a revised wage-rate table was handed back to the XFTU. The union then compiled a standard wage-rate table (*jizhun gongjia biao*) based on the respective tables put forward by the workers' representatives and the XWSMA that produced further internal discussion, meetings and counter-proposals from both sides prior to eventual agreement. A sector-wide meeting of management-approved workers' representatives from 100 enterprises was convened, to which larger enterprises sent two or three representatives while smaller ones sent one. Following a show of hands, the new wage-rate table was agreed and a formal document drawn up and signed by both sides. This was entitled the Wenling City Xinhe Town Changyu Woollen Sweater Sector Workers Wage (wage rate) Consultation Agreement.[10]

The table was included in a more general collective contract, Article 3 of which stated:

> Wages shall be issued on or before the 28th of each month and shall not be less than 800 yuan per month. A lower rate may be negotiated with the trade union if an enterprise is in difficulty but this shall not be less than 560 yuan per month. Piece-rates shall be paid in accordance with the Wenling City

Xinhe Town Changyu Woollen Sweater Sector Workers Wage (wage rate) Consultation Agreement. Rates shall only be adjusted upwards.

(Changyu woollen sweater sector-level collective contract 2003)[11]

The enterprises accepted responsibility for publicizing the agreement in their factories via mass meetings at work and wall posters. The whole process took 55 days from 13 June until 8 August 2003 and involved six formal consultation sessions, 10 meetings and over 500 documents containing suggestions and amendments from concerned parties, mostly workers. Three major adjustments were made to the standard table before agreement was reached. The process I have described makes it clear that at least some bargaining, as opposed to mere consultation, took place. An exceptionally candid press report on the proceedings captured the atmosphere via interviews with some of the participants. Fu Nanbao recalled that, while the initial meeting was calm, tension increased after both sides withdrew to get feedback from their respective constituencies.

> The views of the workers and the bosses differed substantially with a gap of up to one yuan per piece on some work processes. The bosses accepted the workers' rates for top-quality goods but felt that they were too high for the mid-range and bottom-end products.
>
> (Yu Li 2004)

Some of the factory bosses even argued that the whole process should be stopped, a threat that encouraged Fu to appeal to local Party leaders to apply pressure. 'We had no choice but to get the leaders involved. We had to get the bosses on board, even if they were reluctant to do so. Otherwise we would have been unable to push on with the consultation' (Yu Li 2004).

In 2004 and 2005, collective wage consultations again took place, with the XWSTU directly negotiating with the employers' association, albeit under the guidance of the XFTU. The deputy chair of the latter was appointed chairperson of the new sector union and held both posts simultaneously for some time. Following the same format as in 2003, three formal consultations took place over six meetings. Over 800 standardized 'opinion forms' were completed and the standard wage-rate table was adjusted twice during the two-month period of consultation and negotiation. One more work area and six more work processes were included and increases of between five and 10 per cent for 16 work processes were agreed. In July 2005, another round of consultation took place that saw over 1,000 workers – almost 10 per cent – completing an opinion form; three adjustments were made to the wage-rate table; and 67 work processes were included with selected increases of between five and 10 per cent agreed (Case Study Report 2006).

Results

Institutions or systems to manage labour relations are often judged in relation to the degree of acceptance by workers and managers (Oakley 2002: 102) and whether or not they can promote industrial peace (Roberts 2005). The previous chapter on labour unrest discussed the reluctance of the ACFTU to take cases that have previously involved industrial action through formal dispute resolution procedures. The situation in Xinhe was one of sophisticated and powerful labour militancy in small-scale enterprises that would not have sat easily in these formal procedures, even if the union or workers had been prepared to use them.

From the employers' point of view, competition to hire and retain skilled workers was rendering production unsustainable – especially for the small-scale operators. Blunting this competition between employers was the carrot that encouraged them to agree to a standardized wage-rate table. Dealing with strikes that emerged from this situation was taking up an enormous amount of time.

Li Zuqing, the CEO of Century Clothing (*Shiji fushi youxian gongsi*) claimed that '[I]n 2002 and 2003 there were strikes in almost all the factories, big, small, good, bad, they all had strikes and some of them suffered a number of strikes over the year. Some strikes lasted up to 20 days' (Yu Li 2004).

Like most employers fretting about militant workers, Mr Li was probably exaggerating to make his point. The longest strike we found lasted a still significant six days. Nevertheless, the impact was clear and a formula was required that could satisfy the demands of militant and semi-organized workers but also allow employers to control their unit costs and plan for expansion as demand for Xinhe's woollen sweaters continued to increase.

Underlying this situation were non-existent or weak and compromised trade unions on the ground. If another 'strike season' was to be avoided, the unions would have to reach beyond individual enterprises or ineffective VTUFs. The workers' main complaint was wage arrears and the 2003 national government campaign against wage arrears only added to the pressure on the XFTU and therefore its senior, the WFTU. Between 27 August and 6 September 2002 – among the peak days for the busy season in the year preceding the consultation initiative – there were 168 people from eight enterprises involved in collective petitions for wage arrears to the Wenling Labour Bureau. One group of 40 workers even hired a bus to take them to the bureau to present their case (Yu Li 2004). The unrest was taking up most of the XFTU's time. Chairman Fu Nanbao recalled that in 2003 he dealt with 11 petitions involving between 20 and 30 workers each.

Although wage arrears were a problem, this did not necessarily mean that wages were low. Indeed, wages for skilled workers were relatively high, pushing up costs for the employers. A skilled worker at the aforementioned Century Clothing with 10 years' experience in the trade in both Guangdong and Zhejiang pointed out that '[W]ages here are at least twice as much as other places – up to 1,500 per month' (Yu Li 2004). Ms Bo Donghua worked at Xinhe's Tang Gu La company and was making good money at 1800 yuan per month, whereas in Dongguan she had been earning 'just 700–800 per month' (Yu Li 2004). Interestingly, neither the XFTU nor the higher up WFTU made much mention of this aspect of working conditions in Xinhe. For the XFTU, the key point was the relationship between unstable wages – paid out every three months rather than every month as the law required – unrest and consequent unsustainable development.

As far as relations in this sector were concerned, the root of the problem was wages. Due to the lack of [agreed] standards, as soon as the busy season started competition for experienced workers between the enterprises became intense and skilled workers frequently moved jobs for higher wages. This caused stoppages and petitions ... and influenced production. The enterprises were unable to find a solution and the same went for local government organisations. The enterprise-based unions and village trade union federations were even more constrained by the circumstances.

(Yu Li 2004)

The collective consultation does appear to have had an almost immediate stabilizing effect on the situation. In the remaining months of 2003, following the announcement of the new piece-rate wage table in September, there were only two stoppages connected to wages that involved just 17 people, compared with nine similar stoppages involving 103 people in the same period for the previous year. From the end of 2003 until mid 2006, we found no strikes arising from wage arrears. At the same time, the annual consultations have seen rises in the piece-rates of between five and 10 per cent for various work processes. While workers interviewed appeared to be unaware of the details of the actual collective agreements, they were aware of the wage rates and improved environment (Yu Li 2004) and that wages were stable in the quiet season and had remained high in the busy season (Case Study Report 2006; Yu Li 2004). According to Li Yunzi from Henan, the new standards guaranteed her a minimum of 800 yuan per month in the slack season and in January 2005 she earned 2500 yuan (Shao Xiaoyi 2005: 5). Moreover, the agreement signed between the union and employers also stated that piece-rates can only go up, not down. For the employers, the consultation was worth the extra effort and the compromises they felt they had made with regard to not dropping wage rates. Wang Xinfa, president of the XWSMA in 2005, said that the slack season did not see the usual exodus of workers and that '[E]mployers can concentrate their efforts on business management rather than fighting with other companies for skilled workers, or dealing with labour disputes' (Shao Xiaoyi 2005: 5).

Analysis

How can a local trade union operating in actual existing conditions act in defence of the interests and rights of its members and potential members? Or in other words, is trade union reform possible? The case study shows that, in the absence of freedom of association and legal protection of the right to strike, the XFTU's twin task of becalming labour relations to facilitate further economic growth and meet the demands of workers did indeed require innovation. A National People's Congress (NPC) document has recently stated how local law courts and labour arbitration departments have reported that 'collective contracts ... have an important function in protecting workers rights and interests' (National People's Congress Report 2009). The experimental and pragmatic strategy of initiating and implementing a sectoral collective agreement at local level is likely to be replicated in the coming years. Indeed, Article 53 of the new Labour Contract Law directly addresses this development and provides the legal space for further progress away from relying solely on enterprise-level agreements.

The XFTU's departure from traditional practice was not in any sense a democratic, participatory process. This may have a negative impact on the sustainability of such initiatives, although the process appeared reasonably entrenched when our fieldwork finished in 2006. Of course, there is a danger of seeing all trade union reform in China through democratic lenses that measure progress against an ideal of sustainable, grass-roots participatory trade unionism that rarely exists in the real world. Nevertheless, while Xinhe's experiment did not blaze any trails in terms of worker representation and participation and in fact did not meet the standards of Chinese national law, far less ILO standards, this did not rule out a consultation process that included real bargaining. The XFTU's Fu Nanbao told reporters that direct elections for improved worker participation were now a priority for the newly formed XWSTU (Yu Li 2004). As far as I have been able to ascertain, these have not yet taken place and the first chairman of the new sector-level union remains in his post. On the other hand, the process had an 'organic' character to it, echoing Deng Xiaoping's pragmatic reform model of 'crossing the river by feeling for the stones'. As the Chairman of the XFTU explained:

> We were not aware of the details of Document Nine or the Regulations when we began these sector-level consultations. It was only after the inspections and visits by leaders from the relevant departments as well as the press coverage that we learnt about these laws and regulations in any detail.
> (Case Study Report 2006)

This admission surprised experienced researchers conducting my supervised fieldwork on the experiment.

> We were moved by what we found. These so called 'peasants' – the town's trade union chair and prime mover of the experiment was a former infantry soldier – had established a successful experiment. They weren't implementing the law, they were ahead of it!
> (Case Study Report 2006)

The process in Xinhe took on the form of a successful exercise in experimental pragmatism in its striking of agreements at the sector level across small enterprises, whereas at the time established law and practice concentrated on single enterprise-level agreements or vague regional and industrial (sector) agreements. The key was that the trade union recognized that enterprise-level agreements were inappropriate for existing conditions in the Xinhe woollen sector. Given that the lack of legal guidance is frequently employed by ACFTU officials as a justification for inertia, this was indeed a groundbreaking departure. Xinhe's union officials did not base their strategy on a systematic study of the relevant labour regulations – which they admitted they were unaware of – but via a detailed survey of existing local wage levels in the 116 enterprises producing woollen sweaters. Hopefully representing a new work style (*zuofeng*) for a new generation of trade union officials, the chairperson of the WFTU, Zhao Guofeng, was clear that this was about wages and benefits – an approach that may have earned him an accusation of economism just 10 years previously. Zhao told a reporter that 'based on the peculiarities of a given sector, carrying out sector-level consultations in a down-to-earth manner and effectively upholding the economic rights of workers allows the latter to obtain actual material benefits' (Xia Xiaoyin 2005).

When faced with reluctance from some employers to stay involved in the consultation, the XFTU – backed by the WFTU – was able to use its relationship with the local Party-state to part-persuade, part-compel mostly small-scale employers to sign up to a sector-wide agreement that stipulated that workers must be paid monthly and that piece-rates can only go up.

The experiment has since been identified as an example for possible future legal/institutional development and the local trade union press has reported similar exercises in the nearby towns. For example, the Zeguo Town Pump Makers Union was established in late 2004 and has since carried out three rounds of collective consultations (Xia Xiaoyin 2005; Liu Mingwei 2007). The model is also being applied and adapted in other parts of China. Sector-level trade unions have been established in the single industry towns of Laomiao (producing fireworks) and Gongli (building materials). Agreements were concluded in late 2007 at Ducun (glass containers) and Meiyuan (building materials) in Shaanxi's Fuping county (Yi Ming 2007). As news of the Xinhe experiment has spread, approval from senior trade union officials and other government departments followed. In 2006, the MOLSS issued an 'Opinion' encouraging experiments with similar agreements and processes. The MOLSS contextualized its document in a manner that demonstrates the importance of events at Xinhe with regard to the future of collective bargaining in China.

> Following the development of the socialist market economy, the private sector has expanded rapidly. The majority of private enterprises are small in scale and have a high labour turnover and very weak trade unions. Labour violations are frequent and labour relations extremely tense. The evidence from pilot projects' demonstrates that in areas where there is a concentration of small enterprises or enterprises engaged in similar production, sector-level or district-level collective contracts are able to protect the rights and interests of both the enterprise and workers and promote harmony. Such agreements are able to protect workers' legal rights, stabilise labour relations, ensure a good environment for continued and sustainable economic development … and uphold social stability.
>
> (MOLSS 2006)

Completing the process of rolling out a successful local project at national level, Article 53 of the new Labour Contract Law makes legal provision for sector- and district-level collective contracts.

Conclusion

The experiment in Xinhe was essentially an exercise in grass-roots innovation based on a pragmatic assessment of the problems faced – sophisticated labour militancy in a tight labour market. In a sign of the growing importance of the trade unions to social stability, the Party, local government and big employers used the trade union structure to get the information they needed to draw up an administrative solution to their problem. It is clear that the principal advantage of this experiment to both the Party and employers was that it successfully damped down strikes. From the workers' point of view, it brought stable wages in the slack season and ensured that future wage levels only went up.

The crucial point is that it was a response to sophisticated informal mobilization of migrant workers, which, as we have seen, the authorities were not in a position to replace. The militancy suggested that formalistic traditional trade union practices were inappropriate and were demonstrably failing to provide stable labour relations in what was a difficult organizing environment for any trade union, let alone a state-sponsored institution. New practices were required. In this case, it was the existence of militant skilled workers that prevented the experiment from degenerating into wage regulation by an employers' organization.

Politically, the agreement may have laid the groundwork for a collective bargaining framework that until very recently has been confined to the realm of the imagination (Brown 2006: 36). Of course, it was by no means democratic or representative – far less participatory – but the structure in place provides room for the development of collective bargaining that some commentators see as a significant opportunity for the ACFTU. We may even be justified in speculating that the events in Zhejiang have encouraged breakthroughs in collective bargaining elsewhere, even in go-ahead Shenzhen. For example, the Shenzhen implementation measures for the 2006 national regulation on collective consultation formulated by the SFTU refer to 'collective bargaining' rather than the more neutral and traditional term 'collective consultation'. And in late October 2009, the Law Implementation Group of the National People's Congress Standing Committee released a national report on the implementation of the Trade Union Law that gave an example from Shanghai of eight city-level sector trade unions forming a confederation that 'smashed through all restrictions' on this aspect of trade union work (National People's Congress 2009). Of course, freedom of association was – and is – the core issue and in Xinhe we can see its impact on industrial relations as it emerges in embryonic form.

5 Experimental pragmatism II
Trade union rights centre in Yiwu

The rising tide of labour unrest is testament to the inability of trade unions to moderate employer power at enterprise level. This is the main constraint on the ACFTU's capacity to represent workers in a market economy. The root of this failure lies in the dependency of primary trade union cadres on employers which is in danger of becoming an institutionalized shortcoming. It is apparent that left to its own devices the ACFTU has little stomach to tackle this problem at the national level. Frustration at the passivity of union cadres in the private sector has reinforced the argument of those who claim that the ACFTU is incapable of reform.

As we saw from the review in Dongguan cited in Chapter 3, evidence of passivity is not hard to find. The follow-up interviews with enterprise union cadres revealed a profound lack of confidence in their ability to address individual or collective workers' rights violations at primary level. Most of the union officers held the view that where employers seriously violated labour laws – behaviour the interviewees described as including wage arrears, verbal and physical bullying and ignoring their responsibility for health and safety – the enterprise union did not have the power to redress the situation and that it was essentially a matter for local government to resolve. One interviewee was particularly blunt on the union's incapacity to address 'excessive' (*guofen*) attitudes, stating simply that 'the boss has money and power and the workers need to eat' (interview, Case Study Report, 2006). Trade union cadres at enterprise level tend to react to disputes in one of three ways: first, pass the problem on to the higher levels of the union; second, ignore the problem and hope it will sort itself out without union intervention, a reaction to crisis known in Chinese as *buliao liao zhi*, i.e. to solve a problem by not taking steps to solve it; and third, simply side with the employer for fear of the threat to his/her own job and career prospects. In Yiwu – a county-level city in the eastern province of Zhejiang – trade union cadres tended to react by passing disputes to the senior levels to deal with, an approach the chairperson of the Yiwu Federation of Trade Unions (YFTU) described to me as 'generally too little too late' and as a consequence the possibilities of escalation became much higher. He added that 'by the time we got to hear of a dispute in a factory, it was often too late to avoid some kind of incident of some description – stopped production, road block, protest or even violent confrontation' (interview, Chen Youde, Yiwu, 21 March 2006).

The other side of primary-level weakness has been the higher-level unions' lack of direct contact with enterprises and specifically with the workers employed in them. Higher-level unions are legally and politically obliged to work closely with the local government on economic development and scarce staff and resources are channelled in this direction rather than towards the enterprise shop floor. There are two reasons for this privileging of administrative work over building stronger unions: first, it is easier and second, building stronger unions from the bottom up has the potential to bring about conflict with both employers and the local administration. This has reinforced an administratively top-heavy approach by the higher trade unions that were – and generally still are – apt to spend their time on report writing, studying directives from the centre, attending meetings, compiling statistics sent up from the primary organizations and generally passing round pieces of paper to each other. These practices have been described in trade union circles in China as the *xingzhenghua* – literally the 'administratization' – of trade union work (Yi Ming 2004).[1]

Chapter 4 demonstrated that it was possible for a town-level trade union (*zhen gonghui*) to go beyond the restrictions of historical tradition and practice, albeit with the powerful support of Party and local government. The experiment in local sector-wide collective consultation in Xinhe was based on identifying standardized cross-factory piece-rates as being in the interests of the workers employed in the factories and then persuading or cajoling employers that it was also in their interests to negotiate such rates. The main weakness I identified was the lack of direct worker participation in collective consultation. This in turn threatened the credibility and future sustainability of what was essentially an interest-based collective agreement negotiated from above.

In this chapter, we will examine an innovative rights-based experiment in trade union practice aimed at improving union capacity to both solve and reduce the number of enterprise-level labour disputes in the private sector. The Yiwu Workers' Legal Rights Centre (YWLRC) attempted to facilitate a more stable labour relations environment by opening up a new space in which workers could settle complaints and claims against employers. Established by the YFTU and its dynamic chairperson Chen Youde, the YWLRC did not attempt to substitute the work of the union's organizing department – understaffed as the latter clearly was – by attracting workers into the unions. Rather, it took a rights-based approach to tackling the gross labour rights violations that rapid capitalist economic expansion had brought to the city. The frequent petitions, strikes and presence of sometimes violent hometown associations in the city's industrial zones and villages had served sufficient notice to Chen and his team at the YFTU that the union was struggling to fulfil its designated function of channelling disputes into formal juridical procedures. The consequent break with traditional practice has become nationally and even internationally famous, but little is known about how this innovation came into being and what barriers it had to overcome. As the process of innovation can often be as illuminating as the innovation itself, I decided to carry out an in-depth study.

Nationally, a key problem with dispute resolution has been the ACFTU's unwillingness to take on cases that are either collective or not certain winners.

As we saw in the chapter on labour unrest, this less than stalwart approach has been an important factor in the rise – especially in Guangdong and the PRD – of both 'black lawyer' networks and labour NGOs that have set up rights or service centres as vehicles for their work. We might expect that, given its close contacts with both Party and government, it would be pretty straightforward for the ACFTU to follow their lead and set up legal rights centres of its own to support workers – a process that is starting to unfold nationally thanks largely to the YFTU's experiment. However, as a pioneer in this process, the YWLRC demonstrated the considerable contention involved.

YFTU chairman Chen Youde came to believe that a trailblazing (*chuangxin*) approach was required if the tense labour relations in Yiwu were to improve. However, the YFTU was constrained by limited trade union resources and an obligation to remain within the city government's authorized plan (*bianzhi*) for union work.[2] Chen's vision was of a centre for tackling labour rights violations that would also raise the union's capacity to provide direct assistance to workers in dispute as well as offer a better service to the primary trade unions. However, equally important to this project was to experiment with areas of cooperation and work styles traditionally outside the union's modus operandi by employing a targeted strategy of resource borrowing and partnering with other actors relevant to labour relations such as the Justice Department, the local People's Congress and the media. This approach has been labelled the 'socialization' of union work (Luo Xiaojun and Zhou Songqiang 2007: 25–30). As Chen explained:

> We wanted to try out an entirely new approach of working outside the trade union box. We proposed to take advantage of the practices, power and experiences available to us but as yet largely untapped. We dared to blaze a new trail and gradually socialize the practice of this work. This approach has since become known as [a key part of] the Yiwu Model.
>
> (Interview, Chen Youde)

In this chapter, I pose the same question as in previous chapters: How can a local trade union respond to labour unrest and act in defence of the interests and rights of its members and potential members? Or in other words, is trade union reform possible? I have divided the chapter into four sections. The first section describes the developmental model of Yiwu city and the results this has brought. The second section briefly summarizes the development of labour rights centres in China prior to narrating in detail the contentious process of setting up the centre in Yiwu. The third section looks at how the Yiwu centre works and uses statistics and specific case studies to describe its achievements. The fourth section analyses the significance of the YFTU's trailblazing in the light of its own aim to provide a new approach to an important aspect of trade union work and labour relations and returns to the research question itself – the application of experimental and pragmatic methods in union work. In conclusion, I summarize the Yiwu Model from three perspectives: specific innovation, general reform of the ACFTU and comparison with centres run by NGOs.

Methodology

This chapter is based on collaborative research in the city of Yiwu undertaken in 2005 and 2006 concluding in our Case Study Report. As with other case studies in this book, the interpretation of the data are mine alone. I have supplemented the collaborative research with my own interviews with the principal actors involved in the Centre, including an entire day spent with Chen Youde, the chair of the Yiwu Federation of Trade Unions, and extended discussions with academics during my visits to Hangzhou and Yiwu during 2006 and 2007. Where possible, I have triangulated the results of the research data with secondary sources and interviews with rights centre personnel in Zhejiang and Guangdong.

Sugar for chicken feathers: the development of Yiwu city

Yiwu city is on the eastern end of the Jin-Qu Basin in the centre of Zhejiang province. It is classed as a county-level city with 15 towns and eight villages under its jurisdiction. It has a total population of 1.6 million people and a registered local population of approximately 680,000 (Yiwu Government Website 2008). The remaining one million are mainly migrant workers from all over China, but also include comparatively large numbers of capitalists or agents of capital from Greater China, the US and the Middle East as well as almost 20,000 Japanese temporary residents. Of note is that at least a third of the migrant worker population is non-Han Chinese (Case Study Report 2006).

Yiwu was established as a county over 2,220 years ago and has enjoyed a reputation as a cultural hub producing famous sons: from patriotic generals during the Song dynasty to Cheng Wangdao, the first translator of *The Communist Manifesto* into Chinese. Since the reforms, the government has prioritized commercial trading as a keystone of development policy and has actively promoted and facilitated Yiwu's once small commodities market, which is now the largest in China. In 2004, the city's gross domestic product was 28.2 billion yuan (Ding Ke 2006: 4–5).

Generations of Yiwu farmers have passed on trading traditions based on the exploitation of local resources, particularly brown sugar (*hongtang*). 'Exchanging sugar for chicken feathers' is how Yiwu's commercial traditions have been described – literally – in Chinese (*jimao huan tang*). Farmers and merchants made simple sugar products from home-grown and manufactured sugar and exchanged these for chicken feathers which were then used for compost or to make brooms and anything else that could be made out of the feathers. The brooms etc. were sold for cash which was reinvested. In post-liberation China, these traditions earned Yiwu the sensitive reputation as being the 'tail of capitalism' and, despite frequent clampdowns on such entrepreneurial activities, they kept re-emerging, partly as a result of the historical influence of a peddlers' organization known as the *Qiaotang Bang*.

> Gradually, a peddler's organization, which is called Qiaotang Bang, was formed. At its peak in the second decade of the twentieth century, Qiaotang

Bang had 7,000–8,000 members (Zhejiang Province Zhengxie Historical Data Committee, 1997: 301–303). After the PRC was established, Qiaotang Bang was dissolved and their peddling activity was discontinued for a while. However, they started peddling again in 1963, at the latest. In the 1970s, these vendors spontaneously formed two periodic markets in Yiwu.

(Zhang Wenxue *et al.* 1993: 35 cited in Ding Ke 2006: 7)

With the formal launch of the reforms in 1978, the Yiwu government, by and large, skirted the ongoing political debates of the time and moved quickly to take advantage of its trading traditions. In 1982, four years after the household responsibility system was implemented nationally, the Yiwu government took matters a step further by formulating the 'four permissions', allowing farmers and peddlers considerable room to trade in farm and off-farm produce. The 'permissions' were: to engage in business and trade; to transport goods over long distances for sale; to open up urban and rural markets; and to engage in competitive practices. In retrospect, these measures seem moderate but 25 years ago they were at the cutting edge of China's re-engagement with market forces. They were the administrative foundation on which the subsequent substantial expansion in productive and trading activity took place. This growth was largely based on indigenous Chinese capital, as opposed to FDI which, at the time, was largely heading towards the southern provinces of Guangdong and Fujian. Figure 5.1 shows a dramatic shift – even by China's standards – that the reforms have brought to the city's economic structure.

Twenty-five years later, Yiwu is known as the 'supermarket of the world' due to its reputation as the largest small commodities market on the planet. It is not a gentle place and gives the visitor a frontier-town experience.

> Yiwu is a brash, gaudy and ugly place. The Century Shopping Centre is a perfect example. Selling the best Yiwu has to offer, it is carved into one of the city's main parks. It may not be pretty, but it has plenty of foreign visitors. Susan Ali has come from the United Arab Emirates looking for supplies for her clothing and export business. 'We come here because it's the factory of all China', she says. 'They've got good quality, great variety and they're cheaper than any other country.'

(Somerville 2005)

Staying in Yiwu is a cosmopolitan experience. Amongst the city's residents are traders and factory representatives from Pakistan, India, Russia, Europe, Africa and the US as well as every province in China, many of whom have representatives' offices in the city. By the end of 2007, Yiwu's famous small commodities market had more than 50,000 stalls and reported a trade volume of 3.48 billion yuan (Xinhua 2008). Perhaps not surprisingly, due to its position at the low end of the production chain with goods initially aimed at the domestic and Asian markets, the city's dramatic transformation has also been noted for the proliferation of counterfeit goods.

138 *Trade union rights centre in Yiwu*

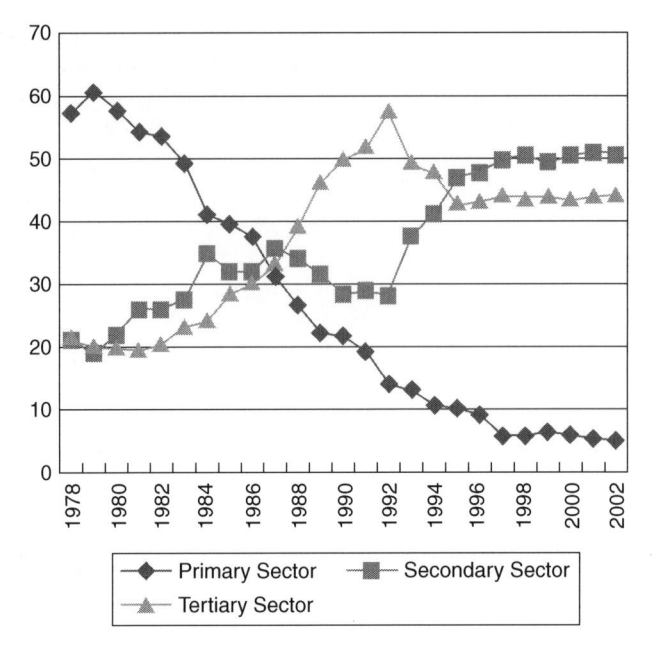

Figure 5.1 Changes in the industrial structure of Yiwu city (per cent)
Source: Liu, Bai and Wang (2003): Yiwu Statistical Yearbook (1978–2002) cited in Ding Ke 2006: 7.

Each day about 200,000 people visit the market to purchase goods from among over 400,000 different varieties of items. About 8,000 foreign buyers visit the market each day. Each day two tons of goods are purchased. The highways and roads to and from Yiwu are heavily congested day and night with trucks coming from the South that deliver counterfeit goods to Yiwu and trucks leaving Yiwu loaded with counterfeits that have been purchased and are bound for locations throughout China.

(Chow 2006: 5–6)

The history of the Zhejiang China Commodities Cities Group Company Limited (ZCCCG) gives us a dramatic illustration of the entrepreneurial energies unleashed in Yiwu back in the late seventies. During the last weeks of 1978, peasant farmers from the towns of Choucheng and Gansanli began setting up stalls and selling produce along the roadsides, which heralded official tolerance of the 'sugar for chicken feathers' trade, gradually transforming itself into a small commodities market made up of small market traders. Trading times and stall places gradually became fixed at the 'main road market'. The nickname was changed to the 'grass hat market' when the area was covered so as to facilitate trading during rainy weather. After the 'four permissions' awarded formal approval to the market in 1982, it began to grow rapidly. In 1982, there were 705 stalls with a total turnover of 7 million yuan and by 1984 this had almost tripled to 1,887 stalls and shops trading 24 million yuan worth of goods. By 2004, the one-time illegal farmers' roadside market had become a large listed company enjoying trading relationships with over 1500 companies all over China (ZCCCG 2007). ZCCCG has also obtained an import and export licence and trades directly with overseas buyers and outlets. This phenomenal growth has not been in isolation and has been accompanied by rapid development of Yiwu itself. In 2003, it was ranked in the top 20 of China's 100 Robust Counties and also named by the provincial Zhejiang government as its most competitive county. The model of 'trading city, industrial towns and specialist villages' (*shangye cheng, gongye zhen* and *zhuanye cun* – Case Study Report 2006) has also helped to produce some startling statistics. The town of Dazhen has over 500 factories producing half a million blouses and shirts every day and has been nicknamed China's 'shirt town' by the China National Garment Association (*Zhongguo fuzhuang xiehui*). Another of the towns under its jurisdiction, Datang, produces over 30 per cent of the world's socks. The Fenli underwear factory produced over three billion pairs of socks for Wal-Mart, Pringle and Disney in 2004, helping to forge Datang's nickname as 'sock town' (Somerville 2005).

Official statistics for *average* incomes in Yiwu are indicative of considerable growth patterns and give expression to Yiwu's transformation. In 2004, the average urban income was 16,383 yuan, three times the average rural income in the county of 6700 yuan, which is nevertheless near the top of the national scale for rural income. The minimum wage in Yiwu is 670 yuan (Wu Xiaoxian 2006), which puts it at the top end of the mid-range for China's county-level cities.

Contextualizing the YFTU experiment: the growth of labour rights centres in China

The city-level trade union in Yiwu was no different from senior levels of unions all over China in finding itself hard put to cope with the challenge of rapid economic transformation. As we saw in Chapter 1, the state has gone to considerable lengths to devise and implement a formal procedure for the resolution of disputes via mediation, arbitration and the courts. But weak or non-existent trade unions at primary level have rendered mediation committees – which are rare in the private sector anyway – easily manipulated by employers. Consequently, a large number of labour disputes go to arbitration and the courts, both of which were – and are – overwhelmed by the increase in their workloads. Despite the national emphasis on channelling disputes into juridical procedures, the union has remained cautious, and at times even reluctant to represent workers. On the one hand, support and representation is generally restricted to cases where there have been flagrant legal violations, and a win can be guaranteed. On the other hand, the ACFTU is much more reluctant to provide support in the case of collective disputes and rarely provides legal advice to workers who have been involved in collective action (Chen Feng 2003b: 1014–6). This partially explains the mushrooming of legal advice centres run by NGOs that help workers to file and pursue the kinds of cases in court that the ACFTU avoids. The new law on labour dispute resolution has added impetus to trade union legal rights work and it is highly likely that the numbers of both trade union and LNGO-run centres will expand in the coming years. There are also significant examples of trade unions working with local LNGOs to establish labour service centres. For example, the New Citizens' Centre in Qingdao is the result of collaboration between the Xiao Chen Hotline and a district branch of the ACFTU with the approval of the Qingdao Federation of Trade Unions (Chen Yuming, interview, Detroit, 12 April 2008).

Labour rights centres are mostly concentrated in export-orientated South China, especially Guangdong province. This is due chiefly to its links with Hong Kong that have facilitated a flood of investment into Guangdong followed by a somewhat smaller flow of people concerned at the labour rights violations this has given rise to. The cluster of centres in the south has shaped the development of the labour rights 'scene' in the province, even if their actual impact on labour relations is harder to measure. These LNGOs have attempted to improve labour rights and labour rights awareness via various methods including corporate social responsibility (CSR) initiatives, worker-training projects, telephone hotlines and drop-in centres. There is no evidence of a direct link between these initiatives and the experiment in Yiwu, although there are mutual indirect influences that stem from a common root: capitalist relations of production in a rapidly expanding private sector.

There are three interconnected factors that have combined to produce the rise of labour rights centres. Firstly, there is the transformation from a *danwei*-centred, administratively controlled model of industrial production in which employment was preconditioned on formal urban status, to a law-based contractual framework that places the rights and obligations of both employer and employee at the heart of a labour relationship that is applicable to all workers regardless, in theory, of their residential status. Secondly, there are considerable conditions and restrictions to the new framework which are often explained as a result of a 'still immature or imperfect market system' (Tao Junyi *et al.* 2003). For example, the relationship between the labour market and local government regulations and even factory rulebooks can render the legal rights that workers are supposed to enjoy very difficult to ascertain in theory and virtually non-existent in practice (interviews, LNGO staff, Hong Kong, 2005–2008). Thirdly, the overwhelming power of the employer in the workplace, usually supported by the local administration, and the concomitant political constraints on independent organizing seriously limit most workers' knowledge of their rights and their capacity to do anything to improve this situation. Confronting these three factors, labour rights centres – sometimes called 'labour service centres' – have offered a wide and varying degree of services from classes and discussion groups on labour and trade union law to OHS and personal health awareness and even English classes. In essence, they are a specific external response – i.e. initiated outside the workplace – to the hardships to which capitalist relations have given rise. It is of note that the target group of almost all China's rights centres has been migrant workers and not the traditional working class who have demonstrated – often literally – a more rigorous understanding of their class position and the changes being visited on it. Charting the progress of South China's LNGOs, Huang An's carefully chosen words echo the three factors described above – transformed employment relations, limited implementation of the law and the absence of freedom of association – and are indicative of the challenges facing labour rights NGOs.

> Migrant workers are a marginal group that has never enjoyed, as an independent social group, formal state protection. And their lack of urban residential permits has excluded them from the corporatist trade unions. Moreover, authoritarian government does not generally encourage workers to actively unite but instead focuses on the dissemination of ideology as opposed to offering support to workers' autonomous expressions of legal struggle.
>
> (Huang An 2007)

While labour rights centres are not 'workers' autonomous expressions of legal struggle' their work highlights the ineffectiveness of primary-level trade unions.

Broadly speaking there are three types of LNGOs operating in China. First are groups – occasionally member-based, or perhaps 'member-enhanced' is the more appropriate term – that are managed by a state institution such as the All China Women's Federation (ACWF). Second are groups established and run by mainland Chinese activists. And third are Hong Kong-based groups active on the mainland via various project-based activities such as running a rights centre, service centre, 'clinic', health and safety bus or the conducting of OHS and labour rights awareness training in mainland factories under the umbrella of TNCs attempting to improve their CSR score. LNGOs in the first two categories are increasingly taking part in these activities, which has at times given rise to mild competition with Hong Kong labour groups. All three categories are legally obliged to register with the Ministry of Civil Affairs (MoC), although many groups get round this by registering as limited companies. There are estimated to be 71 labour groups in China (Wang Kan 2008: 202), the overwhelming majority of them in the south due to Guangdong's position as a leading export promoter and its proximity to Hong Kong facilitating access to funding and solidarity.

The China Labour Education Centre (CLEC) is a Hong Kong-based LNGO that has established a centre in South China and registered as a limited company.[3] The aims of the centre are largely identical to those of other Hong Kong-assisted centres, although they all vary slightly in emphasis. For example, the CLEC concentrates on OHS work, partly because this is perceived to be more neutral territory by employers and the Centre's management whereas another group, Workers' Action, concentrates on rights relating directly to contracts and labour law.[4] At the time of writing the CLEC's work principally involved: promoting OHS and labour rights awareness; assisting workers in identifying solutions to the problems and issues they face in the workplace; and training up peer educators and organizers in order to increase shop-floor participation in OHS issues. A key factor in this work was securing an identity that justified the overall functionality. According to the CLEC's founder:

> One of the main difficulties in setting up the centre was ensuring that we had a legitimate function and, above all, identity (*shenfen*) so as to gain acceptance from the relevant authorities and the workers. There were two important qualifications: that we were not actively involved in trade union organising; and that we were meeting a need – in our case occupational health and safety – the fulfilling of which did not break any laws.
> (Interview, LNGO coordinator, Hong Kong, 6 December 2005)

The main point here is that when a labour rights centre is set up, a chief requirement is clarity in identity and function. As the following narrative recounting the YFTU's experiment with setting up a rights centre demonstrates, the same clarity was required when a powerful state-backed agency – such as the YFTU – embarked on a rights centre project.

The rights centre initiative in Yiwu

In 1999, in response to high and rising levels of industrial conflict, the YFTU organized a major survey of working conditions and migrant workers' demands. They concluded from the results that there were three main problems confronting the official dispute resolution system in Yiwu and, by implication, the YFTU. First, migrant workers' legal rights were violated on a huge scale, and many migrant workers themselves expressed the need for an organization capable of speaking out on their behalf. Second, labour relations in the city were entering a new phase of multiple labour disputes in which the enterprises' bosses preferred to reach out-of-court settlements which, according to the research, usually led to temporary and unsustainable results. On the other hand, the research also showed that migrant workers were willing to use labour dispute resolution procedures but did not have the resources to make use of these channels. Third, the city did not have a sufficient number of lawyers to address the demands of migrant workers to take their claims to the courts (Case Study Report 2006). Moreover, the cases that were accepted by lawyers involved considerable effort for very little financial reward (Luo Xiaojun and Zhou Songqiang 2007: 25–30).

The research also demonstrated the depth of the challenge facing the YFTU. They were working in an environment in which 90 per cent of the enterprises were small scale and privately owned. Since 1997, these enterprises were between them averaging more than 10,000 disputes per year with at least '30 per cent proving, for one reason or another, difficult to solve in a prompt manner' (Case Study Report 2006).[5] Many had been tinged with 'acts of violence, collective protests and even involved threats [by workers] to jump off high buildings, the kidnapping of bosses, as well as collective petitions to government authorities demanding intervention' (interview, Chen Youde).

According to Chen, the situation had been further complicated by the emergence of 'place-of-origin gangs such as the "Anhui Gang", the "Jiangxi Gang" or the "Kaihua Gang" who had a negative impact on the morale of the migrants and often led to inter-gang violence'. The home-town associations (*tongxianghui*) to which Chen was referring can provide a questionable form of protection to migrant workers, usually in return for a compulsory fee. Luo and Zhou described a typical scenario in the town of Suxi, which falls under Yiwu administration.

> The two hamlets of Hu and Jiang had over 8,000 migrant workers each, far outnumbering the local population. Most of these workers had arrived in large groups from the same villages outside the province and, as such, had recourse to powerful hometown 'forces' (*shili*) through which they protected their interests. Some ... paid a 'protection fee' of ten yuan per month to the hometown association which ... engaged in organized criminal activities including violent bullying [of other people] and even terrorizing employers.
> (Luo Xiaojun and Zhou Songqiang 2007: 27)

As we discussed in Chapter 3, Chan came to the same conclusions on home-town associations but, crucially, also acknowledged their capacity to organize strikes and pursue class-based interests that cut across home-town loyalties – at least temporarily (Chan 2009: 60–77). However, while competent at frightening employers to the point of extracting short-term concessions, their organizational structures and norms of operation are, by default, based on home-town loyalties, reinforced through the threat of violence, rather than appeals to class solidarity. As far as the YFTU was concerned, they represented 'a threat to social stability' and the management of large numbers of migrants. As such, they constituted an unwelcome extra dimension to extremely tense labour relations (interview, Chen Youde).

Apart from this unsanctioned and *ad hoc* competition to their work, the YFTU's most basic problem was the lack of union staff and cadres at all levels. By way of historical example, at the beginning of the 1950s there were over 6,000 employees in Yiwu county serviced by eight full-time county level cadres. Half a century later, in 2006, there were approximately 600,000 workers in Yiwu city, but the number of full-time county-level ACFTU cadres had actually gone down to seven. The YFTU had an overall staff of just 30 people, many of whom were town and village cadres doubling up on their posts (Case Study Report 2006). Secondly, there was the problem of the weakness of trade union organization at township, neighbourhood and enterprise levels, which was often further complicated by officials' multiplicity of roles and interests. Although trade union committees were gradually being established in locales where industry was developing fast, they nearly all lacked – and still lack – full-time trained staff. Moreover, the committees' chairpersons were often local government or Party leaders with neither time nor inclination to put union work before the more pressing priorities of job creation and capital accumulation. Where they did exist, primary-level unions suffered from a lack of financial independence that placed serious limits on their ability to hold employers to the law. Even when committees at any of these levels showed an interest in carrying out some kind of union-related protection work, there was limited cash available to fund it (interview, Chen Youde). Financial and administrative impotence was accompanied by the phenomenon of primary-level unions led by managers or even relatives of the boss despite the fact that Article 9 of the revised Trade Union Law (2001) made the latter illegal.

Finally, the horizons of the union's approach to the task of upholding their members' rights were narrowed by the repetition of traditional working practices that concentrated on documentation, meetings and slogans rather than active engagement with the workforce and employers. The YFTU itself lacked legal specialists and looked inwards rather than drawing on wider social resources and as a result, the union came up against structural and operational barriers. Predictably, employers took advantage of the situation.

> We were faced with bosses displaying an extremely negative attitude to their employees. Refusing to pay wages and generally ignoring both the labour and trade union laws. Underlying this behaviour was the bad attitude of many employers towards their workers.
>
> (Interview, Chen Youde)

Meanwhile, 'migrant workers were turning towards informal place-of-origin networks that operated on the basis of intimidation against employers and other workers' (interview, Chen Youde). In the short and mid term, the YFTU did not have the capacity or accumulated experience to 'organize' its constituency characterized, as it was, by a migrant workforce employed in scattered small enterprises. Instead, a 'rights-based' approach was deemed an effective strategy for addressing the multiple violations of workers' rights in the face of what the YFTU itself described as the 'three lacks' (*san wu*): no specialist legal staff, no specific funds for rights work and no specific dedicated organization for rights work (interview, Chen Youde). However, once Chen made the pioneering decision to allocate funds and hire dedicated staff from beyond the usual trade union recruitment fence, the possibilities for an experimental approach opened up. Following the Spring Festival in 2000, the YFTU employed two labour law specialists and on 20 March the union set up the Yiwu City Trade Union Legal Advice Room (*Yiwushi zong gonghui falü guwen shi*) and Trade Union Legal Aid Centre (*gonghui yuanzhu falü zhongxin*). The next day, the city's judicial department issued a notice stating that the use of the characters meaning law (*falü*) in the names of both the Centre and the Advice Room required prior approval from other departments.[6] Moreover, the trade union did not have the authority to establish a legal aid centre, which was the responsibility of the justice department. The YFTU came back with two alternative names that avoided the offending combination of 'trade union' with 'legal aid'. These were: Yiwu City Labourers' Lawyer Office (*Yiwushi laogong lüshi shiwusuo*) or the Yiwu City Labourers' Law Service Office (*Yiwushi laogong falü fuwusuo*), but these too were rejected. Facing apparently intransigent opposition and with no other options available, the union switched tactics and successfully submitted an application to the Department of Civil Affairs to register the proposed centre as a 'social organization' (*shehui tuanti zuzhi*). On 12 October 2000, the Yiwu City Workers' Law and Rights Association (*Yiwushi zhigong falü weiquan xiehui*) was formally established, over six months after the original attempt. It was the first of its kind in China (Luo Xiaojun and Zhou Songqiang 2007: 26). The name has since been changed to include the words trade union and is now known as the Yiwu Federation of Trade Unions Workers' Law and Rights Centre (*Yiwushi zong gonghui zhigong falü weiquan zhongxin*), but the compromise was only successfully signed off after Chen and his supporters lobbied at the highest local level – the Jinhua City People's Congress (JCPC) under whose administrative authority the county city of Yiwu falls.

After the YWLRC was registered under the authority of the Ministry for Civil Affairs, opposition to its existence continued. For those who had invested a political commitment in the Centre, especially the chair of the YFTU, it was essential to obtain the highest possible political backing for the project in order to neutralize opposition from government departments and powerful employers wary of a new channel of recourse opening up for their employees. It was in the light of this opposition that the YFTU chairperson, Chen, decided to use his status as a representative deputy of the nearby JCPC to consolidate the Centre's status and head off new obstacles to its work. He wrote and submitted a proposal to be presented at the fourth plenum of the second session of the JCPC. The proposal – Document 206 – was entitled: 'On establishing new workers' law and rights mechanism(s) in the trade union system'.[7] The motion was a clear attempt to foster closer cooperation between the YFTU and various government departments, especially the Department of Justice. Document 206 made a number of points. First, that the appropriate departments should permit the union to set up organizations such as the Centre in Yiwu city; and second, that the Department of Justice enter into consultation with the trade union in order to establish a baseline condition (*jianli yi ge tiaojian*) with the aim of the justice department formulating appropriate guidelines. Document 206 also proposed that such centres be placed under the overall management and supervision of the Department of Justice but that individual cases should be the responsibility of the trade union. The document framed its suggestions by arguing that both institutions would then be in a position to better serve the workers and poorer sections of society and that the work would be socially and economically beneficial to the whole city. The JCPC Resolutions Department (*yi an chengban bumen*)[8] of the JCPC took a different view:

> There is no basis in law for the establishment of a rights centre or office or similar organization dedicated to the provision of legal services [specifically] upholding workers' rights. Moreover, the current situation is that the [existing] city-wide legal services have been able to meet the basic demand from society in general. The proposal will be retained on file for reference.
> (Case Study Report 2006)

146　*Trade union rights centre in Yiwu*

Clearly not one to give up without a fight, Chairman Chen next garnered the support of 12 People's Congress deputies and issued a response that restated the original arguments for the Centre. On 4 September 2001, they received a second reply from the Department for Congress Motions and Resolutions which stated that 'the matter would be resolved when the right conditions were in place' (*deng chuangzao tiaojian jiejue* – Case Study Report 2006). Chen and the supporting deputies again responded in writing, expressing their disagreement, but this time succeeded in attracting the attention of the leader of the JCPC. On 15 October 2001, a delegation from the JCPC Standing Committee, which included the director of Jinhua's Department of Justice, arrived in Yiwu to conduct an investigation into the work of the Centre. During subsequent meetings, representatives from Yiwu People's Congress Law Committee, *daigongwei*[9] and courts expressed their support for the project. Nevertheless, within three weeks, the JCPC Department for Motions and Resolutions issued a third veto. This time, the trade union chair and supporting deputies forwarded their previous response to the JCPC Standing Committee and its *daigongwei* as well as the Jinhua City Inspection Bureau for Government News and Information (*zhengfu xinxi duchake*). The Standing Committee expressed its support for the Centre and also agreed to meet the proposal's suggestion formally to include its work in the work plan (*bianzhi*) of the Yiwu legal aid system run by the Department of Justice. Following such a dramatic breakthrough, the work of the Centre could now, finally, begin in earnest.

Managing a trade union rights centre in China

Chen instituted a management policy he dubbed the *yi bu san ding* which equates in English to 'the one do not do and the three must dos'. As stated already, one of the experiment's chief aims was to avoid further enlarging the union bureaucracy itself and to draw on wider social resources. Four professionally trained legal graduates were hired and signed individual labour contracts with the YFTU. The point here is that these employees were on labour contracts and, unlike their trade union colleagues, were not formal civil servants appointed from within the union bureaucracy. While the wages of these employees came out of a 300,000 yuan grant from the YFTU to the Centre, they were hired from 'society' and as such part of the process of 'socializing' union work, as opposed to enlarging the union bureaucracy itself. The second half of the *yi bu san ding* arrangement – 'the three must dos' – was aimed at ensuring that new staff members would stay in the job and at overall sustainability. This meant providing training and ensuring the career development of the four new personnel, their basic pay and bonus, and the overall budget of the Centre. The first 'must do' awarded staff the same privileges enjoyed by city-level union personnel. They were to receive the same level of 'political treatment' (*zhengzhi daiyu*), 'political study' (*zhengzhi xuexi*), and 'vocational training' (*yewu peixun*). Second was the economic 'must do', which stipulated that the trade union shoulders the responsibility of paying the new staffers 800 yuan per month plus an end-of-year bonus based on performance and number of cases handled. Thus, remuneration was rooted in market rates and productivity rather than the civil service salary scale that was considerably higher. Excluding the annual bonus, the wages of the four new employees represented less than 12 per cent of the Centre's overall budget. The third 'must do' capped the overall operating budget at 300,000 yuan per annum allocated, as mentioned above, from YFTU funds.

Building on experience gained in the struggle to establish the Centre, the future political security of the Centre was strengthened by the YFTU's actively seeking the support and advice of leading city individuals and departments and locking this support into working practices. As soon as it was formally established, Chen asked leaders from the City Party Committee – the most powerful body in the city – along with leading figures from the Judiciary, Police, Procuracy, Civil Affairs and Legal departments to form an advisory group to support and guide the Centre's work. Regular progress reports were sent to these leaders and they were consulted when major cases came before the Centre.

Building a 'socialized rights network'

Once the political space and backing for the Centre's long-term plans had been won, the next step was to provide the appropriate physical space, supported by an effective process of upholding rights work within the aforementioned budgetary constraints. As Chen explained, '[O]nce we were accepted as an idea, we then had to concentrate on making our Centre work in practice. This meant a process (*guocheng*) of rights protection that drew on resources in society rather than exacerbating confrontation in society' (interview, Chen Youde).

At first, the Centre operated on a membership basis in order to keep costs down and work units, institutions and even individuals could apply for membership. Primary-level trade unions and their members were deemed as 'natural members' and workers in enterprises that did not have unions could apply for membership on an individual or collective basis. Fees were paid in both these membership categories and, although I have been unable to determine what these were, they are likely to have been low as the Centre's status as a social organization (*shehui tuanti*) dictated a non-profit status. If a work unit successfully gained membership, this automatically awarded all employees of the work unit free membership status. By the end of 2001, 275 work units had joined and brought with them 32,870 members. The following year, all union members were deemed members of the Centre, a move which facilitated the 2004 change of name to that by which the Centre is now known – the Yiwu Workers' Legal Rights Centre.

The Centre itself was located on the ground floor of the YFTU building. It is interesting to note that when I took a taxi from the bus station, the driver said he did not know where the YFTU offices were, but he could take me to the YWLRC![10] Four rooms were set aside for dedicated activities based on a process of dispute and/or complaint resolution. On the left as one enters is a reception room for workers, who either phone with complaints and requests for help or arrive in person. This was staffed by one reception worker who explained: 'The main task of this room is to register a case, get it on file and begin the process for dealing with it. We also try to get the workers who come to start thinking about a feasible (*ke zuo de*) settlement rather than just letting off steam (interview, YWLRC staff, Yiwu, 22 March 2007).

The room consisted of one desk, a telephone and various forms for workers to complete. There were no computers, and distractions were deliberately kept to a minimum. Opposite this room was the investigation and procedures room (*diaocha chulishi*). As the name suggests, this room was for investigating complaints from workers registered in the first room and trawling for supporting evidence from mediation of disputes either in the relevant enterprise or at the Centre itself. The third room was the Legal Service Room (*falü fuwushi*) where preparations were made for representing workers at arbitration or in court. It was designed to facilitate a formal arbitration hearing which the Centre had obtained the right to hold (see below) and slightly resembled an English courtroom. There was a high desk at the 'head' of the room for the arbitrator(s) and in front of that two smaller 'docks' and tables were arranged so that they faced each other and were designated for employee and employer respectively. Although I did not witness a hearing, this room did have a somewhat formal atmosphere to it. Opposite this room was an archive office. Detailed records of all cases were rigorously filed in clip box files and these filled shelving that extended 20 feet along the end wall of the room.

External to the Centre itself, there were three initiatives aimed at building support for a socialized rights network. First, the union set about gaining the support of the Department of Telecommunications to establish a city-wide legal rights telephone hotline. The first two numbers of this phone line were '51', deliberately chosen by the union as they represent May Day in Chinese. The caller is greeted with a brief helpful-sounding recorded message offering help and encouraging him or her to follow up the complaint (Case Study Report 2006). In order to avoid an atmosphere of formality, which can be intimidating for migrant workers who often lack confidence when confronted with the official language of government, the caller is initially greeted in the local dialect – which is sufficiently close to standard *putonghua* to be understandable to most Chinese.[11] Second, a great deal of emphasis was placed on mediation at enterprise or local level. Acknowledging that enterprise-based mediation committees were not working effectively, the YFTU lobbied the Department of Justice for permission to set up the YFTU People's Mediation Committee which, in enterprises with more than 100 employees, was to merge with any existing mediation committees under the leadership of the enterprise union chairperson or deputy. In enterprises with no mediation facilities, mediation was organized by staff from the YWLRC representing the YFTU and this usually took place in the Legal Service Room of the YFTU. In smaller but important towns such as nearby Fantang, the Party-government liaison committee (*gong wei*) was asked to act as an outreach office of the Centre itself and assist with mediation cases wherever possible. Third, the Centre organized a major rights awareness campaign in local townships, which involved seminars in trade union law as well as the writing, printing and distribution of materials pertaining to rights awareness. It also organized well-known local lawyers and legal specialists to attend question-and-answer and education sessions on labour rights at various public and semi-public venues, including street level, residential neighbourhoods, migrants' dormitories, enterprises and various community centres and gathering places. A popular slogan for this activity was coined: 'know the law, respect the law and use the law to protect yourself' (*zhi fa, shou fa, yi fa shishi ziwo baohu*).

In keeping with the suggestions in Document 206, on 27 February 2002, the YFTU and the Yiwu Department of Justice issued a joint document that effectively met Chen's goal of coordinating the YFTU legal work with that of the citywide legal aid system under the administration of the Department of Justice. As such, the Yiwu City Legal Aid Centre (Staff and Workers' Section)[12] was formally established and immediately increased the opportunities for workers – especially migrant workers – to finance cases against their employers. Where the reorganized channels of mediation failed and a case went on to court – via arbitration – the union strove to speed up the process by persuading court judges to establish a fast-track 'green channel' for cases being assisted by the YWLRC personnel. This was centred on a pre-trial mediation session, a service that, according to official YFTU sources, has achieved a 90 per cent success rate. The YFTU used the information gained from the Centre's casework to get involved with MOLSS labour inspections wherever possible.

One of the YFTU's most innovative measures in building a socialized rights network was to seek out the involvement of the media in order to publicize violations and pressurize all parties to resolve a dispute. Almost from the outset in 2001, the YFTU and the local provincial edition of the *Workers' Daily* cooperated in setting up a 'rights work station'. In practice, this pro-media policy meant that as soon as a serious dispute emerged, reporters from local TV stations and newspapers were invited to cover the story, as opposed to the usual practice of keeping reporters away. This developed into a regular TV slot called *Trade Union March* (*gonghui zongzheng*), which used YWLRC case studies to highlight trade union law and also encourage public discussion of labour rights. Early experience in one of the Centre's first cases demonstrated the power of the media in labour disputes in which the new Centre faced an intransigent employer. According to Chen:

> Yes, there was opposition from employers at first – and there are still challenges. In fact our first case centered on three women workers at a hotel in the city. The boss owed the girls wages but wouldn't pay so they came to the Rights Centre which they had seen advertised in the press. The boss had a 'dark heart' (*heixin*) and his attitude was very negative, yet we couldn't let the Centre appear overtly confrontational as this was an early case. We decided to challenge the boss to discuss the details of the dispute on the local TV station and let the people decide. This suggestion was made after many hours of negotiation during which the boss showed no sign of compromising. Our challenge to him worked and he gave in. We drew two lessons from this: First, that use of the media is a very interesting yet in some ways quite a traditional approach. It is based on a public opinion approach to justice rather than entirely focusing on the fine detail of the legal points. It is also an effective

negotiating tactic in that it put huge pressure on the boss. After all, he was running a hotel which needs good publicity, not bad. Second, we [the Centre] had to win this case but at the same time we could not afford to create more opposition from local enterprises to the Centre's activities. We had to think of our continuing development and take conditions into account. But in this case, owing to the exceptionally stubborn attitude adopted by the hotel boss, we had to suggest a public exchange.

(Interview, Chen Youde)

The YFTU also cultivated working relationships with two law 'offices', both of which employed lawyers who had experience of labour cases, in order to improve the quality of legal services provided to workers. These were the Tiandi Legal Services Office (*fuwusuo*) in Yiwu and the Zhejiang Siyuanhunlun Lawyers' Office (*lüshi shiwusuo*). Finally, the union worked closely with trade unions from other areas and counties that exported labour to Yiwu. For example, Kaihua County exported over 23,000 migrant workers to Yiwu each year. On 13 October 2002, the YFTU and the Kaihua County Federation of Trade Unions established a work station aimed at dealing with complaints and cases involving migrants from Kaihua. By the end of December 2004, this cooperation had dealt with 36 cases involving 506 migrants with wage and compensation claims totalling 1.2 million yuan. Over one million yuan in wage arrears had been successfully retrieved (Case Study Report 2006). The Centre, via the work station, had represented workers in one case of arbitration and dealt with three cases in court. A network was in place.

Case studies: the centre in action

We have already discussed the ACFTU's cautious response to representing workers in court. I will begin this section by first returning to the issues around formal dispute resolution, prior to discussing details from the YWLRC's caseload. A senior trade union official in Guangzhou explained the union's reticence to take up difficult or sensitive cases.

We can generally only take up cases in which the violations are so bad that the workers will definitely win. We know that this is not an ideal (*lixiang*) policy but it is the only policy that we can effectively employ in the period. At this stage in our economic development it's not going to encourage migrant workers to join if we take up cases which, for one reason or another, we lose.

(Interview, city-level union official, Guangzhou, 12 July 2001)

In recent years, the union has certainly increased its caseload and this trend will continue following the enactment of the Labour Mediation and Arbitration Law (LMAL) on 1 May 2008, but a cautious and constrained approach remains in place. Lawyers and migrant workers in Guangdong province have criticized this policy. A lawyer practising in Guangzhou whose caseload included industrial disputes, sometimes for the Guangzhou Federation of Trade Unions (GFTU), told me that:

> Our office would take on more workers' cases if we could secure the formal backing of the union. It's not a question of organization and everyone knows the union is compromised in the factory. It's more an issue of the higher levels throwing their weight behind specific cases – publicly and much more often – and being prepared to lose. The GFTU blacklist [of bad employers] is not such a good thing from this perspective. It ignores the fact that most employers break the law most of the time!
> (Interview, lawyer, Guangzhou, 6 June 2006)

From a different angle, a worker recovering from benzene poisoning in Guangdong told me that:

> The union won't take up our case as it's complicated. Half of us didn't have contracts and the workers like me who have been hit badly have been talking to the media already and this has not helped our cause with the union. Also the company's claim that the chemical was labelled is partly true. But I didn't even know what benzene was when I started so what difference did a label make?
> (Interview, injured worker, Guangzhou, 7 September 2002)

The YWLRC has taken a different approach. At the same time as cultivating contacts among relevant government departments and conducting labour law education and law propaganda exercises, it has also set out to take on as many cases as possible, encouraging mediation over arbitration and the courts, although these options are certainly not ruled out. This is going against the general direction of development, which has seen a decline in the relative use of mediation by workers and selective intervention by the unions. Chen explained that, even though unions remained weak at enterprise level, the advantage of the Centre was that it could react fast and carried the authority of the YFTU itself.

> Over 90 per cent of the cases we deal with involve a violation of workers' legal rights. Our Centre deals with cases irrespective of their size or degree of complexity. If you can get to a dispute early enough, there is always a way of finding a solution if you try hard enough. The Centre has been of immense help in this respect. Workers are beginning to come to us first and not as a last resort.
> (Interview, Chen Youde)

Chen stressed that thorough investigation by the Centre's staffers was at the core of successful prosecutions but that while the fast-track channel established with the courts was important in bringing pressure on the employers, the preferred approach of the 'Yiwu Model' was compromise through mediation. At a conference on Labour Dispute Resolution in 2007, a deputy director of the Centre, Chen Ji, explained the logic.

Workers are like anyone else, they are prepared to compromise. If we get a case that say involves 5,000 yuan in wage arrears but the boss, following our intervention, is only willing to pay 4,500 yuan, we have found that workers will accept the lower figure as long as it is reasonable rather then go for a long-drawn-out case to get the full amount. At the end of the day, we believe it is in the workers' interests to compromise. We think arbitration and the delays it involves can be a waste of time so we encourage this spirit of compromise.
(Chen Ji, observation, Beijing, 20 January 2007)[13]

There is an irony to this argument in that a rights centre is spending as much time persuading workers to compromise, and in effect to abandon their rights, as it is helping workers pursue employers through arbitration and the courts. Yet, perhaps even more ironic is the criticism that the Yiwu Model occasionally attracts from within the ACFTU, despite the fact that the ACFTU itself has made only limited progress in juridical resolution, as testified by the rise in the number of strikes described in Chapter 2. In a contribution at a seminar in Beijing organized by a Sino-British project on labour dispute settlement procedures, Chen Ji's comments in favour of compromise and mediation over arbitration and legal action was greeted with scepticism by attending academics and was even rebuffed by one participant as a step backwards. In the following section, I narrate how the Centre solved three different disputes that were compiled during the research for this chapter. All three are representative of the Centre's work.

Hu XX was one of 112 carpenters employed on a new recreation park in Yiwu City. On 14 January 2005, Hu and three other representatives of the carpenters, all from the nearby Kaihua county, arrived at the Yiwu-Kaihua Rights Centre Work Station, part of the 'rights network' established by the YFTU. The four representatives had been delegated by their workmates to ask the station for assistance in chasing 290,000 yuan in unpaid wages dating back to August 2004 when their work on the project was completed. The construction of the park was under the overall management of a major construction corporation. Despite the fact that the arrears were over a year old, rendering the facts of the case more difficult to pin down, the Centre agreed to take the case and immediately contacted the project manager at the construction company. A staff member at the Centre embarked on a process of explaining the relevant labour law articles as well as a national government campaign which was prioritizing the problem of wage arrears among construction workers. The Centre also explained that companies which violated these regulations were subject to fines. After claiming that the company was also owed money by the developers, the project manager of the company was persuaded to apply to a special guarantee fund established by the Ministry of Construction for an emergency payout of 300,000 yuan in order to cover the unpaid wages. An explanation for the company's initial reluctance to apply can be found in the sometimes political nature of contract bidding in China's construction industry, where companies applying for government contracts can be penalized if their management record is blemished by such applications that could suggest mismanagement (interview, lawyer, Guangzhou, 6 June 2006). Given the recent attempts by the government to stamp out wage arrears in the construction industry, the dispute would be taken into account when the company put out future tenders in what the local provincial-level trade union has described as an 'immature, unregulated and often chaotic construction market place in which payments to construction companies are delayed as a matter of course and "competition"' (Tao Junyi *et al.* 2003). That the Centre took just an afternoon to solve this case by negotiating on behalf of the workers, even though there was no direct evidence of an employment relationship, is testament to both the reputation of its rights network after just four years in full operation and the leverage a quasi-official body can exercise over an enterprise. From the YFTU's point of view, it also gives a certain amount of credence to the argument for mediation over more confrontational tactics.

The second example is of a dispute involving former SOE workers employed at the now restructured and privatized national department store chain *Baihuodalou*.[14] When the store began restructuring in 1998, it offered its employees the choice to purchase shares in a process known nationally as *gufenhua* or literally 'shareholderization'. Sixty retired and 'internally retired' employees were not included in the offer, even though they were still formal employees and/or pensioners of the company. By 2003, the shares had risen in value by more than 500 per cent. When former employees cashed in and sold their shares to a new corporate buyer, the 60 retirees realized the extent of their losses and launched a campaign of petitioning government up to and including provincial level for compensation for their original exclusion. These protests attracted a great deal of attention as news of the campaign spread beyond Yiwu city. During December 2003, the retirees presented a collective complaint to the YFTU offices. Both YFTU officers and employees from the Centre were duly dispatched to organize dialogue between company managers and the protestors. Acting as mediators between the two sides and working to narrow the difference in opinion, the YFTU gradually edged itself towards a negotiating role on behalf of the workers by urging the company to consider the long years of service and contribution they had made to the store's successful development and eventual restructuring. The company agreed to make a one-off compensation payment of 5,000 yuan to each former employee. This represented approximately eight months' wages, based on 1998 wage rates.

These two cases involved mediation and limited representation in which neither courts nor arbitration committees were involved. The third example is quite different and involved the Centre taking up a case of work injury compensation *after* due legal process failed to result in justice. Mr Xu worked as a lift engineer for the Shanghai Express Elevator Company. In May 1997, Xu was seriously injured in a fall while installing a lift and was classified as having a Category 6 injury by the local government-run occupational injury committee. Between 1998 and 2002, Xu took his employers to three arbitration courts and filed five legal appeals to obtain adequate compensation. Despite hiring a competent lawyer, these efforts did not lead to a fair settlement from Xu's point of view. Five years after the original injury and heavily in debt, he approached the YFTU on 30 May 2002. The case was passed to the Centre.

154   *Trade union rights centre in Yiwu*

The Centre organized a five-pronged strategy to win compensation for Xu. First, there was a thorough investigation into the case, which included gathering as much hard information as possible in order to build up a critical mass of evidence that would stand up in negotiation, arbitration or in court. Second, the Centre compiled and sent reports, backed by supporting evidence, to the arbitration committee and the Department of Justice. This tactic also involved asking these bodies for further instructions (*qingshi*), keeping open channels of communication on the case and even lobbying for support. Third, Chen Youde personally wrote a document entitled 'Award or revoke, long delay or speedy solution' which he submitted to the Jinhua People's Congress – in his capacity as a People's Congress deputy – as well as the senior judge of the People's Intermediate Court and various government leaders in Yiwu. Fourth, the Centre drew on its contacts at law offices and appointed legal representatives to organize a sixth appeal. Finally, steps were taken to ensure that the case received widespread attention via the media. A year later, on 6 May 2003, the Yiwu City Intermediate Court awarded Xu damages of 106,835 yuan. This case demonstrated the multi-pronged strategy that the union had employed to win acceptance for the Centre's right to exist: a combination of lobbying, political appeals and tactical use of the media.

Between 2002 and 2006, the Centre dealt with a large number of individual cases, collective protests and carried out educational activities. The following is a summary of these activities which, according to senior officials of the YFTU, have significantly contributed to improving labour relations in the city. These statistics are from the YFTU itself and I have been unable to verify them independently. Cases received: 3,112, of which 2,831 were solved; 266 collective petitions involving 4,337 people; 2278 enquiries to the legal rights telephone hotline answered; 29 serious incidents have been settled without 'further escalation or conflict'. The Centre has made 113 free representations in arbitration committees; 114 free representations – by lawyers – in court; 52 broadcasts of the *Union March* TV programme on Yiwu TV; 32 legal training sessions involving 16,770 workers; and wages and losses retrieved for workers totalling 9.01 million yuan (Case Study Report 2006).

Significance of the YFTU experiment

Given the lack of competition from alternative trade unions, it is difficult to conceive of the ACFTU behaving as an independent trade union whose power is rooted in the collective will of its members. Therefore, much of the pressure to change must inevitably derive from external factors: namely, increasing working class militancy and the Party itself. By the same token, successful reforming initiatives that aim to improve workers' rights via union activity must also include external agencies. According to the *Zhejiang Workers' Daily*, this was one of the prime lessons of the Centre's initial achievements:

> In order to seriously undertake rights work [the union] must actively go after the support of both the Party Committee and the government. Only by blending

in with the wider situation facing the Party and government, can the right kind of space for developing [rights work] be opened up.

(*Zhejiang Workers' Daily* 2005)

Political constraints apart, restrictions on the YFTU's access to resources, as dictated by the local government's overall administrative plan (*bianzhi*), ruled out a full-blown legal assault on employers' violations. In this sense, the YFTU differed little from most county-level city trade union federations. The key weapon in the struggle to establish the rights centre in Yiwu can be found in the fact that Chen Youde possessed the will to do something about the plight of migrant workers. Indeed, unusually for a local union official, Chen has become something of a local hero.

> In Yiwu city many migrant workers are aware that the trade union has a rights centre that specializes in speaking out for migrant workers and solving the difficult problems they face. The trade union Chairman is Chen Youde who migrant workers call 'Old Uncle [Chen]'.
>
> (Liu Shen 2006)

The experience of walking around the streets near the YFTU with Chen certainly backs up this approachable and down-to-earth image that this 'peasant's son' (Liu Shen 2006) has acquired. As we walked to a nearby restaurant for lunch, Chen stopped to talk to people he appeared to know – shopkeepers, a building security guard – and the driver of a passing bus sounded his horn and waved in greeting when he saw Chen. After spending time with Chen, it became clear that he was the driving force behind the experiment and indeed this conclusion was backed up by interviews with some of the project's advisers (interview, labour researcher, Hangzhou, 21 March 2007). Once a leading union official – in this case at city (county) level – with the political will to innovate or 'trailblaze' (*chuangxin*) was appointed, barriers to action were at least breached if not removed altogether.

To demonstrate that their strategy would work to sceptical government officials, often hostile employers and victimized workers alike, the YFTU and its Centre had to be seen to make a difference to the general climate of industrial relations. Early intervention in disputes via rights work was prioritized and the 'borrowing' of resources was the key strategy.

> Faced with these problems, the YFTU put the upholding of rights at the forefront of its work and set out to achieve this by the concept of 'carrying out trade union work outside the trade union'. The road to [successfully] upholding rights was to 'make use of policies, make use of external strengths and make use of logic and experience' (*jie feng jie li jie li*).
>
> (Case Study Report 2006)

This meant taking aspects of trade union work and 'socializing' it by turning to wider social and governmental resources. At the same time, it should not surprise us that the YFTU did not deem it appropriate to 'borrow' from their constituents' only available resource – collective class power! Such radical departures from policy and practice were off the radar even in the blazing of new trails. In the struggle to set up the YWLRC against sustained opposition, the YFTU made no attempt to break from its constitutional acceptance of Party leadership and guidance – indeed Chen Youde was – and is – a loyal servant of the Party and as such provided an important anchor of authority and continuity to the experiment. And while it attempted to improve the YFTU's capacity and reputation as a defender of workers, it did so by relying on China's trade union and labour laws, which can equally serve as a passport for trade union passivity simply due to their non-implementation. To his credit, Chen took these laws seriously and thought out a creative strategy for at least partially enforcing them. Thus, the starting point for the YWLRC experiment was not Chen's close links with the 'grass roots' or inspiration derived from the traditional trade union pantheon of class interests and solidarity. It was the law, specifically the Trade Union Law, Article 2 of which stipulates: 'The All-China Federation of Trade Unions and all the trade union organizations under it represent the interests of the workers and staff members and safeguard the legitimate rights and interests of the workers and staff members according to law' (ACFTU 2001).

We can see that an important function of the Centre was to provide a channel through which workers could take grievances justified by trade union and labour law. The strategy and tactics adopted to achieve this aim were both experimental – the socialization of union work – and pragmatic – the emphasis on mediation over formal legal action. While the law served as an important reference point for developing the project against strong opposition, mediation, persuasion and garnering influence in high places was preferred to ruthless pursuit of the implementation of the law in the name of inalienable rights. As Chen Ji told me during a conversation at the aforementioned symposium on dispute resolution in Beijing:

> Our job is not to terrify employers with the law. Our job is to get the best possible deal for workers in a difficult labour relations environment. Before the Centre was set up, workers, migrants especially, had virtually no accessible channels of recourse and the union had very few full-timers! Remember our industrial areas are full of small companies where employees have no chance of actively influencing the boss, short of just leaving the job. We were not in a position to organize all these workers effectively. Our best option was to try and hold employers to their most basic obligations and remind them that these are the law. But this also requires workers to compromise. We cannot spend all our time and resources in the courts. We have to be more imaginative than that and this is why we stress that effective mediation can still work.
> (Chen Ji, personal communication, Beijing, 20 January 2007)

Part of this imaginative work came in the form of increased, flexible and improved mediation services. The YFTU set up the Yiwu City Federation of Trade Unions People's Mediation Committee with the – hard-won – backing and authority of a 'borrowed' resource, namely the Department of Justice. While there are no independent statistics available, it is interesting to document the results of this emphasis on mediation and compare it with trends in not-too-far-away Shanghai. Between October 2000 and autumn 2004, the Centre dealt with 3,112 cases and achieved a 91 per cent success rate via various channels of mediation (*Zhejiang Workers' Daily* 2005). In Shanghai, enterprise-level mediated disputes dropped dramatically in foreign-owned or invested enterprises between 1996 and 1997 from 55,000 to under 8,000 and flatlined in the first years of the new century (China Labour Statistical Yearbooks 1997–2002). Gallagher found a total of just 698 mediated disputes in the whole of Shanghai for the year 2000 (Gallagher 2005b: 31–54). In 2004, the new mediation committee in Yiwu dealt with 425 cases and avoided 93 per cent of these going on to formal arbitration.[15] In one case, involving a trade union chairperson dismissed early from his post, the YWLRC obtained his successful reinstatement after 10 rounds of mediation (Case Study Report 2006). For Chen Ji, the compromise that mediation usually entailed was worthwhile if it meant avoiding 'clogging up courts and arbitration committees' in drawn-out battles. On the other hand, the Centre did not exclude arbitration or court representation from its programme. As I have shown, it broke new ground in getting official backing from the Yiwu Labour Arbitration Committee for its mediated arbitration work as well as openly drawing on the experience of foreign trade unions in directly engaging the services and reputation of law firms, offices and centres.[16] Again, the emphasis was on drawing on wider social resources and official support and avoiding expanding the budget or work plan (*bianzhi*) of the YFTU itself. Indeed, Chen Youde was keen to point out that:

> The Centre's employees were all hired via the market. They are not civil servants. This is very important and in fact experimental. If our example is going to be applied elsewhere, it will simply not work if it is expensive or involves reassessing administrative work plans (*bianzhi*). This is all part of what we meant by 'doing union work outside the union' – we are breaking out of traditional union practices and trying to adapt to the new conditions.
> (Interview, Chen Youde)

The *Zhejiang Workers' Daily* reminded union cadres studying its discussion of the Yiwu Model of the experiment's limits. According to the newspaper, which is owned by the Zhejiang Federation of Trade Unions, going out on a limb and solely relying on the trade union to protect workers' rights was 'far from enough' and the model demonstrated the centrality of government and Party support to the YFTU strategy – as well as 'aid from all corners of society' (*Zhejiang Workers' Daily* 2005). Indeed, a legal adviser employed at the Centre pointed out to me that one of the challenges they had faced at the outset was persuading officials from 'relevant government departments' to accept that they themselves should be part of a 'socialized rights network', i.e. that their department was part of the process of upholding rights as well. The *ZJWD* article stated that 'practice has demonstrated that the YFTU's socialization of rights work is in keeping with the trade unions becoming socio-political organizations' (*ZJWD* 2005). One labour researcher interpreted this as meaning that unions are no longer restricted to serving as transmission belts for Party and government policies (interview, labour researcher, Beijing, 23 January 2007).

Political decision making in China is an opaque process and as such it is a challenge – particularly at local level – to map clearly the arguments that inevitably lie behind the acceptance or rejection of a new strategy or policy initiative. But, as I have shown, the fieldwork in Yiwu did afford a reasonably detailed snapshot of the protracted lobbying campaign by the YFTU and its chairman to get the YWLRC up and running. Interestingly, this contention has been entirely bypassed by both the senior leaders of the ACFTU and the media in their public discussions and endorsement of the Centre's work. In fact, the contention offers us a clear example of how, as it edges towards a more representational role, the ACFTU's labour rights work can 'upset people' (interview, Chen Youde). The 'people' ranged from individual employers, heavies from home-town associations to what appear to be arguments over turf with government departments. In fact, it is in the struggle to get the Centre accepted that the YFTU entered into truly experimental territory. This was characterized by two major decisions. First, by hiring staff outside the traditional channels of union employment, the YFTU was taking direct responsibility as an employer, and second, by placing these employees in an organization registered under the Ministry of Civil Affairs as a non-profit making group that fits into the first of three NGO categories I discussed in the second section, the YFTU was going well and truly beyond the union fence. The crossover of responsibilities and authority that these measures implied was initially a step too far for some related government departments. The Department of Justice saw in the YWLRC a challenge to its legal aid work and the implication that established legal mechanisms of labour dispute resolution were failing workers, not just on the grounds of union incapacity but by the procedures themselves.

Conclusion

To return to the research question: How can a local trade union act in defence of the interests and rights of its members and potential members? Or, more broadly, is trade union reform possible? The evidence suggests that we can judge the work of the YWLRC from three angles: first, as an example of changing union work practices; second, as an example of the changing nature of the ACFTU itself; and third in comparison with similar work carried out by civil society's new kids on the block: LNGOs.

What the ACFTU does well is draft laws, carry out research and maintain contacts with government departments. More recently, it has grown in influence in the international union world, reflecting an investment and upgrading of its international department that has facilitated its re-election to the Governing Body of the ILO in 2008. On the other hand, it is not doing well at negotiating effective collective contracts, organizing from the bottom up and activating its primary levels to reduce violations of workers' rights. These failures are a direct historical legacy from its role in the command economy and the work practices that this role produced over time. The YWLRC broke the mould. It used its own resources to go beyond the usual parameters and borrowed from other resources to ensure at least partial success in attempting to create a rights network serving not only migrant workers but also weak enterprise-level trade unions. In Chen Youde, the YFTU happened on a trade union official with empathy for the plight of workers and the initiative to draw up a workable and legal strategy (*jie feng jie li jie li*) to improve it. This translated into 'political will' and as a result resources not normally associated with the trade union bureaucracy became available.

The YWLRC also reflects the changing nature of the ACFTU itself, though progress is sometimes excruciatingly slow and erratic. The institution is being called on to stabilize labour relations in a market economy, and yet it remains largely ineffective in the workplace, where the higher levels have little or no leverage. It is still too early to say if the YFTU has found an interim solution to this contradiction even if the results so far represent an improvement. Much more important to the bigger picture, however, is that the experiment was indicative of reform that eventually gained approval from the chairman of the ACFTU, Wang Zhaoguo (*Workers Daily* 2005b).

Finally, the case study also shows how a state agency – albeit in transition – with responsibility for upholding workers' rights differs from non-state agencies – LNGOs – which are attempting to do the same thing. While the work of LNGOs is vital, results are hard to measure except in terms of general influence. And in contrast with LNGOs, the YFTU was able to make use of its status as essentially a government agency in order to exercise political and administrative leverage to persuade employers to back down. For their part, LNGOs have to tread a sensitive path in which employers are under little obligation to accept their role as mediators and, as Huang Qingnan's injuries demonstrate, are occasionally prone to resorting to direct violence to discourage LNGOs from their work. On an optimistic note, recent developments in Guangdong province perhaps herald the next step in the evolution of labour rights centres in China – and one with the potential to widen the employers' goalposts in favour of workers. In the wake of the attacks on Huang and others, the SFTU made approaches to LNGOs in October of 2007 and convened a meeting with 16 representatives of both LNGOs and so-called 'black lawyers'. At the meeting, the SFTU proposed working with these networks to establish a township-based system of rights centres throughout Guangdong. This important development has given rise to considerable debate in the NGO community, especially as the proposal ruled out those LNGOs with direct overseas funding. In this light, the experiences, strategies and tactics of Yiwu are of great relevance to both the LNGOs and the SFTU, the differences between Zhejiang and Guangdong notwithstanding.

6 Trade union elections
From dependency to democracy?

This chapter examines the more sensitive issue of 'direct' trade union elections at enterprise level. Using evidence from case studies, interviews and secondary sources, I will explore different procedures for candidate selection and voting to elect trade union chairpersons, deputy chairpersons and committee members at enterprise level. Traditional practice has been for the enterprise party committee to appoint trade union officials via a generally non-competitive, consultative procedure that prioritized ideological commitment, class background, education level, administrative skills and an unblemished personal file as preferred qualities for such a post. The quandary that arose out of this system was not unique to China. Writing on the former Soviet Union, Ashwin and Clarke positioned unions as being strung between the Party and enterprise management (Ashwin and Clarke 2003: 18–19). Both Chinese and Russian union cadres were *supposed* to keep managers and workers to the Party line, but they were more likely to serve management, which did not necessarily represent Party or national interests. Traditional practice has continued into the reform era and in the more polarized environment of the private sector, the impotency of trade union cadres became far more apparent. As far back as the early 1980s, protagonists of direct trade union elections advocated pilot projects as part of a long-term strategy to improve enterprise unions' capacity to meet the challenges of a new economic environment (Howell 2006: 11).

As we saw in Chapter 2, the ACFTU's room for manoeuvre during the restructuring of the state sector was constrained by its politically defined institutional incapacity to mount a challenge to government policy. As the reforms deepened and began to impact on workers' lives, feelings of abandonment and disappointment among those losing out were sometimes directed at the trade union and its cadres across the country.

> What the hell have you come here for? We've got nothing here! The mines have shut down and those bastards in their offices [where the union office is housed] are corrupt to the bone! We had a strike, but there's no way of controlling them. It's not like the USA where everyone's rich and you've got democracy. Shulan Town? It's a joke.
> (Interview, miner, Shulan, 22 October 2001)

> The union did not explain the full consequences of severing our relations with Petrochina and that's been a big disappointment for us. I think the union should help us get our jobs back, not direct us to casual work in society.
> (Interview, laid-off oil worker, Daqing, 25 March 2002)

> Now our factory is bankrupt and the overwhelming majority of its workers have been reduced to the level of unemployed vagrants and we are furious. Most of us here have met with disaster and, as we have no other option, we address this open letter to you in order to recount the events leading up to, and since, the bankruptcy.
> (Open Letter to President Jiang Zemin, 5 March 2002 cited in Human Rights Watch (HRW) 2002: 38)

The feeling of being abandoned and under-represented in the state sector was also felt by workers who had transferred to the private sector. A former SOE worker who had found a new job in the Shenzhen Shangri La hotel explained that she saw no point in a union on the basis that there was nothing for it to do!

> There is no union here. I am not sure that management would allow it anyway. The guy who runs this place is a capitalist from Malaysia. It is different working here. The pay is better but the work is much harder and there are no benefits. If he [the Malaysian manager] won't talk to the unions and there are no benefits, what's the point in having one?
> (Interview, hotel worker, Shenzhen, 11 February 2006)

Against the background of increasing labour unrest, this mix of despair and apathy deeply worried Party leaders and has served as an impetus to strengthen senior Party and ACFTU leaders' appetite for improved union representation and more generalized reform. Following the trauma of 1989, the momentum for reform began to gather speed in the mid to late 1990s, continuing into the build-up and aftermath of the ACFTU's Fourteenth Congress in 2003. In Chapter 4, we noted former ACFTU chairman Wei Jianxing's lambasting union cadres for their poor performance at the turn of the century. Following the Congress, some in the leadership were beginning to interpret the challenges posed by the private sector as an opportunity to rebuild the legitimacy lost as a result of the ACFTU's inability to protect jobs and status during restructuring.

> We must give China's unions a backbone. We must understand how to organize the working masses in unions within China's socialist market economy, and particular attention should be given to private sector workers and migrant workers. We must learn how to truly represent the working class masses, and staunchly uphold the legal rights of workers ... We must transform the Party's leadership of unions, and allow for union workers to reflect their true conditions and engage in legal and proper struggle.
> (Liu Shi 2003)

Key to understanding the dynamic for reform, especially with regard to trade union elections, is that the ACFTU and the Party remain profoundly concerned that trade unions should anticipate worker grievances and unrest in order to curb growing militancy. As we saw in Chapters 2 and 3, this militancy has been evolving since the mid 1990s as well-organized strikes and picket lines have replaced demonstrations outside government offices. Thus, the supporters of trade union elections in China have posited elections as a strategy aimed at strengthening primary unions by improving their representational credibility in a transformed environment. Guo Wencai, head of the ACFTU's Department for the Establishment of Primary Organizations (EPO), has argued:

> The degree of democratization and 'massization' (*qunzhonghua*) of primary level trade unions determines their degree of vitality or weakness. Practice has shown that enterprise unions with high levels of democratization and close links with ordinary workers are more active and enjoy much higher levels of approval and satisfaction from their members. There are many reasons why some primary unions are weak and inactive, but the failure to prioritize democratization and 'massization' remains, universally, the crucial explanation.
>
> (Guo Wencai and Gao Jie 2007)

Primary-level union cadres in the market economy require different skills than those needed to survive the command economy and the argument that directly elected officials can provide the right people has gradually gained credibility. The risk for the Party is that more effective may well mean more outspoken cadres and this could have a detrimental effect on investment or social stability and the ACFTU's recent release of the Method on Election of Trade Union Chairpersons (2008b) reflects these concerns. The Method excludes senior company administrators, business partners and their close relatives, employees responsible for human resource management, and foreign nationals from standing as candidates for chairpersons. Arguably it leaves enough space – just – for the type of local experiments in loosening and even removing constraints on candidature examined in this chapter.

This chapter is structured as follows: the first section briefly reviews the Western literature on trade union elections as a background to discussion of some of the issues and social relations pertaining to elections; and in the second section, I present and analyse two case studies involving different electoral procedures. I conclude that while trade union elections are important, they are not sufficient on their own to make a radical difference to the ACFTU's overall operational effectiveness and credibility. This would require not just more accountable enterprise-level union chairpersons and committees but a more supportive, interactive and, at times, directive relationship between the higher trade unions and their enterprise-level subordinates.

Methodology

The main fieldwork for this chapter consists of collaborative fieldwork undertaken in late 2005 and 2006 in two enterprises in Zhejiang province, which has a reputation for being a trailblazer of direct trade union elections. It involved observation, questionnaires and interviews. I conducted follow-up interviews and discussions with trade union researchers and union officials in 2006 and 2007. Gaining access to sufficient data and materials to provide a full narrative of trade union elections was not a straightforward matter, and, as other researchers have pointed out, evaluating trade union elections is a sensitive endeavour (Howell 2008: 845). However, our work was able to draw on primary data from fieldwork that I have used as part of a generalized evaluation. This included a review of attitudes to elections in a prosperous township of Zhejiang provincial town where the local town-level trade union (*zhen gonghui*) had an exceptionally well-established network of enterprise-level trade unions. In 2002, the first elections were held in 10 relatively large enterprises. In 2005, 300 questionnaires were distributed to trade union members across the town and 144 were returned. When conditions allowed, my colleagues also distributed questionnaires to other trade union committee members and chairpersons during the course of the fieldwork in 2005–2006 and the data from these more recent pilots is included in the discussion. This chapter also draws on data – cited in previous chapters – from the review of the attitudes of 60 enterprise-level trade union cadres that included 24 interviews conducted in Dongguan in 2006.

Contextualising trade union elections

The literature

For Taylor and Li, the continued practice of appointments is one of three factors that undermine the ACFTU's legitimacy as a trade union, the other two being its constitutional role as protector of the entire working class, i.e. 'national' interests, and its monopolistic status. Acknowledging that the appointment of trade union officers is hardly unique to China, Taylor and Li nevertheless argue that the absence of an 'effective electoral system for union office holders' makes too large a hole in the ACFTU's trade union credentials (Taylor and Li 2007: 707).

Howell positions trade union direct elections as a component in a broader one-step-forward-two-steps-backwards-one-step-forward-again trajectory of political reform and improved accountability in government. The legal institutionalization of the latter in 1987 via the enacting of the experimental Organic Law of Village Committees – reaffirmed in 1998 – has increased interest in 'the idea of electing leaders from below rather than appointing them from above' (Howell 2006: 853). Discussing the progress of elections in general and trade union elections in particular, Howell argues that '[A]nother aspect of the move towards more responsive and inclusionary governance is the widening spaces for citizens to articulate views, express interests, and form organizations with varying degrees of independence from government' (Howell 2006: 24).

Discussing the success of village elections and the concepts of democracy and accountability in China, Schuter has cautioned against employing a Westernized 'ideal type' of democratic model. Instead, insights into Chinese modernity can be gleaned 'by carefully analysing the internal innovation potentials of this system – i.e. its institutional flexibility and adaptability – to generate elite accountability and regime legitimacy'. For Schuter, Western democratic theory is not relevant here. Instead 'Chinese Democracy' 'assumes that democratic participation in the PRC at the lower administrative levels is possible without automatically putting the CPC's power monopoly into jeopardy, but even stabilising it' (Schuter 2003).

Schuter's observations notwithstanding, these scholars tend to approach the issue of trade union elections solely from the perspective of democratic credibility and accountability. Important though they are, democratization is not the central issue per se. More important for the ACFTU is the creation of effective workplace trade unions that can forestall unrest and head off challenges to the ACFTU's monopolistic status. As such, elections are not simply a means to make unions more democratic. Equally valid is their potential to render their primary organizations more responsive to workers' grievances and more effective in negotiating a peaceful resolution of those grievances.

Framing representational credibility

In this light, Guo Wencai's case for democratic work practices as one of three essential requirements for effective unions is especially important to our inquiry. In fact, there is a political and regulatory history behind Guo's views that senior leaders have made use of in order to dampen down the expectations of reformers. At the dramatic 11th Congress of the ACFTU in 1988, the official trade union work report outlined the need to improve the work of primary-level unions (*jiceng gonghui*). Chairman Ni Zhifu's report on trade union work to the delegates emphasized the centrality of grass-roots work 'if the ACFTU was to become a genuine workers' organization'. Ni argued, 'that primary level trade unions do not exist to serve the higher levels, but rather leaders at all levels of the union are there to serve the primary levels' (Ni Zhifu 1988: 70). Change was in the air and it appeared that many people in the unions could not wait for the law to catch up with the progress capital had been making since 1978. Chairman Ni Zhifu, who had delivered the work report at the 11th Congress, was dismissed after Tiananmen, following the ACFTU's hesitancy in condemning the student protestors. Nevertheless, during an interview in *Workers' Daily* over 15 years later, ACFTU Deputy Chairman Su Liqing returned to the theme of trade union elections by quoting from an important document from the very same Congress entitled 'Tentative Plan for Trade Union Reform'.[1] The tentative plan contained frequent references to democracy and transparency. In the interview, Su quoted Point 43 from the document.

> All levels of the trade union leadership should be elected via strict democratic procedures. Elections must be democratized (*minzhuhua*), opened up (*gongkaihua*) and give full play to the will of the voters. Candidates in primary-level democratic elections can be proposed from grassroots level upwards and candidates [should] put their arguments directly to the workers.

In the right conditions, primary-level trade unions can gradually implement the direct election of leaders by the members.

(Wang Jiaoping 2003)

However, Su also points to a complicated and as yet incomplete legal framework guiding elections that has done as much to restrict their expansion as to encourage it. It includes: Article 9 of the Trade Union Law (2001); Article 10 of the ACFTU Constitution (2001); Article 43 of the 'Tentative Plan for Trade Union Reform' quoted above; the 'Provisional Regulations for Primary Level Trade Union Elections' (Provisional Regulations 1992); Article 15 of the ACFTU's 'Opinion on Questions Arising from the Implementation of Trade Union Reform and Construction' (1997), which recommended that elections should be restricted to small- and medium-size enterprises; the 'ACFTU Decision on the Further Strengthening of Primary Level Trade Unions' (2004), and finally the 'Method on the Election of Trade Union Chairpersons' (2008b). While the latter document, issued after Su's interview, does give more room for union innovation in general, the Method signals that 'sea elections' (open candidacy) popularized in village elections and employed in one of our case studies are not appropriate.

In practice, the ACFTU has not recommended elections in situations characterized by a high degree of industrial conflict, its main concern being to avoid the election of militant representatives prepared to go beyond the restrictions of the Party's social harmony project. In contrast to the two purely local and genuinely innovative initiatives discussed in the previous two chapters, direct elections are not regarded as an appropriate strategy for stabilizing labour relations in areas of unrest in the short term, but rather as a tool for consolidating an existing stability.

Union cadres and union members

The relationship between enterprise-level union cadres and their members is defined chiefly by social, political and economic disparities that in turn feed into doubts over representation and credibility. Although not institutional in themselves, traditional trade union practices carry the weight and characteristics of an institutional barrier to improvements in these areas. While Wang overstates the extent of ACFTU rejuvenation in the private sector, his contrasting of the traditional appointments system in 'official trade unions' in China's remaining SOEs with the 'new direction of trade unions in private enterprises' illustrates the problem well. He argues that the latter increasingly boast primary-level officials who are able, ready and willing to respond to their members, while old style union officials in SOEs are better described as 'responsible persons in mass organizations' who fall under the orbit and treatment of 'leading cadres selected via a limited democracy directed by Party organizations' (Wang Jinhong 2005). The implication is that the trade union agenda in SOEs is fixed by the Party-state and this is a major constraint on their representational credibility. While Wang is largely correct in his positioning of traditional SOE unions, the case studies I present – one of which was at the cutting edge of direct elections in terms of democratic credentials – will enable us to test Wang's assertion of an emerging 'new direction' in the private sector.

The term 'treatment' (*duidai*) refers to the pay, conditions and a less measurable but equally important degree of political influence enjoyed by trade union cadres largely as a result of their civil servant status. Issued in 1981 by the ACFTU, Document 24 stated that enterprise-level trade union cadres should receive the same levels of treatment as a Deputy Party Secretary or Deputy Director in an SOE.[2] At the time, this meant access to larger accommodation and occasional use of a company or Party car. But following the gradual dismantling of SOEs over the 27 years since Document 24 was issued, the income gap between frontline workers and company deputy directors has grown dramatically, effectively separating trade union officials from the everyday financial concerns of their members. Article 19 of the 2008 Method shores up the privileges of primary level union chairpersons in SOEs by confirming they receive the same pay and conditions as a deputy manager and that in the private sector (*gongsi zhi qiye*) they are admitted to the board of directors. My reading of the Method is that it is unclear on the actual pay and conditions stipulated for private sector union chairpersons, but the privileges for their brothers and sisters in SOEs are sufficiently lucid to provide a material basis for opposition to direct elections. For example, one provincial trade union official interviewed by Howell argued that elections can threaten the status and conditions of appointed union officials in SOE enterprises who are paid as union cadres, having undergone the formal process of civil servant recruitment and training (Howell 2008: 859). Thus, a strategy for improved union intervention that at the very least facilitates the election of a growing corps of 'untrained' workers as union officials inevitably implies that union officials at primary level need not be qualified civil servants and therefore need not be awarded the superior income and privileges concomitant with such status and qualifications. Basing his conclusions on a case study analysis of trade union direct elections, Wang concludes that two quite separate types of trade union function and operation have emerged.

> On the one hand there is the new type of trade union in the non-state sector. Basically, they do not have a governmental background, are set up under the initiative of workers themselves and their leaders are elected by workers' representatives to whom they are directly responsible. They do not have an administrative grade and do not enjoy any political privileges [as civil servants do – author]. On the other hand are the traditional administrative state-managed (*guan ban*) trade unions in which [enterprise-level] union leaders are elected in a process that lacks a democratic component. These trade unions do not excel at upholding the rights and interests of workers and are excluded from their [traditional] right to participation in democratic management and democratic supervision [of enterprise leaders].
>
> (Wang Jinhong 2005)

Not surprisingly, Wang concludes that the future of representative trade unionism in China lies in the private sector.

Union cadres and management

A second barrier to effective primary trade unions has been the relationship between enterprise-level union officials and their employers in the private sector and here my research suggests that Wang's conclusions are overstated. Most primary trade union leaders in the private sector are part-time, combining trade union work with a regular (usually managerial) job (or, if full-time, they are usually seconded from their regular job). They are dependent on, and identify with, management and the manner in which they find themselves in the job is not usually a relevant factor. Moreover, since the job of a trade union president is traditionally deemed as managerial, workers think that it is appropriate for a manager to take the position and tend to vote for managers. Interviews with part-time primary-level union cadres in Guangdong demonstrated how their managerial 'day job' was much more important than their union work and that there was no incentive for them to take the side of workers in a dispute with management. Moreover, there was little impetus for them to prioritize union work as their income and future career were entirely dependent on the employer. Similar attitudes encouraged the pilot elections in Yuhang where, prior to elections,

> most trade union chairpersons listened to the senior managers of an enterprise and were unenthusiastic about trade union work. They would not speak out on behalf of the workers and were not generally trusted by the workers and as such they could not adequately uphold the legal rights of workers.
>
> (Case Study Report 2006)

Workers and workers

As we have discussed, Chinese migrant workers often join home-town or place-of-origin organizations, usually operating outside formal state recognition, and indeed these organizations have a long history in China (Hershatter 1986). Some researchers have identified links between the ACFTU's experimenting with elections and its fears of alternative organizations. Howell listed anxiety about them as the second reason why some provincial-level trade union leaders are prepared to tolerate elections, despite ambivalence at the top because '[D]irect elections, too, can, they argue, increase workers' consciousness of being both a trade union member and part of the working class and so dilute the influence of a place-based identity that hinders the development of class consciousness' (Howell 2008: 853).

As we will see from the case studies, local trade union leaders take great care to identify enterprises where conditions are deemed compatible with pilots. And even then permission to proceed is required from officers at the next level up in the union hierarchy, who instigate the process and carry responsibility for its results and consequences. This generally rules out large enterprises and enterprises or areas that have been prone to unrest simply because the consequences of anything going 'wrong' would have a much greater impact. Thus, in Yiwu

168 *Trade union elections*

(see Chapter 5), the activities of influential place-of-origin organizations was one of the factors that persuaded the chair of the YFTU of the urgent need for innovative action, but elections appeared to be ruled out as the risk of either gangsters or militants being elected was too high (interview, YHFTU officer, Hangzhou, April 2006). Likewise in Xinhe, labour militancy, high labour turnover and the presence of skilled workers with experience of organizing for better wages ruled out the possibility of holding direct elections in what was deemed too unstable an environment.

ACFTU, the party and external pressures

The absence of democratically elected enterprise-level trade union representatives has encouraged some CSR initiatives to conduct worker trainings that aim to contribute towards the election of workers to a representative committee. These have provided a framework within which NGOs such as the British Ethical Trading Initiative and the Dutch Fairwear Foundation have tried to improve worker representation often under the noses of the ACFTU. For the most part, these have been isolated instances and there is no evidence that they have had any substantial impact on the overall progress of trade union elections, which are driven by different concerns. Nevertheless, Chan has found that as well as being instrumental in the exploitation of Chinese workers, multinational corporations (MNC) can provide fertile ground for improving the performance of trade unions at enterprise level. Citing experiments with elected trade union committees at two Reebok contract factories, Chan argues that the key problem was Reebok's failure to follow through a 'pioneering' position by fully employing their leverage over two supplier factories and by implication, the local government authorities. Above all, the newly elected committees needed time and nurturing. This should have come via further training from Hong Kong-based LNGOs and support from Reebok. Chan concludes that the pilot programme 'could have worked had Reebok taken a stronger stand vis-à-vis the suppliers and had it continued to provide support to the fledgling union branches' (Chan 2009: 314).

On the other hand, the ACFTU has been quick to reject foreign pressure on its trade unions, whether from capital, LNGOs or CSR-inspired projects. In the field of trade union elections, progress has for the most part been presented as the logical outcome of legal reforms and regulations that the union itself was instrumental in bringing about. While not altogether rejecting the daring plans for democratizing the union that emerged from the 11th Congress in 1988, the ACFTU leadership that emerged following the post-Tiananmen purge in 1989 has been far more at home with framing direct elections in a legally based step-by-step approach inspired by Deng's call to cross the river by feeling for the stepping stones. From this perspective, elections are not about democratization as such, but about making primary trade union organizations more responsive to the grievances of their members. ACFTU Deputy Chairman Su Liqing encapsulated this approach in his aforementioned *Workers' Daily* interview in July 2003, following apparently heated debates on the subject at the five-yearly union congress when he reminded readers that '[T]he relevant trade union documents [provide] clear regulations for the direct election of primary level (*jiceng*) trade union chairpersons' (Wang Jiaoping 2003). As far back as the 1980s, some primary-level trade unions started exploring and practising such direct elections.

The point Su is really making is that the election pilots have a history and should be seen in a Chinese context, and not as a consequence of foreign pressure, as even some local-level trade union cadres had stated in the media. Just a month before Su's interview, the *Hangzhou Daily* ran a report entitled 'Yuhang leads the upsurge in trade union direct elections: Foreigners' emphasis on labour rights leads to a change in Yuhang bosses' attitudes'[3] which stated that trade union elections in Yuhang, the location of one of the case studies presented below, were in part a consequence of foreign pressure. Chairman Mo of the Yuhang Federation of Trade Unions (YHFTU) backed this up in the aforementioned article.

> Mo Bingfo told us that Chinese enterprises were subject to two basic pressures regarding union elections: firstly from foreign companies, especially given new international regulations related to membership of the World Trade Organisation; and secondly from domestic regulations.
>
> (IHLO 2004)

During an interview with a senior YHFTU official who had been instrumental in promoting the elections in Yuhang, I raised the question of foreign influence on the pilots, as suggested by the Hangzhou newspaper report. This elicited a robust answer which explained the elections in Yuhang as a continuing national experiment that had first surfaced in the mid 1980s and as such could not convincingly be attributed to foreign influence. The alacrity of this response and its replication of Su Liqing's line as expressed in *Workers' Daily* in 2003 further demonstrated the sensitive nature of elections and indeed, this nervousness is not entirely without cause. While CSR initiatives in the MNC supply chain follow a different trajectory to the much more numerous ACFTU-sponsored direct elections, there is an indirect relationship between elected worker representatives and corporate social responsibility as evidenced by the inclusion of elected worker committees in many CSR initiatives. However, in the grand scheme of things, these have hardly had a direct impact on the ACFTU's reform path.

Summing up these arguments, we can say that the ACFTU is concerned about its position as a mass organization in the Party-state hierarchy and this concern is heightened by its inability to head off industrial unrest. On a national scale, its solutions to date have been to reverse its membership decline and experiment with measures to contain conflict. Some see elections as a means to improve the quality of cadres – or at least get rid of dead wood – and so more effectively contain conflict.

The evidence presented in the two case studies that follow demonstrates that the goal of local union officials is to use elections as part of a long-term process of 'massization' (*qunzhonghua*) of the union i.e. to foster a more intimate and connected relationship between union cadres and their members. This in turn, it is expected, will lead to increased levels of commitment among primary-level union cadres to uphold the legal rights of their members and consequently improve their record of curtailing the worst of employer abuses.

Piloting direct elections

By the turn of the century, both the Yuhang District of Hangzhou city and Yuyao city (county), which falls under the administration of Ningbo city, had succeeded in establishing a comprehensive union presence in their respective private sectors. However, union dependency on management and a lack of trust between primary-level union officials and their members remained key obstacles to union work (interview, YHFTU official). In 2000, the YHFTU began preparations to run pilot direct elections of trade union chairpersons and committee members in an attempt to improve the standards of union work at enterprise level. The success of these pilot projects facilitated a cautious spread of direct elections first in Yuhang and then across other selected districts in Zhejiang province. This progress was – and is – guided by 'opinion' and 'trial opinion' documents. In 2000, the YHFTU supervised elections in 31 enterprises, 48 in 2001, 175 in 2002 and 332 by mid 2003, representing 40 per cent of trade union chairpersons in the district (Case Study Report 2006). From 2001 to April 2005, 200 trade union chairpersons were directly elected in a pilot organized by the Yuyao (city) Federation of Trade Unions (YYFTU). On 4 December 2003, the Ningbo Federation of Trade Unions (NFTU) issued an 'Opinion' entitled 'Ningbo City Trial Opinion on the Direct Election of Enterprise-level Trade Union Chairpersons' based on Yuyao's experience (Ningbo Opinion).[4] Article 3 of the Ningbo Opinion recommended an expansion of the project to enterprises in Ningbo city in which trade union work was 'relatively established, the workforce relatively stable, the cohesiveness of the enterprise relatively strong, and the democratic consciousness of managers and/or owners relatively robust'. In 2003 in Zhejiang's Tongxiang city, 70 trade union chairpersons and committees were directly elected by the staff of the city's 75 schools (Case Study Report 2006). In December 2003, the trade union chair of a major auto electrical components factory was directly elected in Wenzhou – the first of its kind in the city. Most of the employees were migrant workers from the provinces of Hunan, Hubei, Guizhou, Sichuan and Jiangsu and, according to a provincial trade union journal, over 11 trade union members stood as candidates (*Zhejiang Gongyun* 2004). This gradual expansion of direct elections stems from the pilots described below (interview, YHFTU official).

Yuhang district federation of trade unions

In March 2000, the Organizing Department of the Yuhang District Party Committee and the YHFTU jointly issued the 'Yuhang City Trial Implementation Opinion on the Direct Election of Enterprise-level Trade Union Chairpersons' (Yuhang Opinion hereon).[5] The Yuhang Opinion excluded owners, managers and their relatives from standing in the elections and advocated enterprise-level Party committee leaders and members, where they existed, as ideal candidates. Article 2 of the document stated the standard requirements of adherence to the Party line and acceptance of national laws. It also stipulated that candidates should be active supporters of reform and possess the 'spirit of innovation' (*you kaituo chuangxin jingshen*). Otherwise, the conditions of candidacy were based on the requirements for the post of trade union cadre as stipulated in Article 31 of the ACFTU Constitution at the time (1998).

The initiative for this document did not come from an enterprise-level union but from the YHFTU itself i.e. it was top down. In 1999, the union presented a tentative proposal to the Yuhang Party Committee in which it argued for the piloting of direct elections in targeted enterprises that demonstrated stability and relatively low levels of labour turnover. Having secured Party support, the YHFTU contacted the Yuhang Party Committee Department for Organizing and together they drafted and issued the formal opinion. The Yuhang Opinion lays down eight procedural steps to guide elections. First, the trade union at the pilot enterprise must request permission, in writing, to hold a direct election to the next level up in the union hierarchy, in this case, the YHFTU. Once permission has been granted, the primary union can go ahead and organize a preparatory meeting of trade union representatives, or all union members depending on the number of employees. This meeting elects – or confirms – trade union representatives on the basis of factory site, workshop and administrative or technical areas with worker-representative ratios that broadly reflect the employment structure of the enterprise, for example 25 per cent of representatives being ordinary frontline workers; 20 per cent skilled workers or administrative staff; 20 per cent middle or senior managers and the remaining places taken by women or young workers. The third stage of the process requires vetting (*shencha*) the elected representatives in enterprises deemed too large for workers to vote directly. This is carried out by an unspecified small group of members known as the 'representatives' qualifications examination group' (*daibiao zege shencha xiaozu*), whose task is to check that all the workers' representatives meet the relevant conditions set out in the trade union constitution and the relevant regulations. It was hard to get an idea of what these checks entailed or how they compared to the standards set out in the ACFTU's 'Certain Provisional Regulations of the System for Implementation of a System of Primary Level Trade Union Representatives' Meetings' (1992).[6] In a reference book recently published by the ACFTU's EPO, Li Jianping summarizes Point 121 of this document that stipulates the following qualifications for representatives: union membership; support for the basic line of the Party; and to enjoy a degree of trust by fellow workers and demonstrate a willingness to speak out for them (Li Jianping 2005: 88–9). The actual process of checking appears to involve a 'representatives qualifications examination group' compiling a report confirming or rejecting representatives for the union's chairperson's group (*zhuxi tuan*) and recommends another vote for new representatives where necessary (Li Jianping 2005: 88–9). In Yuhang, the process generally appeared to be aimed at weeding out managers, people with affiliation to home-town associations, people with a criminal record, and people without an understanding of union work as well as the political background checks (interview, YHFTU official, Hangzhou).

The Yuhang Opinion stated that the names of all workers' representatives must then be posted in a public place in the workplace at least three days prior to the direct election. Stage four was to produce a list of candidates to stand for election to the trade union committee. Candidates for trade union committee election could be selected via four channels: as part of a slate presented by the trade union or trade union group for a factory site, workshop or technical/administrative office; a recommendation from the enterprise Party Committee or the next level up of the trade union and/or its standing committee; by putting oneself forward as a candidate; or by other methods of recommendation that are in keeping with the relevant regulations.[7] There must be more candidates than committee places and when there are 'comparatively too many' candidates, the Opinion stipulated that a preliminary election meeting be held at which workers or workers' representatives vote and the least popular candidates are removed from the list. The fifth stage was to hold a secret ballot for the election of the trade union committee and also the union treasury committee (*jingfei shencha weiyuanhui*). This must be a multi-candidate election with the number of candidates for each committee being in accordance with the Provisional Regulations for Primary-Level Trade Union Elections (1992). Once the trade union committee has been elected, each new committee member willing to stand as trade union chair and/or deputy chairperson(s) must deliver a mandatory speech on why he or she is the best person for the job. Speeches are followed by questions from the floor. Votes are then cast and the chair and deputy chair(s) elected on a first-past-the-post basis. All voting is by secret ballot, the votes must be counted on the premises at the time of the meeting and the results announced at the meeting. Acceptance speeches are delivered by the new chairperson and deputy chairperson(s). Finally, the results of the election must be passed on to the next level up of the trade union. The Yuhang Opinion also reminds employers that, in accordance with the CPC Central Committee's Document 12, issued in 1989, trade union chairpersons at enterprise level are entitled to pay, conditions and authority in parity with deputy party secretaries, deputy directors of government departments and middle managers in enterprises.

Yuyao city federation of trade unions

Noting the developments in Yuhang, the YYFTU drafted its own independent pilot opinion at the end of 2001.[8] The document was entitled: 'Trial Opinion on the Step-by-Step Practice of Democratic Direct Elections of Trade Union Chairpersons and Committees in Non-State Sector Enterprise-level Trade Unions Across the Entire City' (Yuyao Opinion hereon).[9] The title of the document and its addition of the word 'democratic' suggested a more open process than the Yuhang Opinion. The Yuyao Opinion was followed up with a 'Reference Opinion' (*cankao yijian*) which stressed that elected trade union chairpersons and committee members should possess the ability to respond to workers' demands and enthusiasm for union work. Entitled 'Reference Opinion on Implementing the Democratic Direct Election of Trade Union Chairpersons and Committee Members at Enterprise Level'[10] (Yuyao Reference Opinion hereon) it stressed that the posts required

> enthusiasm for trade union work, dedication and a sense of responsibility. A strong empathy for the masses and [the courage] to dare to speak out for workers in order to get things done on their behalf as well as uphold their legal rights and interests. [The chairperson and committee members] should also have a relatively democratic working method and understanding of [democratic] concepts. They should be able to accept the collective critical supervision of the workers.
> (Yuyao Reference Opinion cited in Case Study Report 2006)

The Yuyao Opinion stipulated that elections should follow one of three formats. Smaller enterprises with fewer than 100 union members could organize a plenary meeting (*dahui*) of all union members for the purpose of holding a direct vote. These plenary meetings should be organized by a previously established election preparatory group whose members were either appointed by the next level up of the trade union or, in the case of new union branches, the Party committee in the enterprise – if there was one – along with recommendations from the workers themselves. During the meeting, two rounds of voting were to take place. The first to elect the trade union committee in which successful candidates – entirely nominated by the members themselves – were required to obtain at least 50 per cent of the vote. A second round of voting elected the union chairperson following mandatory speeches by the newly elected committee members who stood – if willing – as candidates. The second format was designed for larger enterprises with more than 100 union members where candidates were elected by workers' representatives. The representatives themselves were elected and not subject to the post-election checks that are standard practice nationally and were applied in Yuhang. Their numbers were determined via a simple ratio to the number of employees. For example, by Yuyao's standards large enterprises with approximately 2,000 employees had 200 representatives elected on the basis of 10 workers for every representative. They then voted in a plenary meeting according to the same procedures outlined for smaller enterprises. The third method was used in split-site or multi-site enterprises or those running 24-hour shifts. A 'roaming' ballot box was used to collect votes. At least three appointed election workers (*xuanju gongzuoyuan*) took the box to workshops and offices so that workers could vote. To ensure that these voting procedures were both public and transparent, the YYFTU also announced that elections should be accompanied by five public announcements (*zhangbian gongbu*). These were respectively: a notice informing workers of the formation of a democratic direct election preparatory committee (*minzhu zhixuan choubei xiaozu*) that named its members, the election procedures, the appointment conditions (*renzhi tiaojian*) for the post of trade union chairperson, the names of the election workers (*xuanju renyuan*) and the results of the election itself.

Clearly, the title and language used in the YYFTU documents suggested a greater emphasis on candidates' ability to represent workers' interests rather than ensuring a 'safe' result. For example, candidates should ideally possess the courage to 'dare to speak out' and to 'be able to accept personally the collective critical supervision of the workers' as well as the 'ability to organize and consult' (Case Study Report 2006). This more relaxed approach crystallized into a much looser hold on candidacy, facilitating the sea elections (*hai xuan*) pioneered in rural village elections. Casting aside the pre-vote checks and vetting procedures that candidates had to go through prior to a vote in the Yuhang pilot, the Yuyao Opinion allowed for much more leeway and its practical application centred on 'two direct election models' based on the procedures above. First, union members or representatives anonymously wrote the names of their preferred trade union chair and/or trade union committee members on the ballot paper. Those with the most votes were elected as chair and committee members (according to the number of selections), as long as they received over half the total number of votes cast. Second, union members or representatives wrote the names of their preferred trade union chair and trade union committee members on separate ballot papers in order to determine a candidate list. When necessary, union members or representatives then voted again to decide on a chairperson and committee (Case Study Report 2006). One researcher confirmed that 'these are the people-to-people sea elections. Period!' (*jiu shi minjian suoshou de 'hai xuan!'*) (Interview, researcher, March 2006).

Research in the field also involved observing two democratic direct elections in Yuyao. One was in a small enterprise with 67 union members involving two rounds of voting. The first round elected the trade union committee. Each worker wrote down his or her preferred slate of seven union members. The five people with the most votes formed the new committee and a second round of voting was held to decide which of these five should be chairperson. This process 'produced 47 candidates in the first round! All those who took part in the meeting were very positive, fully participated in the process and felt this was the first genuinely democratic union election they had taken part in' (Case Study Report 2006).

In the second example, there was some procedural confusion in which it appeared that initially voters could not grasp that there really was an open vote i.e. that there was no candidate list. Consequently, the 52 union members mistakenly assumed that the election preparation committee members were the actual candidates and almost all the votes went to these people. Once the results were in and the misunderstanding became obvious, the committee immediately explained that there was no prearranged slate of candidates and workers could vote for whoever they liked. A new round of voting followed and a slate of 16 members emerged, all of whom had been selected by at least 50 per cent of the members. These 16 then stood for the post of trade union chairperson on a first-past-the-post basis (Case Study Report 2006).

These examples demonstrate that in practice voting procedures outlined in the Yuyao Opinion and Reference Opinion were flexible and also that the newness of the project gave rise to the confusion that the YYFTU was eager to avoid.

The YYFTU also provided a template for competitive elections aimed at avoiding such confusion descending into chaos. The document was entitled 'Main Work Points for Democratic Direct (competitive) Elections'[11] (Work Points hereon) and, apart from reiterating the main points from the Yuyao Opinion and Reference Opinion, it also included solutions for potential difficulties. The document concentrated on practicalities, including ensuring transparency and consensus in the formation of the election preparation committee and stating that the committee was only confirmed after all objections to its members had been smoothed out. With regard to voting and the absence of a candidate list (sea elections), Work Points recommended that union members write their preferences for committee members and chairperson either on two separate ballot papers or that one ballot paper may be used with the person getting the most votes automatically deemed chairperson. Members or members' representatives may not recommend the same person more than twice i.e. once for chairperson and once for committee membership. In cases where a second round of voting was required to decide the post of chairperson, Work Points stressed that speeches were required and gave guidelines for the format of speeches: personal background; views and visions of trade union work; and question and answer sessions etc. No personal attacks were permitted in the speeches and if the roaming ballot box method was used, election preparation committee members must arrange an appropriate time and place for as many workers as possible to listen and ask questions. In the event of disputed results and related difficulties, discussion and another round of voting was stipulated.

Elections at S enterprise

Round one: the committee

A newly established enterprise trade union distributed to its members a series of notices that served as a guide to a two-round 'sea election' for the trade union committee and chairperson at S Enterprise, a limited company in Yuyao. The first notice announced to the workers that, on the suggestion of the local township-level trade union – itself galvanized by the YYFTU – the newly established enterprise trade union would hold a democratic direct election for the trade union committee and chairperson. The notice included the names of a four-person preparation committee and requested that any members who were not happy with the make-up of this committee contact the township-level union. Mobile and landline telephone numbers were included in the notice, although the members were given just 24 hours to make their views known. The second notice, released three days later on 10 May 2004, announced the procedure for the election itself. The preparation committee decided that the number of employees merited a three-person union committee and a roaming ballot box to be taken round the various workshops. There would be no formal candidate list and each member was asked to write down his or her preferences for the three members. To be elected, committee members had to garner the votes of at least 50 per cent of the total number of employees. Once three committee members had been elected, a second round of voting to elect the chairperson would take place within two days. The committee itself recommended three names for the committee: Zhu Renmu, Shao Zuda and Wang Yalian.

On 12 May, ballot papers with voting guidelines on the back were distributed for the committee elections. Anyone who wrote down more than three names would immediately invalidate their vote. Members putting themselves forward for the committee were permitted to write their own name down three times. All union members had the right to vote except the enterprise manager/owner and his or her relatives. The third notice listed the results. Of the 29 members' names submitted, Shao Zuda obtained the most votes with 77 nominations. Next was Wang Yalian with 53 nominations, then Chen Fuliang with 44 votes and tied for fourth place were Zhu Renmu and Shao Duohua each with 39 nominations. Shao Zuda was duly declared a committee member but as neither Wang, Chen, Zhu or Shao obtained the minimum 50 per cent (i.e. 68 votes), a second round of voting was held to elect the remaining two committee members. Members were asked to vote for two out of the four runners-up from the first round, or alternatively put forward two new names. Fresh ballot papers with the four names on them plus two blank spaces were provided. Members were asked to write an 'O' next to their first two preferences and an 'X' next to the remaining two. If they were not happy with these candidates, they could use the blank spaces to write the names of up to two new choices adding the required 'O' alongside each new name. The results were announced on 15 May and were as follows: Zhu Renmu obtained 75 votes, Wang Yalian 73, Shao Duohua 69 and Chen Fuliang 53 votes. Zhu, Wang and Shao Zuda agreed to stand as candidates for the position of chairperson in a result that obviously pleased the senior township trade union and was testament to the caution with which enterprises are selected for pilots.

Round two: the chairperson

Apart from announcing the results of the run-off for the committee elections, the union's fifth notice provided more detailed background of the three candidates for trade union chairperson. The information included their respective age, educational level and a detailed employment history. Zhu Renmu was the most highly educated and the only member of the Party among the three candidates. He had worked as an accountant at the company for over a year and was 45 years old. Shao had previously worked at a nearby reed mats factory for 11 years and started work at this company in 2002. He was 37 years old. Wang was the same age as Zhu and had previously worked in the same factory as he had – making latex products for hospitals from 1984 until 2001. Before that she had graduated from middle school in 1975 and then worked the land. She started working at S Enterprise in 2002. The notice also gave details of the voting procedure for the next round. Members were only allowed to vote for one candidate by marking an 'O' against his or her name on the ballot slip but also, to reduce the possibility of vote tampering, adding an 'X' next to the names of the candidates they were not voting for. Shao Zuda won with 93 votes with Zhu and Wang garnering 33 and 11 respectively.

Evaluating direct elections

The provincial Zhejiang Federation of Trade Unions (ZFTU) has been relatively pleased with the results of the elections to date (interview, researcher, 2006). However, the relative lack of mainstream media coverage to what was obviously a successful pilot perhaps echoes similar reticence noted by others (Chan 2009: 293–317; Howell 2008: 857). I believe that up until January 2008, when the first national Method on election candidature was released, this reflected wider uncertainties and ongoing debates about the strategy in general (Li Jianping 2005: 61). It is likely that we will see more press reports on trade union elections in the coming years.

To date, it has not been possible to interview voters in Yuyao and Yuhang on how the elections have impacted on pay and conditions, and this is clearly an important next stage in the research on union reform. However, I have been able to draw on assessments of the views of workers and managers in various Zhejiang towns and townships that help us gauge the opinions of both workers and managers – see section above on methodology for details. I have analysed the results as follows.

Replacing the bosses' relatives: the emergence of official 'activism'

It was clear that despite continuing constraints on local trade unions, in particular the lack of financial independence and union dependency on employers to approve activities, the election of union chairpersons has raised the profile, status and effectiveness of trade unions in both Yuyao and Yuhang. In answer to the question: 'Has a directly elected trade union chairperson proved to be any more effective in meeting your demands, promoting your democratic rights and protecting your interests?' 131 out of 144 respondents replied positively. When asked their views on the legitimacy of the election, 138 said that they had taken the election and their participation in it very seriously (*shenzhen di canyu xuanju*); and when asked about future elections, 129 said that based on their experience of the election they would stand as candidates for a future trade union committee should the opportunity arise. In Yuhang, a senior YHFTU official gave his judgement on the emergence of more proactive primary-level chairpersons:

> A few of those elected were staff or workers who were more intimately connected to the feelings and wishes of the workers in general. Whether they were [frontline] workers or not, elected chairpersons and committee members have tended to be more courageous in speaking out, even disagreeing with the employer. We concluded that this was because they wanted to take part, and not because they had been told or appointed to do it. These guys had more influence (*hao zhaoli*) among the workers.
>
> (Interview, YHFTU official)

The fieldwork reflected these sentiments, especially where the 'sea election' method of candidacy had been applied. We found that these elections successfully

178   *Trade union elections*

jettisoned union chairpersons who were close relatives of the boss and that these people were being replaced by younger union committee members and chairpersons who took the view that 'I was elected by the workers so I must try to work on their behalf' (Case Study Report 2006). These words also mirror press reports of direct elections, although we should bear in mind that negative stories are unlikely to be published. In a brief article reporting '[O]ld Xia's' re-election to a second term as union chairman of a metal factory in Hangzhou, the reporter had asked workers why they voted for 'Old Xia':

> One worker replied enthusiastically that '[O]ld Xia speaks up for workers. Now we've got accident insurance and pensions at our factory'. Another worker named Ms. Zhang said that 'the trade union negotiates on our behalf and because of this the average wage has hit 1,300 yuan. Frontline workers can earn as much as 2,800 yuan'.
>
> (Shao and Luo 2003)

In April 2008 – three months after the Method was released – the ACFTU website carried an English language account of elections from Dalian that announced

> [T]he trade union chairperson of a joint venture company in Dalian Economic Development Zone in Northeast China's Liaoning Province sought a second term, but the trade union council in the development zone refused to confirm him in office. The reason: The majority of workers were dissatisfied with his performance during his tenure. It is reported that since direct elections were introduced [in Dalian] in 2003, thirteen trade union chairpersons have come up for re-election but not a single one of them got elected.
>
> (ACFTU 2008b)

The report does not specify so we must assume that the 13 trade union chairpersons who lost their posts were previously appointed rather than elected! Either way, the 'back story' is clear: some current trade union cadres at primary level are not up to the job of negotiating with the employer. Although media reports on elections emphasize that a 'win–win' scenario exists in which both employers and employees benefit from proactive enterprise unions, the risks are nevertheless never far way. An assessment of the views of 200 workers participating in recent elections in Yuyao found that nearly a quarter of the respondents answered that elected representatives *did* lead to more fraught labour relations. For sure, most workers felt that this was not the case, but a significant minority of workers believed that direct elections would produce more confrontations between union and employer, and, as the positive responses to the democratic elections in Yuyao made clear, were quite happy with this outcome. On the other hand, a separate assessment of employers' attitudes in Yuyao found that most of them were prepared to trade off the risk in the hope that elections would produce a more effective channel for everyday grievances.

Thus we can see how the debates on the advantages and risks of direct elections come to life in practice. On the one hand, this increased potential for militancy arising from elections is precisely why the ACFTU and the Party are proceeding with such caution. On the other hand, for the reformers who wish to use trade union elections as a long-term strategy to improve the quality of trade union officials, the boldness and willingness to speak out was – and is – very important (interview, YHFTU official).

Qualified accountability

Practically all the post-Tiananmen trade union documentation (Opinions, Regulations, Methods, etc.) emphasized that candidates for the election of a trade union committee – who in turn become candidates for chairperson – must be vetted prior to a vote. For example, Articles 10 and 11 of the 1992 Provisional Regulations on Trade Union Elections stipulate that suggested candidates for the committee are named by trade union groups within the enterprise, i.e. according to shop, office or other work area, and a slate is then compiled by the enterprise trade union election committee based on who gets the most selections. However, this slate must be approved by the equivalent-level party committee and submitted to the higher-level trade union for examination and approval (*shencha tongyi*). Thus, aside from the fact that they took place at all, the pilot elections conducted by the YHFTU are significant only insofar as they were a practical manifestation of the existing regulatory regime that places considerable constraints on union members' electoral choices. On the other hand, workers were permitted to self-nominate or nominate others. This option was not provided for in the 1992 regulations but is provided for in Article 8 of the new Method, subject to approval by the outgoing committee, the next level up of the trade union or the election committee members who, in turn, must base their decision on the majority views of the workers. As noted, these procedures were not just about excluding militants, although that was clearly a consideration in Yuhang.

> The reforms have brought significant changes to the Chinese working class. Although we have a well-established union network in our private enterprises [in Yuhang], we have issues with unity due to the variation in the backgrounds of migrant workers. Some people exercise a disproportionate influence over others from their villages which may be enforced by threats of violence. We would like to see more frontline workers elected but it is also a question of finding the balance between development and the consciousness of the workforce. These are complex issues for us. In the short term we need to retain some influence over candidature in order to ensure stability.
>
> (Interview, YHFTU official)

Despite these concerns over home-town associations, it is significant that the new Method clearly states that in the non-state sector, non-local candidates (*waiji zhigong*) may stand as chairperson candidates.

In contrast to the traditional practice of opaque trade union appointments, the Yuhang elections were conducted in public and considerable efforts were made both to publicize and generate enthusiasm for the event beforehand. Public notices were put up in the enterprises by the election preparatory group, broadcasts were made over factory loudspeaker systems, and it was made clear that the election was conducted by a secret ballot. The Yuhang Opinion also insisted that elected committee members who agreed to stand as candidates for the post of chairperson must deliver speeches in person to a workers' election meeting and that the voting that followed these speeches be competitive. For the YHFTU, improving representational accountability was a long-term process that required both 'debate, caution and transparency' (interview, ACFTU researcher, 2006). At the time, the emphasis was on feeling for the proverbial stones in reasonably calm waters.

> We are just starting on a process and are not in a position to recommend 'sea elections' at the current time. So far, our results have been impressive and although we deliberately selected enterprises that were basically stable, we have found that the elections have even reduced strikes, stoppages and incidents in general.
>
> (Interview, YHFTU officer)

Democratic innovation

'The key issue is not the staging of elections, but whom members are permitted to elect, and, even more importantly, whom they are not permitted to elect' (interview, ACFTU researcher). In this light, if Yuhang was a significant step in openness and participation – as opposed to democratic practice – Yuyao was a daring and innovative democratic stride. Although enterprises were carefully selected, the Yuyao pilot was far more experimental in terms of improving representational credibility and pushing the democratic envelope. Moreover, the successes in Yuyao have led to the NFTU drafting a city-wide 'trial opinion' aimed at gradually rolling out the Yuyao pilot model across the city as a whole.[12] The 'Trial Opinion for the Direct Election of Primary Trade Union Chairpersons in Ningbo City' (Ningbo Opinion hereon)[13] appears to have cast caution aside and 'jumped into the sea' as well – even if the drafters donned a life-jacket in insisting that membership of an election preparation committee was approved by the Party and/or the next level up of the trade union based on the wishes of the members or their representatives (Ningbo Opinion, Article 2). On paper and in practice, the direct election pilots coming up the transmission belt from Yuyao and, beginning in 2004, Ningbo, are way ahead of the regulatory guidelines that were sent down the same belt back in 1992. This has turned out to be a 'pilot project that is promoting the process of democratising the trade unions' (Case Study Report, 2006). I will use both the Ningbo Opinion and the Yuyao Opinion to demonstrate how.[14]

First, although Article 2 of the Ningbo Opinion does not go further than existing regulations, it emphasizes that the election of the trade union chairperson and deputy chairperson(s) is to be achieved via direct voting at a union meeting of workers or their representatives and that this method 'is different from the method of electing a trade union chairperson and deputy chairpersons(s) via a full meeting of the trade union committee'. Second, Clause 4 of Article 8 in the Ningbo Opinion stated that procedures for the election of a trade union chairperson can 'also include a no candidate list' (*ye ke bu she houxuanren*) method. In Yuyao, the YYFTU permitted 'sea elections' and as a consequence of their success, the Ningbo Opinion has left room to emulate them. Article 9 of the Ningbo Opinion recommended that in small enterprises where the union does not present a candidate list, there should be two ballot papers, one in which the members write down their preferences for trade union committee members and on the second, their choice for chairperson. In larger enterprises adopting this 'no candidate list' method, all the elected trade union committee members are automatically rendered candidates – if they are willing to stand – for the post of chairperson and a meeting of workers or workers' representatives casts their votes. The Yuyao Opinion stated that voting must be anonymous and the chairperson and committee members elected on a first-past-the-post basis. No matter whether there is a candidate list or members simply list their choices on ballot papers, neither the Yuyao Opinion nor the Ningbo Opinion made any mention of candidate checks or vetting procedures. Article 12 simply states that '[A]ll candidates put forward are [treated on] an equal footing and only have to meet the conditions necessary for such a post (*zhiyao jubei renzhi tiaojian*)'. On the other hand, Article 2 states that the members of the election preparation committee must be agreed upon via negotiation between the enterprise and the next level up of the trade union. If the enterprise has a Party Committee, i.e. it is an SOE or former SOE, this committee and the senior trade union must approve names of those on the election preparation committee and their decision based on the members' or their representatives' meeting and approval. Nevertheless, the space left by the absence of direct candidate vetting has been described by one union researcher as 'an important break with current practice' (interview, ACFTU research officer, 2007).

Conclusion

Both the case studies and supporting secondary evidence demonstrate that direct elections possess considerable potential in bringing about a change in attitudes towards the union and even influencing its direction. While more conservative, the YHFTU nevertheless recognized and argued the need for elections with the Yuhang Party Committee, a policy that put it ahead of other areas of the country. There is no direct evidence, but it is highly likely that the Yuhang Opinion was consulted during the drafting of the nationwide Method (2008). Yuyao shows that if appropriate conditions prevail, there is the space within the current political system to push the boundaries of democratic participation and candidacy and that, as in Yuhang, this can produce a more active and effective layer of trade unionists as well as considerable enthusiasm from organizers, participants and – ominously – even bosses! The case studies also indicate the extent of diversity in the ACFTU even within a single provincial federation. They carry with them an implicit call for follow-up research especially now that there is a new national Method, the effect of which will require measuring.

The research further illustrates that the issue of direct elections is of profound importance to the ACFTU and the Party itself, namely due to the risk of increased labour militancy and foreign interference. Evidence from some of Yuyao's townships revealed a substantial number of people who thought that the more muscular trade union committees and chairpersons that had emerged from the pilots were likely to intensify conflict between labour and capital. Official announcements from the centre, such as Su Liqing's interview in 2003, demonstrated how important 'ownership' of the pilots is for the ACFTU. On the other hand, elections also create an internal dynamic. For example in 2004, the *Hunan Workers' Daily* complained that 'in Hunan only 500 union branches out of a total 80,000 primary-level unions have directly elected officials' and cited, among other provinces, Zhejiang as being ahead of the game (Ceng Ying 2004). Moreover, the material conditions of labour relations in SOEs and large joint ventures under local management possess the capacity to foster opposition to the new layer of unqualified 'young Turks' that Wang claims has already emerged (Wang Jinhong 2005). As we saw earlier in this chapter, Wang's argument, based on evidence from case studies of elections, is that the private sector provides the conditions in which a new type of democratic union representative can develop. Inevitably, this represents an implicit threat to the established cadres and their practices and privileges in the state sector.

Finally, to return to the wider themes of this book: union reform and the challenge of labour unrest. At present, there is not enough evidence to support the argument that elections can make a radical difference to pay and working conditions, or indeed the overall effectiveness of the ACFTU. The chief issues remain dependency on the employers, inactive primary-level unions and an unwillingness of the higher levels to mount a systematic challenge to employers either in support of workers already doing so or on their own initiative. Employers are certainly not going to be a source of inspiration for direct elections, despite Chan's admiration for Reebok's innovations (Chan 2009: 309). Existing appointed union officers are hardly going to welcome elected rivals with open arms, given the privileges they may stand to loose. And while there are senior figures in the ACFTU who argue for more elections and provincial leaders who tolerate them, fear of provoking further unrest is likely to see the current caution remain in place for some time to come.

All this takes us back to the workers themselves. As labour organizing and unrest continues to develop, it is likely that this will increase pressure on the ACFTU to further improve its effectiveness in representing workers' legitimate rights and interests. Given the risks that open elections carry, it is by no means certain that more open direct trade union elections will be a central plank of the ACFTU's national response, as the caution in the 2008 Method suggests. At the same time, this same militancy will encourage more pilots in relatively stable areas to experiment with electoral procedures and the record demonstrates that these will contribute to the overall debate and direction of reform. Although nuanced and often not straightforward, these links are real and help us to understand the complexities of the ACFTU's response to the challenge of labour unrest.

7 Constraining capital in the era of globalization

In this book I have sought to contribute to a deeper understanding of the changing character of trade unionism in China. I have done this by putting forward case studies of innovative reforms undertaken by ACFTU officers at local level in response to increasing worker unrest. The chapters preceding the case studies serve as an historical context that demonstrates both the turbulent history of trade unions and industrial relations in post-liberation China, and how the ACFTU has evolved from a 'left-for-dead' state institution to an organization that is playing a central role in the development of Chinese society. My principal argument has been that, despite the passivity associated with state-sponsored trade unionism, the ACFTU is nevertheless in a process of reform and that the impetus for reform has been workers' own actions. It is clear that class struggle not only exists in what the Chinese government calls the 'socialist market economy', but that the struggles of working people play a crucial role in the ongoing development of Chinese industrial relations. As capitalism recovers from its recent dramatic crisis, the case for further developing a policy of targeted engagement with the ACFTU by the international trade union community based on knowledge is a strong one. In this final chapter, we revisit the main points and conclusions of the preceding chapters and look at the prospects for further trade union development as recovery from the global recession of 2008–9 gathers steam.

In Chapter 1, I described the development of labour relations from 1949 until the present day. By the mid 1950s, the role of the ACFTU was fixed as a conduit for state policy and for workers' reaction to such policy, but the ACFTU's prioritizing of national reconstruction and development narrowed the trade unions' potential to represent workers' interests. By 1957, following the more or less full nationalization of the economy, the ACFTU had been thoroughly anaesthetized. At enterprise level, its role was to administer the not inconsiderable welfare benefits of the *danwei*, organize campaigns to boost production, develop health and safety and occasionally intervene in administrative disputes between individual workers and enterprise managers. The Cultural Revolution shattered this scenario and the unions shut down in the face of Red Guard violence, ideological attacks from the Centre and the emergence of army-dominated Revolutionary Committees to restore order and production in the enterprises. They were resurrected with the onset of economic reforms in 1978 when the ACFTU's rapid return to its former

184 *Constraining capital in era of globalization*

role was assisted by the revamping of the Staff and Workers' Congress and the Party's cautious step-by-step approach to withdrawing from direct intervention in industrial management. As the state pulled back, pressure on the trade unions to improve their performance built up and the question of constraints on trade union effectiveness – chiefly the absence of competition from other union federations and the related issue of autonomy – were the major preoccupations of delegates to the 11th Trade Union Congress in 1988. The traumatic events of 1989, which included the emergence of WAFs in major industrial cities, led to a three-year period of stasis in which reforms were put on hold even as some workers in the state sector gained concessions from a shell-shocked Party and government. Deng Xiaoping's Southern Tour in 1992 served as the starting gun for the next stage in economic reform that was to have major – and apparently irreversible – implications for industrial relations.

The CPC's historic decision in 1997 to restructure, bankrupt or privatize SOEs and China's subsequent membership of the WTO, dramatically upped the stakes for trade union reform chiefly because the return of capitalist labour relations elevated the potential of labour unrest to impede capital accumulation. The mass lay-offs of the late 1990s and early years of the new century, combined with the emergence of labour shortages from 2003, set the stage for increasingly sophisticated workers' militancy that required a more proactive response from the trade unions if stability was to be maintained.

In Chapter 2, I traced the historical impact of labour unrest on policy and practice in China's industrial relations. The chapter demonstrates how the partial integration of interests between manager and managed during the command economy had the effect of politicizing labour militancy into a contest between workers and the Party. The absence of freedom of association facilitated state control over workers' daily lives but only served to intensify conflict when it broke out – as it did on a major scale at least four times during the first 40 years of the PRC. In the face of increasingly dominant private and foreign sectors, the 1997 decision to go ahead with full-scale restructuring at the CPC's 15th Congress removed the last vestiges of permanent employment known as the 'iron rice bowl'. I argued that the state's phased redundancy policy (*xiagang*), supplemented with targeted detention of workers' leaders, ensured that the widespread resistance remained largely atomized and rarely went beyond the boundaries of a single enterprise. In keeping with the nature of unemployment and its removal of up to 30 million trade union members and cadres from the point of production – and therefore power – there was little room for the ACFTU left to manoeuvre in without provoking a decisive and almost certainly disastrous split with the Party itself.

In the non-state sector, scholarly literature and newspaper reports from the early reform years fretted about labour unrest in the SEZs. However, in Chapter 3, I argued that, compared with the present-day levels, protest was scattered, short and mostly spontaneous. The advent of a national labour law in 1995 and widespread reporting of labour violations heralded the gradual development of private and foreign sector protests into the often sophisticated class struggles against employers that are commonplace in China today. In response, the state has pressured the

ACFTU to channel unrest into juridical labour dispute resolution procedures that the union has helped to establish, while simultaneously acting as a constraint on the establishment of effective and representative primary unions for fear of exacerbating the unrest. These well-documented tensions at policy level have set the scene for innovative union pilot projects on the ground, which are the subject of the following chapters.

In Chapter 4, I demonstrated how the union responded when skilled garment workers took advantage of local labour shortages to organize strikes and marshal demonstrations that threatened collective labour flight. In the town of Xinhe, these actions had the potential to devastate the local economy that was heavily dependent on 116 private enterprises employing 12,000 seasonal migrant workers. Anxious to avoid another season of strikes, the town-level trade union, together with the local manufacturers' association and the labour bureau, launched China's first localized sector-level collective consultation that stabilized wages and reduced strikes. A sector-level trade union specifically for woollen garment sector workers was established to ensure the process was sustainable, although workers' representatives were selected by management and not elected by workers. Following a contentious process of consultation, and even bargaining, the project produced a wage table for 59 work processes. While the union mediated this process, rather than directly taking up the cudgel on behalf of the workers, our research demonstrates that it was willing to consult with workers and back their views. Although the results were announced by the higher city-level union as a 'win–win' situation in keeping with legal guidelines, the clear conflict of interests between workers and employers, and between employers in urgent need of skilled workers, was more a testament to the organic, bottom-up nature of the initiative itself. Our research also demonstrates that the trade unions' access to state power can be a resource as well as a constraint. The Xinhe Federation of Trade Unions was able to use its relationship with the Party to keep employers at the table when many threatened to abandon talks over the rates for less-skilled work processes. Here was an innovative response to sophisticated informal mobilization of migrant workers that the authorities wanted to contain within bureaucratic channels. The high level of worker activism prevented the experiment from degenerating into wage regulation by an employers' organization. Despite the lack of formal channels for worker participation, we can see initial stages of freedom of association developing in practice.

In Yiwu, the city-level (county) trade union launched a research project to identify the reasons behind increasing and sometimes violent labour unrest. The results yielded evidence that migrant workers were willing to use formal channels of labour dispute resolution – as opposed to settling scores via home-town associations – but that resources were scarce and costs were prohibitive. The chairman of the Yiwu City Federation of Trade Unions was also faced with budgetary constraints, aggravated by a shortfall in full-time staff able to exert an influence at enterprise level. On paper, federations of primary unions covered a third of the often rural enterprises scattered across Yiwu's complex supply chains, but these were constrained by conflicts of interests – to the extent that the owner of an enterprise was sometimes the trade union chair – or a crippling dependency on the employers. As chairman of the YFTU, Chen Youde's innovative response was to go beyond the traditional parameters of the trade union bureaucracy. Chapter 5 talked us through the lobbying and alliances he forged with other government departments, some of which were initially less than impressed with his goal of 'socializing' trade union work. For Chen and his supporters this meant drawing on resources from society that were not normally associated with the trade union bureaucracy, including non-ACFTU media, lawyer offices, government departments and the courts. Hiring staff outside the traditional pool of civil service-trained graduates enabled the YFTU to keep within budget and at the same time provide legal services to migrant workers willing to pursue their claims via mediation, arbitration or the courts. The establishment of the Yiwu Workers' Legal Rights Centre registered under the Ministry of Civil Affairs as a social group (*shehui tuanti*) broke new ground in that it demonstrated that trade unions could work with external partners. In Yiwu's case, this was chiefly with government departments and legal agencies, but there are already examples of trade unions dipping their toes into civil society itself and the YWLRC will surely be emulated elsewhere with regional variations suited to conditions on the ground. For example, the Qingdao city-level trade union has jointly set up a workers' legal advice centre with an LNGO already experienced in this work. And in the Pearl River Delta, the Shenzhen Federation of Trade Unions has acknowledged the contribution of paralegal networks to stabilizing labour relations and even offered to work with them – albeit with strings attached.

The tension between improved worker representation and the risk of exacerbating labour unrest has played a major part in the stop–start character of the policy of direct elections for trade union chairpersons and committee members rather than the traditional method of appointment of officials. In Chapter 6, I surveyed the literature on this issue and unpacked the politically sensitive arguments with regard to the development of trade union democracy. Despite various pilot projects, progress has been slow. The experiment was not – and generally is not – deemed appropriate in enterprises recently the subject of strikes or other labour actions. Large enterprises were also excluded on the grounds that the repercussions of elections producing militant leaders were potentially too grave. Reformers have presented direct elections as a device to *maintain* stabilized labour relations – as opposed to producing them – by improving the quality of trade union officials. Elected officials are supposed to be more likely to respond to their members on account of their being elected and in turn members would – in theory – be more likely to trust elected representatives. Practice has shown that this has indeed been the case, with the caveat that more responsive enterprise-level union officials are still prone to dependency on their employers and can always be sacked, transferred to more distant posts or bought off. There is also the central question of electoral procedures. As I illustrate in this chapter, the crux lies with the method of candidate selection and this is where the ACFTU is still performing a delicate balancing act. On the one hand, there is no point in going through the hassle of conducting elections if candidacy is not monitored in order to prevent employers from manipulating the event. On the other hand, completely free 'sea elections' popularized in the countryside risk the election of militants who could easily bring about labour unrest. The YYFTU opted for 'sea elections' that were then provided for – though hardly recommended – in guidelines for trade union elections in the important coastal city of Ningbo. Nationally, the ACFTU stepped back from permitting open candidature when it released its first national Method aimed at guiding such elections. On the other hand, management has been excluded from standing, a further recognition that capitalist labour relations are forcing a departure from long-held notions of integrated interests. It is also significant that the strikes by Yantian crane operators in 2007 and Honda car parts factory workers in 2010 (discussed in Chapter 3) included demands for elected trade union officials that were largely met despite the aforementioned regulatory constraint that elections should only be held in enterprises where there is relative industrial harmony. While it is too early to judge if this demand will become more widespread, its importance will not have been missed by any of the parties concerned.

Taken together, the case studies demonstrate four points. First, the ACFTU is not monolithic and the strategy of testing new policies via pilot projects provides fertile ground for innovation in trade union practice. Second, innovation is often specific to the concrete conditions in a given locality and the personalities that operate in it. Third, it is labour unrest that is the most serious challenge facing the ACFTU and providing the impetus for trade union reform, especially in the private sector. Indeed, it is a sad irony that the myth of 'victimhood' that surrounded Chinese migrant workers was, by the turn of the century, more appropriate to the laid-off SOE workers, despite militant traditions and their adoption of class conscious language. Fourth, the general level of worker organization is not at the stage of presenting an organized challenge to ACFTU's monopoly on representation. Indeed militant workers are usually very careful to avoid such a dangerous challenge in favour of calling for the open election of worker representatives. As the case studies show, the ACFTU is capable of responding to militancy at the local level, where the challenge has been most acute, by developing structures and practices that by no means overcome the limitations of state-sponsored trade unionism, but which provide building blocks for the future.

How will these blocks be placed? On the one hand, the caution adopted by the leadership when promoting local innovation to national policy remains very important and is entirely in keeping with Deng Xiaoping's strategy of 'crossing the river while feeling for the stones'. On the other hand, the return of full-blooded capitalist labour relations and the attendant rise in militancy continues to intensify the need for innovation. Apart from the case studies presented, my central argument is supported by evidence from the first three chapters, including more worker-friendly labour laws, the 'normalization' of strikes, the gradual acceptance of LNGOs as players in Chinese industrial relations and the Wal-Mart episode.

These developments are of practical importance to the international trade union movement and its evolving policy towards the ACFTU. The international trade union community has sharply criticized China and the ACFTU for the absence of freedom of association. However, since the Change To Win split from the AFL-CIO and the merger between the World Confederation of Labour and the ICFTU, the newly formed ITUC has moved towards engagement with the Chinese unions. Whether by accident or design, they have begun to connect with the ACFTU just at a time at when embryonic forms of autonomous association are emerging in China and the ACFTU is responding to it in ways that go way beyond its traditional reliance on state intervention. Although the possibilities of international solidarity actions against predatory capitalist behaviour remain a long way off, accusations of job stealing and protectionism motivated by national rather than class interests are heard much less frequently, despite the advent of a global recession when one would expect the clamour arising from such prejudices to increase in volume.

Finally, it appears that the tsunami of job losses caused by the financial crisis has begun to recede. At the outset of the crisis, Chinese worker militancy transformed into a more defensive struggle for fair compensation for early dismissal as factories closed or reduced output and millions of migrant workers headed back to the countryside. However, China posted an 8.9 per cent growth in gross domestic product for the third quarter of 2009 and as order books have filled up some areas are once again reporting labour shortages. This suggests that the material conditions for intensified labour militancy and concomitant trade union reform are again in place. Of course, the state may instead adopt a retrogressive policy of repression over concession. However, it is more likely to continue to build institutions that can resolve labour unrest peacefully.

Taking the more optimistic scenario as our starting point, we can see that space is gradually opening up for further practical research in three areas. First, our knowledge of the process via which the ACFTU upgrades local pilot projects into national policy remains inadequate. Second, the constraints on effective collective bargaining are gradually loosening as strikes are normalized and the space for more varied agency – such as specialist negotiators – has widened. Unlike a decade ago, we can now envisage collective agreements in Chinese joint ventures that exceed legal minimum standards and even fall into line with regional framework agreements negotiated between TNCs and regional GUFs. Third, the ability to provide relatively cheap labour remains a core reason for China's ability to attract foreign investment. To maintain its supply, restrictions on *hukou* are likely to continue to relax, and the slow convergence in the interests of private and state sector workers that Sargeson (1999) imagined in Hangzhou nearly two decades ago will inch closer to reality. All these fields of research are of direct practical importance to the wider challenge of building an effective internationalized constraint on capitalist globalization on the foundation of an organized working class.

Notes

Introduction

1 With the qualified exception of the Great Leap Forward, the stated aim of which was to increase production dramatically.
2 Two experienced labour researchers from Africa recently informed me that this myth is currently widespread among African workers, some of whom are faced with migrant workers from China on short-term contracts and long working hours.
3 The results of this project were published by Palgrave in 2010.

1 Industrial relations in the People's Republic of China

1 Workers sarcastically dubbed the security of tenure enjoyed by CPC cadres working in industry as the 'golden rice bowl'.
2 The other two being the integration of government and enterprise budgets and profitability of the state sector as a whole; and the work unit as a locus of political organization and social control (Hussain 2000: 58).
3 Real estate was owned by the enterprise, although 90 per cent of investment in public housing came from the state (Lü and Perry 1997: 10).
4 This was the title of a big character poster written by Mao himself.
5 In 1978, the government formally allowed urban youths to return to the cities, facilitating the homecoming of 20 million youths (Hu Teh-Wei and Elizabeth Li Hon-Ming 1993: 156).
6 The term was a somewhat ironic use of an expression that had previously applied to the tripartite Revolutionary Committees of the later Cultural Revolution period!
7 Naughton footnotes one anecdote from 1984 in which a group of disgruntled workers turned up outside their manager's home every evening to discuss various workplace grievances. The workers succeeded in inducing the manager to agree to their demands by 'at first delaying, and ultimately sharing in, the family dinner' (Naughton 1995: 343).
8 Although SWCs have had little impact in the private sector, this remains the case in the state sector. In August 2008, the authorities in Henan conceded to protesting workers calling for a halt in the privatization of the Linzhou Iron and Steel Company Limited. Practically on the eve of a hotly contested buyout by the Fengbao Iron and Steel Company Limited, officials announced after five days of protest that '[I]ssues regarding the future of Linzhou Iron and Steel and benefits for its workers should be decided by its workers' congress' (*Shanghai Daily* 2009).
9 *Zhonghua renmin gongheguo xiangcun jiti suoyouzhi qiye tiaoli 1990.*
10 China rejoined the ILO in 1971, replacing Taiwan, and set up a tripartite delegation in 1983 (Ng and Warner 1998: 74) in which CEDA was nominated as the employers' representative.

11 There are many fancy restaurants in Datong. Occasionally I was invited to eat in some of them, which were often full of newly enriched mine bosses controlling newly sub-contracted or privatized mine shafts who spent tens of thousands of yuan on exotic dishes and alcohol. To be fair, there is not much else to do in Datong.
12 I met a number of laid-off workers who had taken up dog breeding. The breeds were invariably large and fierce. During a visit to the dog market one breeder explained to me that some of the buyers were mine bosses who bought them to use as guard dogs; or restaurant owners who kept them at the back ready to release into the dining room 'if there was a fight'. While he was probably exaggerating out of bravado and humour, Datong is nevertheless a tough mining city in which such a scenario was not altogether unlikely. I was also told that illegal dog fights were organized and well attended by laid-off workers who enjoyed a flutter.
13 The interviewee said that being sacked from his job would have excluded him from unemployment benefit anyway. Moreover, as demonstrated by the next quotation, there was a reticence and confusion over what one was entitled to.
14 As we will see in the next chapter, the dramatic protests in Daqing were in fact induced not by *xiagang* but by one-off redundancy deals that the workers rejected when they realized the full consequences of their decision to sign redundancy deals.
15 Of course, senior union officials no doubt lobbied for such measures in private and occasionally sanctioned articles in the official workers' press pointing out the absence of real wage increases in Shenzhen for over a decade. However, this is not the same as a proactive campaign.

2 Labour unrest in the state sector: the rise and demise of decent work with Chinese – and some Russian – characteristics

1 Nevertheless, that stereotype has persisted in some circles and was employed by the AFL-CIO when it joined forces with US manufacturers to lobby the US government to investigate labour abuses in China under Section 301 of the Trade Act (1974). The goal was to persuade President Bush to, as AFL-CIO president Sweeney put it, 'make a choice' and apply trade sanctions to China. The accompanying and quickly shelved report pandered unashamedly to the historical stereotype of Chinese workers undercutting wages and conditions in the US.
2 Harris refers to these regulations as the Model Outline of Intra-Enterprise Discipline Rules (Harris 1978: 91).
3 '*Zai gedi siying qiye zhong sheli lao-zi xieshang huiyi de* zhishi' (Guidelines for the establishment of labour-capital consultative conferences in private enterprises in all areas) cited in Xu Xiaohong, 2003: 19–20.
4 On this occasion being 'air-planed' involves having one's arms outstretched sideways, legs tied together and being carried aloft through the air like an aeroplane. After 15 minutes, the pain in the arms becomes excruciating.
5 Composite nationwide strike statistics are treated as *jimi* or classified information by the government.
6 As noted below, Daqing too remains a wealthy city but this did not prevent large numbers of workers protesting their redundancy deals.
7 For example, the April 2002 meeting of the ICFTU's China Working Party was devoted in its entirety to the unrest, especially in Daqing.
8 The Liaoyang authorities admitted the bankruptcy process had been corrupt and the Director of the Liaoyang Ferroalloy Factory, Fan Yicheng, was eventually arrested (HRW 2002).
9 Of course, at the level of actual implementation, there were mistakes, exceptions and degrees within this overarching policy of caution.
10 This is not to say there weren't any. A media blackout made it extremely difficult to obtain and verify information on arrests.

Notes 191

11 The workers I spoke with in Daqing described themselves as laid off, although legally speaking they had signed away their relationship with PetroChina.
12 '*Zhonghua zong gonghui guanyu jianli kunnan zhigong bangfu zhongxin de* yijian'.

3 From victims to subjects: the long march of migrant labour

1 These figures do not include employees in institutions and government administrative organs (*shiye danwei*).
2 I have placed this word in inverted commas as factory conditions dictate that even outbursts of collective violence require minimum planning of some sort. For mysterious reasons, the term remains widely used.
3 When I first began working on Chinese labour relations in 1996, typing the Chinese word for 'strike' in a search engine invariably produced no results. Using the less contentious terms of 'labour-capital dispute' (*laozi jiufen*) or 'labour dispute' (*laodong jiufen*) returned a few newspaper articles but nothing that might be called a trend. I have just typed '*bagong*' (strike) into Google and it came back with over four million references! Although hardly a scientific methodology, it is a measure of how times have changed.
4 Observation from the Asia Pacific Research Network, *China and the WTO* conference, 4–6 November 2002, Guangzhou.
5 Depending on the Party faction in the ascendancy, the sale of produce from private plots was another method of income generation, although the latitude given to such entrepreneurial activity varied considerably in the pre-reform decades.
6 Civil agency in China recognizes the lack of qualified lawyers and legal aid in China and therefore provides for non-qualified persons to represent 'clients' in court. Wary of the impact that civil agency was having on investment, the Dongguan government effectively banned the practice in labour dispute cases involving more than three people in September 2009 (*Dongguan* [news] *Net* 2009).
7 The station was built in 1979 to separate the inner SEZ from the outskirts.
8 *Guangdong sheng qiye minzhu guanli tiaoli*.

4 Experimental pragmatism I: collective consultation in Xinhe town

1 Karl Marx paraphrasing Dante in the preface to the first German edition of *Capital, Volume One*.
2 Dramatic policy shifts can also be reactive, the most famous being the Party's endorsement of the practices of peasant farmers in Anhui province who began selling their surplus produce at private market stalls in the mid 1970s. The consequent increase in production and productivity precipitated the sea change in agricultural policy represented by the household responsibility system introduced in 1978. A local government's pressing ahead with market practices and policies form part of the background to my second case study in union 'experimental pragmatism' discussed in the next chapter.
3 This information is derived from personal communication with a senior labour academic in Beijing. I use it solely to illustrate my point.
4 In 2000, Wei Jianxing led the CPC's Central Committee for Discipline and Inspection and was number four in the Politburo Standing Committee's hierarchy, the most powerful political body in the land.
5 The Labour Contract Law (2008) has six articles on collective contracts (51–56). This law was not in force at the time of the experiment in Xinhe.
6 Such 'Regulations' have an incomplete legal status and are meant as a reference for a court or arbitration committee dealing with a collective contract dispute. However, if a provincial people's congress – local parliament – has passed local regulations concerning collective contacts, these are legally enforceable.

192 *Notes*

7 Industrial-level collective contracts are notorious for simply regurgitating the law and are a reflection of the weakness of industrial unions and their formalistic practices.
8 It is interesting to note that, despite the importance of the US market, corporate social responsibility does not appear to have played a role in the events in Xinhe.
9 A trade union small group is a trade union preparatory committee established to pave the way for a formal primary level union.
10 *Xinhezhen Changyu yangmaoshan hangye zhigong gongzi* (*gongjia*) *xieshang xieyishu*.
11 The full name of the document was – and is – Zhejiang province, Wenling city, Xinhe town, Changyu woollen sweater sector-level collective contract (*Zhejiang sheng Wenling shi Xinhe zhen Changyu yangmao chen hangye jiti hetong*).

5 Experimental pragmatism II: trade union rights centre in Yiwu

1 In English, the term used would more likely be 'bureaucratic' – '*guanliao*' in Chinese. However, the word 'guanliao' has serious political implications in Chinese, not least as a result of it being a term of accusation employed by Red Guards against union cadres during the Cultural Revolution.
2 Brødsgaard ingeniously translates 'bianzhi' as the 'establishment of posts' albeit 'loosely' (Brødsgaard 2002: 361). For the sake of clarity in the context of this chapter alone, I would add 'at the expense of a government or government institution's formal budget'.
3 For security reasons, the name I have given this organization is not its real name.
4 Again, the name is fictitious but the management strategy isn't. The danger of its more direct approach is shown by the fact that this group has attracted the attention of bosses' thugs who have carried out extremely violent attacks on their staff.
5 This figure was taken from YFTU records that attempted to cover *all* reported disputes no matter how minor. Luo and Zhou reported 1,210 'labour contradictions' among which 17 cases involved one or more violent deaths (Luo Xiaojun and Zhou Songqiang 2006: 26).
6 The department was initially referred to anonymously as a 'relevant department' but I was told during an interview with a contact in Hangzhou in 2006 that this was the Department of Justice (*sifaju*).
7 *guanyu jianli gonghui xitong zhigong falü weiquan xin jizhi*.
8 This department has a mandate to monitor and enforce resolutions from the People's Congress. The implication here is that the Resolutions Department was challenging a motion that was accepted by the JCPC.
9 The full name of this committee is *renda changweihui daibiao xuanju lianluo ren shiren mian gongzuo weiyuanhui*. Its basic job is to act as the secretariat of the standing committee of the local People's Congress. It supports and monitors the work of congress members and is responsible for elections-related business.
10 In fact, they are in the same building.
11 One government-sponsored survey across China found that 51 per cent of Chinese people were not comfortable speaking formal *putonghua*. See 'Greater Numbers Speak Mandarin', *China Daily* 26 December 2004.
12 *Yiwushi falü yuanzhu zhongxin zhigong gongzuobu*.
13 The International Symposium on the Legislation of The Labour Dispute Resolution Law, Renmin University, 19–20 January 2007.
14 I worked as a part-time counter sales staffer in the Kunming branch of the Baihuodalou for six months in 1994 while studying at Yunnan University. Wages for temporary workers were low at eight yuan for an eight-hour day. However, conditions for permanent workers (*zhigong*) were comprehensively good and even included subsidized haircuts. I returned to the store to visit colleagues and friends in 1999 and found it had been divided up into franchised outlets. Some of my former colleagues were still there – though

many had left or been laid off – and told me that contracts were now limited to one year and while wages had gone up, all subsidies had been cut and the previously excellent canteen shut down.

15 It should be noted that Gallagher's figures refer to mediation *in the enterprise* whereas the figures from Yiwu refer to mediation conducted at the Centre and/or at enterprise level. However, they are valid here as Gallagher's point is to stress the decline in mediation due to weak representation, whereas the YWLRC goal is to keep mediation alive by improving the overall environment in which mediation takes place, including representation.

16 Chen Youde could not say from which countries the experience was drawn.

6 Trade union elections: from dependency to democracy?

1 '*Gonghui gaige de jiben shexiang*'.
2 This document was strengthened when the Central Committee of the CPC issued Document 12 reasserting these conditions.
3 '*Gonghui zhixuan Yuhang quanguo lingchao: laowai zhuzhong laogong baohu Yuhang laoban guannian zhuanbian*'.
4 '*Ningboshi jiceng gonghui zhijie xuanju gonghui zhuxi shixing yijian*'.
5 '*Yuhang shi qiye jiceng gonghui zhuxi zhixuan shidian shishi yijian*'.
6 '*Guanyu jiceng gonghui huiyuan daibiao dahui daibiao shixing changrenzhi de ruogan zhanxing guiding*'.
7 Among other matters, this is a reference to the recent practice of appointing trade union chairpersons from outside the traditional trade union/civil service system – see Chapter 5.
8 This appears to have been written independently i.e. not in conjunction with the local Party Committee. However, I have been unable to confirm this, or its significance.
9 '*Guanyu zai quanshi fei gongyouzhi qiye gonghui zhong zhubu tuixing gonghui zhuxi, weiyuan minzhu zhixuan zhidu de shexing yijian*'.
10 '*Qiye gonghui tuixing minzhu zhixuan gonghui zhuxi, weiyuan zhidu de cankao yijian*'.
11 '*Minzhu zhixuan (jingxuan) gongzuo yaodian*'.
12 Yuyao is a county-level city under the administration of Ningbo city, a major port.
13 '*Ningbo shi jiceng gonghui zhijie xuanju gonghui zhuxi shixing yijian*'.
14 On the matter of candidate vetting, the Yuyao and Ningbo documents do not reflect the Method released in 2008. Article 9 of the latter states that the enterprise Party organization and the next level up of the trade union must carry out a check (*kaocha*) on the candidates and remove those who 'do not meet the conditions for holding a post'.

Bibliography

ACFTU (1990) *ACFTU Eleventh Congress Documents*, Beijing: Economic Management Publishing House.
—— (2001) 'Trade Union Law'. Online. Available HTTP: <http://www.acftu.org.cn/template/10002/file.jsp?cid=56&aid=30> (accessed 5 January 2008).
—— (2005) *Chinese Trade Unions Safeguarding of the Legitimate Rights and Interests of Workers and Staff Members 2004*, Bluebook edn, Beijing: Statistics Publishing House.
—— (2006) *Chinese Trade Unions Statistics Yearbook 2005*, Beijing: China Statistics Publishing House.
—— (2007a) *Chinese Trade Unions Statistics Yearbook 2006*, Beijing: China Statistics Publishing House.
—— (2007b) 'Work statistics of the Chinese Trade Unions in 2006'. Online. Available HTTP: <http://english.acftu.org/template/10002/file.jsp?cid=68&aid=239> (accessed 23 August 2008).
—— (2007c) 'Quan zong: jianjue zhizhi yongren danwei weifa zaiyuan "quan ci" zhigong' (ACFTU: firmly prohibit employers from 'persuading' workers to resign), *ACFTU Trade Union News online*. Online: Available HTTP: <http://acftu.people.com.cn/GB/ 6601452.html> (accessed 22 August 2009).
—— (2007d) 'Chinese trade unions strive to safeguard the labour safety and health rights and interests of the workers'. Online. Available HTTP: <http://www.acftu.org.cn/template/10002/file.jsp?cid=51&aid=241> (accessed 20 August 2009).
—— (2008a) 'Constitution of the Chinese Trade Unions'. Online. Available HTTP: <http://www.acftu.org.cn/template/10002/file.jsp?cid=48&aid=469> (accessed 20 August 2009).
—— (2008b) 'Direct elections for union leaders'. Online. Available HTTP: <http://www.acftu.org.cn/template/10002/file.jsp?cid=57&aid=405> (accessed 10 April 2008).
ALII (Asian Legal Information Institute) (2010), Law on the prevention and control of occupational diseases (2001). Online. Available HTTP: <http://www.asianlii.org/cn/legis/cen/laws/pacoodl477/> (accessed 1 November 2010).
Ashwin, S. and Clarke, S. (2003) *Russian Trade Unions and Industrial Relations in Transition*, Basingstoke: Palgrave Macmillan.
Bai Xumin (2007) 'Nuli tuidong gonghui lilun chuangxin he gongzuo chuangxin Zhongguo gonghui xinwen' (Work hard to encourage trade unions to make practical and theoretical innovations), *Trade Union News Online*. Online. Available HTTP: <http://acftu.people.com.cn /GB/67584/4774329.html> (accessed: 6 November 2007).
Barboza, D. (2006) 'Shortage of cheap labor in China', *New York Times*, 2 April 2006.
Becker, J. (1996) *Hungry Ghosts: China's Secret Famine*, London: John Murray.

Beijing Federation of Trade Unions (2005) 'Zhonghua zong gonghui guanyu jianli kunnan zhigong bangfu zhongxin de yijian' (ACFTU opinion on the establishment of Workers Support Centres). Online. Available HTTP: <http://www.bjzgh.gov.cn/template/10002/file.jsp?cid=134&aid=757> (accessed 21 August 2009).

Black, G. and Munro, R. (1993) *Black Hands of Beijing*, New York: John Wiley & Sons.

Blecher, M. (2002) 'Hegemony and workers' politics in China', *China Quarterly*, 170: 283–330.

—— (2003) *'China Against the Tides: Restructuring Through Revolution, Radicalism and Reform*, London: Continuum.

Bo Yibo (1991) *Ruogan zhong da juece yu shijian di huigu* (A review of major policy decisions and practice), Beijing: Central Party School Publishing House.

Branigan, T. (2009) 'Downturn in China leaves 26 million out of work', *Guardian*, 2 February 2009. Online. Available HTTP: <http://www.guardian.co.uk/business/2009/feb/02/china-unemployment-unrest> (accessed 14 October 2009).

Brødsgaard, K. E. (2002) 'Institutional reform and the bianzhi system in China', *China Quarterly*, 170: 361–86.

Brown, E. (2006) 'Chinese labour law reform: guaranteeing workers' rights in the age of globalism', *Asia Pacific Journal Japan Focus*. Online. Available HTTP: <http://www.japanfocus.org/-Earl-Brown/2280> (accessed 21 August 2009).

Brown, R. (2006) 'China's collective contract provisions: can collective negotiations embody collective bargaining?' *Duke Journal of Comparative and International Law*, 16 (1): 35–77. Online. Available HTTP: <http://www.law.duke.edu/shell/cite.pl?16+Duke+J.+Comp.+&+Int'l+L.+35> (accessed 3 June 2009).

Buhmann, K. (2005) 'Corporate social responsibility in China: current issues and their relevance for implementation of law', *Copenhagen Journal of Asian Studies*, 22: 62–91.

Burawoy, M., Krotov, P., Fairbrother, P. and Clarke, S. (1993) *What About the Workers?*, London: Verso.

Cai Fang (2007) 'How to deal with future obstacles in the labor market', *China Daily*, 9 March 2007. Online. Available HTTP: <http://en.chinaelections.org/newsinfo.asp?newsid=3942> (accessed 1 September 2009).

Cai Yongshun (2002) 'The resistance of Chinese laid-off workers in the reform period', *China Quarterly*, 170: 327–44.

Caijing (2009) 'Shang bannian Zhongguo laodong zhengyi anjian jingpen taishi' (Labour disputes explode in the first half of this year), *Caijing*, 13 July 2009. Online. Available HTTP: <http://www.caijing.com.cn/2009-07-13/110196787.html> (accessed 2 September 2009).

Case Study Report (2006) 'Post socialist trade unions, low pay and decent work: Russia, China and Vietnam'. Online. Available HTTP: <http://www.warwick.ac.uk/fac/soc/complabstuds/russia/ngpa/cases.htm> (accessed 3 January 2009).

Ceng Ying (2004) 'Gonghui zhixuan renzhong er daoyuan' (The long and difficult road to trade union direct elections), *Hunan Workers' Daily*, 2 February 2004. Online. Available HTTP: <http://mt.rednet.cn/Articles/04/02/11/419279.HTM> (accessed: 6 August 2008).

Chan, A. (1998) *China's Workers Under Assault: The Exploitation of Labor in a Global Economy*, London: M.E. Sharpe.

—— (2000) 'Chinese Trade Unions and Workplace Relations in the State-owned and Joint-venture Enterprises', in Warner, M. (ed.), *Changing Workplace Relations in the Chinese Economy*, London: Macmillan, pp. 34–56.

—— (2001) *China's Workers Under Assault: Exploitation and Abuse in a Globalizing Economy*, Armonk: M.E. Sharpe.

196   Bibliography

—— (2009) 'Challenges and possibilities for democratic grassroots union elections in China: a case study of two factory-level elections and their aftermath', *Labor Studies Journal*, 34 (3): 293–317.
Chan, A., Rosen, S. and Unger, J. (eds.) (1985) *On Socialist Democracy and the Legal System: The Li Yizhe Debates*, Armonk: M.E. Sharpe.
Chan, C. (2008) 'Emerging patterns of labour unrest in South China', paper presented at Alternative Futures and Popular Protests Conference, Manchester, 17–19 March 2008.
—— (2009) 'Strikes and workplace relations in a Chinese global factory', *Industrial Relations Journal*, 40 (1): 60–77.
Chan Kam-wing and Zhang Li (1999) 'The *hukou* system and rural urban migration in China: processes and changes', *China Quarterly*, 160: 818–55.
Chang Dae-oup and Wong, M. (2005) 'FDI in China: the actors and the possibility of a new working class activism', in Chang Dae-oup and Shepherd, E. (eds.) *Asian Transnational Corporation Outlook 2004: Asian TNCs, Workers, and the Movement of Capital*, Hong Kong: Asia Monitor Resource Centre, pp. 105–06.
Chang Kai (2004) *Laodong lun* (*Workers' Rights Theory*), Beijing: Ministry of Labour and Social Security Press.
—— (2005) *Laodong guanxi xue* (*Labour Relations Science*), Beijing: China Labour and Social Security Publishing House.
—— (2007) 'Guanyu laodong zhengyi chuli lifa de zongti gouxiang' (General conceptions [underlying] labour dispute law), paper presented at International Conference on Labour Dispute Resolution Law, Beijing People's University, 19 January 2007.
Che Jiahua and Qian Yingyi (1998) 'Institutional environment, community government, and corporate governance: understanding China's township-village enterprises', *Journal of Law, Economics, and Organisation*, 14 (1): 1–23.
Chen Feng (2003a) 'Industrial restructuring and workers' resistance in China', *Modern China*, 29: 237–62.
—— (2003b) 'Between state and labour: the conflict of Chinese trade unions: double identity in market reform', *China Quarterly*, 176: 1006–28.
—— (2006) 'Privatization and its discontents in Chinese factories', *China Quarterly*, 185, 42–60.
Chen Ji (2007) 'Yiwu moshi' (The Yiwu model), paper presented at International Symposium on the Legislation of The Labour Dispute Resolution Law, Beijing, Institute of Labour Relations of Renmin University of China, 19–20 January 2007.
Cheseaux, J. (1969) *The Chinese Labor Movement*, Stanford: Stanford University Press.
China Daily (2006) 'Wal-Mart to allow workers to join unions in China', *China Daily*, 11 August 2006.
—— (2007), 'China to enact law on labor disputes arbitration', 27 August 2007. Online. Available HTTP: http://www.chinadaily.com.cn/china/2007-08/27/content_6058495.htm> (accessed 29 October 2009).
China Labour Bulletin (1998) *Reform, Corruption and Democracy: Dialogue Between Han Dongfang and Chinese Workers*, Hong Kong: China Labour Bulletin.
—— (2001) *Gaige yu geming: Han Dongfang yu Zhongguo gongren duihua Reform or Revolution: Discussions Between Mainland Workers and Han Dongfang*, Hong Kong: China Labour Bulletin.
—— (2002) 'Hebei Shengli oilfield workers sue employer over retrenchment'. Online. Available HTTP: <http://iso.china-labour.org.hk/iso/article.adp?article_id_1888> (accessed 12 December 2005).

—— (2005) 'Xianyang textile workers detained for leading historic seven-week strike are released without charge'. Online. Available HTTP: <http://www.clb.org.hk/en/node/8503> (accessed 28 August 2009).
—— (2007) 'Breaking the impasse'. Online. Available HTTP: http://www.china-labour.org.hk/en/files/share/File/general/collective_contract_report.pdf> (accessed 3 August 2008).
—— (2007) 'Disputes over new Labour Contract Law, foreign business groups threaten to withdraw investments'. Online. Available HTTP: <http://iso.china-labour.org.hk/en/node/38245> (accessed 5 September 2009).
—— (2010) 'Swimming against the tide: How the government has tried to control labour conflicts in China'. Online. Available HTTP: http://www.clb.org.hk/en/node/100897 (accessed 14 October 2010).
China Labour News Translation (2008) 'The "migrant worker commander": Zhang Quanshou and Quanshou Labour Dispatch Company'. Online. Available HTTP: <http://www.clntranslations.org/article/40/the-migrant-worker-commander-zhang-quanshou-and-the-quanshun-labor-dispatch-company> (accessed 13 October 2009).
China Labour Statistical Yearbook (2007) Beijing: China Statistics Press.
China Net (2008) 'Yiwu market sees first drop in export to US'. Online. Available HTTP: <http://www.china.org.cn/business/news/2008-04/19/content_14980904.htm> (accessed 10 May 2008).
China Review (2009) 'China's rural migrant workers top 225 million'. Online. Available HTTP: <http://news.xinhuanet.com/english/2009-03/25/content_11072242.htm> (accessed 1 September 2009).
China Statistical Yearbook (1995) Beijing: China Statistics Press.
Chinese Academy of Sciences (2009) *Quan min suo you zhi gongye qiye zhigong daibiao dahui tiaoli* (Regulations on Staff and Workers Congresses in Industrial Enterprises Owned by the Whole People). Online. Available HTTP: <http://www.ihep.cas.cn/dj/ghgz/mzgl/200908/t20090817_2404351.html> (accessed 30 October 2009).
Chinese Education, Scientific, Cultural, Health and Sports Workers' Union (2008) 'Weihu nongmingong quanyi gui zai xingdong' (Upholding the rights of migrant workers requires more initiative). Online. Available HTTP: <http://jkwwt.acftu.org/template/10001/file.jsp?cid=90&aid=1081> (accessed 12 June 2008).
Chow, Daniel C. K. (2006) 'Counterfeiting and China's economic development'. Online. Available HTTP: <www.uscc.gov/hearings/2006hearings/written_testimonies/06_06_08wrts/ 06_06_7_8_chow_daniel.pdf> (accessed 12 May 2008).
Cieri, H., Zhu Jiuhua Cherrie and Dowling, P. (1998) 'The reform of compensation in China's industrial enterprises', Center for Advanced Human Resource Studies, Working Paper 98–05.
Clarke, S. (2006) 'The Development of Industrial Relations in Russia', Report for ILO Task Force. Online. Available HTTP: <http://www.warwick.ac.uk/fac/soc/complabstuds/russia/documents/ilorep.doc.> (accessed 6 July 2007).
Clarke, S., Chang-hee Lee and Li Qi (2004) 'Collective consultation and industrial relations in China', *British Journal of Industrial Relations*, 42 (2): 235–54.
Clarke, S. and Pringle, T. (2009) 'Can Party-led trade unions represent their members?', *Post Communist Economies*, 21 (1): 85–101.
Constitution (1982) 'Constitution of the People's Republic of China'. Online. Available HTTP: <http://english.people.com.cn/constitution/constitution.html> (accessed 20 November 2007).
Cooney, S. (2007) 'China's labour law, compliance and flaws in implementing institutions', *Journal of Industrial Relations*, 49 (5): 673–86.
CPPCC (1949) *Important Documents of the First Plenary Session of the Chinese People's Political Consultative Conference*, Beijing: Foreign Languages Press.

—— (2001) 'Xiagang diaocha baogao – xin yingxi renmin neibu maodun yanjiu 2000–2001' (China Survey Report – A Study on Internal Conflicts of the People under the New Circumstance 2000–2001), Beijing: Central Compilation Press.
CPCCC and MOLSS (2002) 'Jin yi bu zuohao xiagang shiye renyuan zai jiuye gongzuo xuanchuan tigang' (Improve publicity and information in re-employment work for unemployed and laid-off workers). Online. Available HTTP: <http://www.12351.org.cn/template/ 10002/file.jsp?cid=36&aid=105> (accessed 6 October 2009).
Dali L. Yang (2005) 'China's looming labour shortage', *Far Eastern Economic Review*, 168 (2).
Davin, D. (1999) *Internal Migration in Contemporary China*, Basingstoke: Macmillan Press.
Deng, K. (2002) 'China's actual unemployment rate has reached a critical point', *Southern Weekend*, 13 June 2002.
Deng Xiaoping (1985) 'There is no fundamental contradiction between socialism and a market economy'. Online. Available HTTP: <english.people.com.cn/dengxp/vol3/text/c1480.html> (accessed 29 May 2008).
Ding Ke (2006) 'Distribution system of China's industrial clusters: case study of Yiwu China Commodity City', *Institute of Developing Economies*, Discussion Paper 75, 4–5.
Dongguan Net (2009) 'San ren yishang laodong zhengyi an bie zhao "gongmin daily" ren' (Don't use civil representatives for labour disputes involving more than three or more people). Online. Available HTTP: <http://www.dg.gd.cn/dgnews/view.asp?ID= 132901757 DBCE1YKJQPGXBN2> (accessed 13 October 2009).
Dore, R. P. (1987) *Taking Japanese Seriously: A Confucian Perspective on Leading Economic Issues*, London: Athlone Press.
—— (1973) *British Factory–Japanese Factory*, Berkeley and Los Angeles: University of California Press.
Economist (1995), 'Yangzi rising', *The Economist*, 336 (7931), 9 September 1995.
Field, J., Garris, M., Guntupalli, M., Rana, V. and Reyes, G. (2006) 'Chinese township and village enterprises: a model for other developing countries'. Online. Available HTTP: <http://www.umich.edu/~ipolicy/china/5)%20Chinese%20Township%20and%20 Village%20Enterprises,%20A%20Model%20for%20Oth.pdf> (accessed 9 October 2009).
Gallagher, M. (2005a) *Contagious Capitalism, Globalization and the Politics of Labor in China*, Princetown: Princetown University Press.
—— (2005b) '"Use the law as your weapon": institutional change and legal mobilization in China' in Diamant, N., Lubman S. and O'Brien, K. (eds.), *Engaging the Law in China: State, Society and Possibilities for Justice*, Stanford: Stanford University Press, pp. 31–54.
Gipouloux, F. (1986) *Les Cent Fleurs à l' usine – Agitation ouvrière et crise du modèle Soviétique en China 1956–1957* (The Hundred Flowers in the Factories – workers agitation and the crisis of the Soviet model in China 1956–1957), Paris: Éditions de l'École des hautes Études en sciences socials.
Globalization Monitor (2009) *No Choice But to Fight: A Documentation of Chinese Battery Women Workers' Struggle for Health and Dignity*, Hong Kong: Globalization Monitor.
Gluckstein, Y. (1957) *Mao's China*, Boston: Beacon Press.
Greenfield, G. and Leung, A. (1997) 'China's Communist Capitalism: the real world of market socialism', *Socialist Register*, 33. Online. Available HTTP: <http://socialistregister.com/index.php/srv/issue/view/432> (accessed 20 August 2009).
Greenfield, G. and Pringle, T. (2002) 'The challenge of wage arrears in China', ILO, *Labour Education Online*, 128. Online. Available HTTP: <http://www.ilo.org/public/english/dialogue/actrav/publ/128/index.htm> (accessed 1 September 2009).
Guangdong Labour Dispute and Arbitration Network (2009) 'Laodong zhengyi tiaojie zhongcai fa shishe yi zhou nian zuotanhui zai Shenzhen zhaokai' (Meeting to discuss

one year of implementation of the Labour Mediation and Arbitration Law convened in Shenzhen). Online. Available HTTP: <http://www.gd.lss.gov.cn/ldtzw/zc/sy/zcdt/t20090522_100971.htm> (accessed 23 August 2009).

Guillermaz, J. (1972) *A History of the Chinese Communist Party*, New York: Random House.

Guo Wencai and Gao Jie (2007) 'Jiaqiang gonghui jiceng zuzhi jianshe de "san yaosu"' ('Three essential elements' to strengthening primary level trade unions). Online. Available HTTP: <http://www.acftu.org/template/10005/file.jsp?aid=64646&keyword=> (accessed 15 October 2008).

Hangzhou Daily (2003) 'Gonghui zhixuan Yuhang quanguo ling chao'(Nationwide surge in trade union direct elections led by Yuhang), 25 June 2003.

Harper, P. (1971) 'Workers Workers'? participation in management in Communist China', *Studies in Comparative Communism*, 3: 111–40.

Harris, N. (1978) *The Mandate of Heaven: Marx and Mao in Modern China*, London: Quartet Books Limited.

Hart-Landsberg, M. and Burkett, P. (2004) 'China and socialism: market reforms and class struggle', *Monthly Review*, 56 (3).

He Qinglian (1998) *Zhongguo de xianjing: dangdai Zhongguo de jingji shehui wenti* (China's Pitfalls – Socio-economic Problems in Modern China), Beijing: Jinri Zhongguo Publishing House.

He Weifang (2004) 'Help or hindrance to workers: China's institutions of public address'. Online. Available HTTP: <http://www.clb.org.hk/en/files/share/File/research_reports/Help_or_Hindrance.pdf> (accessed 20 August 2009).

Hershatter, G. (1986) *The Workers of Tianjin, 1900–1949*, Stanford: Stanford University Press.

Hobsbawm, E. J. (1964) *Labouring Men, Studies in the History of Labour*, London: Weidenfeld and Nicolson.

—— (1998) *Uncommon People: Resistance, Rebellion and Jazz*, New York: New Press.

Hong Yung Lee (2000), 'Xiagang, the Chinese style of laying off workers', *Asian Survey*, 40 (6): 914–37.

Howell, J. (1998) 'Trade unions in China: the challenge of foreign capital', in O'Leary, G. (ed.), *Adjusting to Capitalism: Chinese Workers and the State*, New York, Sharpe, pp. 150–174.

—— (2003) 'Trade unionism in China: sinking or swimming', *Journal of Communist Studies and Transition in Politics*, 19 (1): 102–22.

—— (2006) 'New democratic trends in China? Reforming the All China Federation of Trade Unions', IDS Working Paper 263, Centre for the Future State/Institute of Development Studies. Online. Available HTTP: <http://www2.ids.ac.uk/gdr/cfs/drc-pubs/summaries/summary%2020-Howell-ACFTU.pdf> (accessed 1 June 2008).

—— (2008) 'Beyond reform? The slow march of direct elections', *China Quarterly*, 196: 845–63.

Hinton, H. C. (1986) *The People's Republic of China 1979–1984: A Documentary Survey*, Wilmington, Del: Scholarly Resources.

HKCTU (2004) 'Chinese labour and the WTO', Hong Kong: HKCTU.

Howe, C. (1973) 'Labour organization and incentives in industry, before and after the Cultural Revolution' in Schram, S. (ed.) *Authority, Participation and Cultural Change in China*, London: Cambridge University Press, pp. 233–56. <http://www.hrw.org/en/reports/2002/08/02/paying-price> (accessed 2 August 2008).

Hu Teh-Wei and Elizabeth Hon-Ming Li (1993) 'The labor market', in Galenson, W. (ed.) *China's Economic Reform*, South San Francisco, CA: The 1990 Institute, pp. 147–176.

Hua Jinyang, Miesing, P. and Li Mingfang (2006) 'An empirical taxonomy of SOE governance in transitional China', *Journal of Management Governance*, 10: 401–433.

Huang An (2007) 'Quanqiuhua beijing xia de laogong zijiu' (Workers' self-defence under the background of globalisation), *Nanfang chuang*, 15 November 2007. Online. Available HTTP: <http://news.sina.com.cn/c/2007-11-15/122014311592.shtml> (accessed 4 January 2008).

Huang Kun (2004) 'Reform of China's legal system on resolving labor disputes', paper presented at *Conference on International Labour Law Forum: Reform and Development*, Beijing University, 26–28, February 2004.

Human Rights Watch (2002) 'Paying the price: workers unrest in Northeast China', *Human Rights Watch*. Online. Available HTTP:

Hurst, W. and O'Brien, K. (2002) 'China's contentious pensioners', *China Quarterly*, 170: 346–60.

Hussain, A. and Stern, N. (1994) *Economic Transition on the Other Side of the Wall: China*. London: STICERD.

Hussain, A. and Zhuang Juzhong (1998) 'Enterprise taxation and transition to market economy', in Brean, D. J. S. (ed.) *Taxation in Modern China*, London: Routledge, pp. 43–68.

ICEM (2002) 'China's protesting oil workers get global unions' backing'. Online. Available HTTP: <http://www.icem.org/en/7-Asia-Pacific/960-China%27s-Protesting-Oil-Workers-Get-Global-Union-Backing> (accessed 12 August 2009).

IHLO (2004) 'Trade union direct elections: a labour rights reform as promoted by foreigners'. Online. Available HTTP: <http://www.ihlo.org/LRC/ACFTU/000704.html> (accessed 22 September 2009).

Jiang Hong (2002) 'Weihu zhigong quanyi, gonghui ze wu pang dai' (Upholding workers rights: the trade unions must not shirk responsibility). Online. Available HTTP: <http://news.xinhuanet.com/fortune/2002-01/14/content_236653.htm> (accessed 21 August 2009).

Jiang Kaiwen (1996) 'Gonghui yu dang-guojia de chongtu: ba shi niandai yilai de gonghui gaige' (Conflicts of trade unions and Party-state: Chinese trade union reform since 1980s), *Hong Kong Journal of Social Science*, 8: 121–58

Jingji Cankao Bao (2005) 'Xiagang xiang shiye baoxian binggui, shi'er sheng guanbi zaijiuye fuwu zhongxin' (Twelve provinces have closed down all re-employment centres and lay-offs to be integrated into unemployment insurance), *Jingji Cankao Bao*, 12 February 2005.

Karnow, S. (1984) *Mao and China: Inside China's Cultural Revolution*, New York: Viking Penguin.

Kessler, D. (2009) 'The structure of Chinese employment protests: pulling migrants out of the trends', unpublished paper, Hong Kong.

Korzec, M. (1992) *Labour and the Failure of Market Reform in China*, New York: St. Martin's Press, Inc.

Kwok, King-lun (2008) 'The changes of Chinese labor policy and labor legislation in the context of market transition', *International Labor and Working Class History*, 73 (spring): 45–64.

Laodong baozhang tongxun (Labour Insurance Bulletin) (2000) 'Laodong baozhang tongji baogao 1998–1999' (Report on 1998–1999 labour insurance statistics), 3: 35.

Law Bridge (2006) *Labour Law of the People's Republic of China 1994*. Online: Available HTTP: <http://www.law-bridge.net/english/LAW/20065/1322462357270.shtml> (accessed 5 January 2008).

Lee Ching-kwan (1999) 'From organized dependence to disorganized despotism: changing labour regimes in Chinese factories', *China Quarterly*, 157 (3): 44–71.

—— (2000) 'Pathways of labor insurgency' in Perry, E. J. and Selden, M. (eds.) *Chinese Society: Change, Conflict and Resistance*, London: Routledge, pp. 41–61.

—— (2007) *Against the Law: Labor Protests in China's Rustbelt and Sunbelt*, Berkeley: University of California Press.
Left Forum (2009) 'Can the Chinese labor movement reverse the "race to the bottom"?' panel discussion at *Turning Points* conference, New York, 17–19, April 2009.
Leung Wing-yuk (1995) 'The politics of labour rebellions in China', unpublished thesis, University of Hong Kong.
Leys, S. (1977) *The Chairman's New Clothes*. London: Allison and Busby.
Li Jianping (2005) '*Zhonghua quanguo zong gonghui guanyu ji yibu jiaqiang jiceng gonghui gongzuo de jueding' xiangguan wenti jianda* (*Answers to Questions Relating to the 'ACFTU Decision on Strengthening the Work of Primary Level Trade Unions'*), Beijing: China Workers Press.
Li Kungang (2000) 'Lun laodong guanxi de wending xing he liudong xing – jian lun woguo hetong zhidu de wanshan' (On stability and mobility in labour relations: completing China's labour contract system), *Fa shang yanjiu*, 6: 94–9.
Li Peilin, Zhang Yi, Zhao Yandong and Liang Dong (2005) *Shehui chongtu yu jieji yishi* (*Social Conflicts and Class Consciousness in China Today*), Beijing: Social Science Publishing House.
Li Shi (2008) 'Rural Migration in China', a paper presented to the Workshop on Understanding Rural Migrant Workers in China Beijing August 2007 cited in 'Rural Migrant Workers in China: Scenario, Challenges and Public Policy', Working Paper 89, ILO: Geneva. Online. Available HTTP: < http://www.ilo.org/wcmsp5/groups/public/—dgreports/—integration/documents/publication/wcms_097744.pdf > (accessed 19 May 2010).
Liang Guosheng (1996) 'Looking back on the Beijing massacre', *Green Left Online*, 26 June 1996. Online. Available HTTP: <http://www.greenleft.org.au/1996/236/14141> (accessed 30 October 2009).
Liaoning Statistical Yearbook (2001) Beijing: China Statistical Publishing House.
Lindblom, C. (1959) 'The science of muddling through', *Public Administration Review*, 19: 79–88.
Liu Aiyu (2005) *Xuanze: guo qi bianqe yu gongren cunzai* xingdong (*Choices: State-owned Enterprises Reform and Workers' Subsistence Actions*), Beijing: Social Science Publishing House.
Liu Kaiming (2005) *A Social Structure of Lost Entitlements*, Shenzhen: Institute of Contemporary Observation.
Liu Mingwei (2007) 'Union organizing in China, swimming, floating or sinking?', paper presented at Warwick-ILR Brettschneider PhD Seminar, University of Warwick, 4 May 2007.
Liu Shang (2004) 'Sifa gaige qianzhan: rang sifa jiguan buzai zhizao minyuan' (Looking ahead to judicial reform in 2004: judicial organs must no longer be allowed to cause popular discontent), *Falü yu Shenghuo*, 1: 2–4.
Liu Shaoqi (1988) [1949] 'Zai Tianjin zhigong daibiao dahui shang de jianghua' (Speech to the Staff and Workers Congress of Tianjin), *Zhonghua quanguo zong gonghui bian, Liu Shaoqi lun gongren yundong* (*ACFTU Documents, Liu Shaoqi on the Workers Movement*), Beijing: Central Committee Documents Publishing House. Online. Available HTTP: <http://www.marxists.org/chinese/liushaoqi/marxist.org-chinese-lsq-19490428.htm> (accessed 30 October 2009).
—— (1988) [1951] 'Zai quanzong kuoda de weiyuanhui shang de jianghua', *Zhonghua quanguo zong gonghui bian, Liu Shaoqi lun gongren yundong* (*ACFTU Documents, Liu Shaoqi on the Workers Movement*), Beijing: Central Committee Documents Publishing House. Online. Available HTTP: <http://www.people.com.cn/GB/shizheng/8198/30513/30515/33959/2523679.html> (accessed 30 October 2009).

202 Bibliography

—— (1984) *Selected Works of Liu Shaoqi Volume 1*, Beijing: Foreign Languages Press.
Liu Shen (2006), 'Wei nongmingong da pao buping de "lao niangshu"' ('Old Uncle [Chen]': fighting injustice for migrant workers), *China Youth Daily*, 30 April 2006. Online. Available HTTP: <http://zqb.cyol.com/content/2006-04/30/content_1374271.htm>. (accessed 6 June 2007).
Liu Shi (2003) 'Current condition of China's working class'. Online. Available HTTP: <http://chinastudygroup.net/2003/11/current-condition-of-chinas-working-class/> (accessed 19 September 2009).
Liu Yufang (2002) 'Zhongwai jiti hetong zhidu bijiao' (Comparing Chinese and foreign collective bargaining systems), *Gonghui xinxi*, (22): 23.
Lü Xiaobo and Perry, E. J. (1997) 'The changing Chinese workplace' in Lü Xiaobo and Perry, E. J. (eds.) *Danwei: The Changing Chinese Workplace in Historical and Comparative Perspective*, London: M.E. Sharpe, pp. 3–17.
Lü Xiaobo (1997) 'Minor public economy: the revolutionary origins of the danwei' in LüXiaobo and Perry. E. J. (eds.) *Danwei: The Changing Chinese Workplace in Historical and Comparative Perspective*, London: M.E. Sharpe, pp. 21–41.
Luo Xiaojun and Zhou Songqiang (2006) 'Zai zhengfu he nongmingong zhijian: shichang jingji xia gonghui shuang zhong shen xi de pingwei' (Between the government and migrant workers: Evaluating the twin role of trade union in a market economy), *Labour Union Bimonthly*, 6: 25–30.
Maitan, L. (1976) *Party, Army and Masses in China*, London: NLB.
Maitland, A. (2002) 'Sowing a seam of worker democracy in China'. *Financial Times*, 12 December 2002.
Mao Zedong (1949) 'On the people's democratic dictatorship'. Online. Available HTTP: <http://www.marxists.org/reference/archive/mao/selected-works/volume-4/mswv4_65.htm> (accessed 30 October 2009).
—— (1950) 'Don't hit out in all directions'. Online. Available HTTP: <http://www.marxists.org/reference/archive/mao/selected-works/volume-5/mswv5_07.htm> (accessed 10 November 2009).
—— (1953) 'Refute the right deviationist views that depart from the general line'. Online. Available HTTP: <http://www.marxists.org/reference/archive/mao/selected-works/volume-5/mswv5_28.htm> (accessed 20 August 2009).
—— (1957) 'On the correct handling of contradictions among the people'. Online. Available HTTP: <http://www.marxists.org/reference/archive/mao/selected-works/volume-5/mswv5_58.htm> (accessed 10 October 2009).
Marx, K. (1867) *Capital: Volume 1* (Preface, German Edition). Online. Available HTTP: <http://www.marxfaq.org/archive/marx/works/1867-c1/p1.htm> (accessed 5 June 2008).
Ministry of Public Security (2000) 'Regulations concerning the public security organs' handling of collective incidents that affect public order'. Online. Available HTTP: <http://www.china-labour.org.hk/en/fs/view/research-reports/mass_incident_regulations.pdf> (accessed 12 August 2009).
Mo, J. (2000) 'Probing labour arbitration in China', *Journal of International Arbitration*, 17 (5): 19–83.
MOLSS (2003) 'Guanyu tuoshan chuli guoyou qiye xiagang zhigong chu zai jiuye zhongxin youguan wenti de tongzhi' (Notice on the proper arrangements for laid-off SOE employees leaving re-employment centres). Online. Available HTTP: <http://ldbz.qzfz.gov.cn/zcfg/myshowatc.asp?id=395&s1=&s2=> (accessed 6 October 2009).

—— (2004) *Jiti hetong guiding 2004 (Regulations for Collective Contracts 2004).* Online: Available HTTP: <http://www.jincao.com/fa/12/law12.46.htm> (accessed 29 October 2009).
—— (2006) 'Guanyu kaizhan quyu xing hangye xing jiti xieshang gongzuo de yijian' (Opinion on the expansion of district- and sector-level collective contracts). Online. Available HTTP: <http://w1.mohrss.gov.cn/gb/zt/2006-10/24/content_140631.htm> (accessed 5 June 2008).
—— (2008) *Laodong zhengyi tiaojie zhongcai fa (Labour Dispute Mediation and Arbitration Law).* Online.Available HTTP: <http://www.molss.gov.cn/gb/ywzn/2008-01/10/content_219148.htm> (accessed 20 August 2009).
Nanfang Daily (2007) 'Dagongzhe zhongxin dezui le shui?' (Who did the Dagongzhe workers centre upset?), 11 December 2007. Online. Available HTTP: <http://www.nddaily.com/H/html/2007-11/28/content_322157.htm> (accessed 6 May 2008).
Nanfang Times (2008) 'Buyao ba bagong kan de tai mingan' (No need to be overly sensitive about strikes). Online: Available HTTP: <http://epaper.nddaily.com/A/html/2008-04/12/content_438127.htm> (accessed 1 September 2009).
National People's Congress (2009) 'Quanguo renmin daibiao dahui changwu weiyuanhui zhifa jiancha zu guanyu "zhonghua renmin gongheguo gonghuifa" shishi qingkuang baogao' (Report of the Law Implementation Group of National People's Congress Standing Committee Report on the implementation of the Trade Union Law). Online. Available HTTP: <http://www.npc.gov.cn/npc/zfjc/ghfzfjc/2009-10/30/content_1524883.htm> (accessed 2 November 2009).
Naughton, B. (1995) *Growing Out of the Plan: Chinese Economic Reform 1978–1993*, Cambridge: Cambridge University Press.
—— (1997) 'Danwei: the economic foundation of a unique institution' in Lü Xiaobo and Perry, E. J. (eds.) *Danwei: The Changing Chinese Workplace in Historical and Comparative Perspective*, London: M.E. Sharpe, pp. 169–94
Ni Zhifu (1988) 'Tuijin gonghui gaige; tuanjie yiwan zhigong; zai quanmian shenhua gaige zhong faihui zhulijun zuoyong'(Push forward with trade union reforms, unite the hundreds of millions of staff and workers and bring into play the main force for strengthening the overall reforms), in *Zhonghua quanguo zong gonghui wenjian xuanbian 1988 (Selected ACFTU Documents 1988)*, Beijing: Economic Management Publishing House, pp. 52–75.
Nichols, T., Chun Soonuk, Zhao Wei and Feng Tongqing (2004) 'Factory regimes and the dismantling of established labour in Asia', *Work, Employment and Society*, 18 (4): 663–85.
Ng Sek-Hong and Warner, M. (1998) *China's Trade Unions and Management*, Basingstoke: Macmillan Press Ltd.
Ngok Kinglun (2008) 'The changes of Chinese labor policy and labor legislation in the context of market transition', *International Labor and Working-Class History*, 73: 45–64.
Oakley, S. (2002) *Labour Relations in China's Socialist Market Economy*. Westport: Quorum Books.
OECD (2003) 'Investment policy reviews: China 2003 progress and reform challenges', OECD Publishing.
O'Leary, G. (1998) 'The making of the Chinese working class' in O'Leary, G. (ed.) *Adjusting to Capitalism*, London: M.E. Sharpe, pp. 48–74.
Pan Yue (2005) 'Quanguo zong gonghui 2006 yuandan chunjie song wennuan huodong qidong' (ACFTU's charitable activities on the eve of the 2006 Lunar New Year), *People's Daily*, 12 December 2005.

People's Daily Online (1979) 'We can develop a market economy under socialism', 26 November 1979. Online. Available HTTP: <http://english.peopledaily.com.cn/dengxp/vol2/text/b1370.html> (accessed 23 January 2008).

—— (2008), 'Migrant workers' life under city roofs in China'. Online. Available HTTP: <http:// english.people.com.cn/90001/90776/90882/6525710.html> (accessed 13 October 2009).

Perry, E. J. (1993) *Shanghai on Strike*, Stanford, Stanford University Press.

—— (1997) 'From native place to workplace: labor origins and outcomes of China's *danwei* system' in Lü Xiaobo and Perry, E. J. (eds.) *Danwei: The Changing Chinese Workplace in Historical and Comparative Perspective*, London: M.E. Sharpe, pp. 42–59.

Philion, S. (2007) 'Workers' democracy vs. privatization in China', *Socialism and Democracy*, 21 (2): 37–55.

Pioneer Monthly (2002) 'Mai duan gongren huainian lingxiu Mao Zedong' (Retrenched workers cherish the memory of Chairman Mao), *Xianqu Jikan* (*Pioneer Monthly*), 63: 17.

—— (2002): 'Daqing dangju jiajin zhenya, kangyi qunzhong shiqi diluo' (Authorities tighten repression in Daqing as mass protests weaken), *Xianqu Jikan* (*Pioneer Monthly*), 64: 5–7.

PLA Daily (2004) 'Woguo xianzai chengzhen fei zhenggui jiuye renyuan jun 8000 wan, chengwei jiuye zhongyao qudao' (China's informal sector hits 80 million workers and has become an important path to employment), *PLA Daily*, 8 May 2004.

Pringle, T. (2001) 'Industrial unrest in China: a labour movement in the making?'. Online. Available HTTP: <http://www.hartford-hwp.com/archives/55/294.html> (accessed 20 August 2009).

—— (2004), 'Trade union elections in China', *IHLO*. Online. Available HTTP: <http://www.ihlo.org/LRC/ACFTU/000504.html> (accessed 5 January 2007).

Pringle, T. and Frost, S. (2003) 'The absence of rigor and failure of implementation', *International Journal of Occupational and Environmental Health*, 9: 309–16.

Pringle, T. and Leung, A. (2006) 'Causes, implementation and consequences of xiagang', paper presented at International Conference on Labour Relations and Labour Standards under Globalisation, Beijing University, 1–2 April 2006.

—— (2009) 'Causes, Implementation and consequences of "xiagang"' in *Xiagang: the Sacrifice in the Transformation of Labour Policy in China from State to Market*, Luk, P. (ed.), Hong Kong: Asia Monitor Resource Centre.

Pun Ngai (2005) *Made in China: Women Factory Workers in a Global Workplace*, London: Duke University Press.

Qiao Yu (2005) 'Zujin zai jiuye (Encourage re-employment)', *Workers' Daily*, 19 January 2005.

Richman, B. (1969) *Industrial Society in Communist China*, Toronto: Random House of Canada.

Roberts, D. (2005) 'A new China for organized labor', *Business Week*, 22 August 2005. Online. Available HTTP: <http://www.businessweek.com/magazine/content/05_34/b3948435. htm?chan=search> (accessed 15 February 2008).

Sargeson, S. (1999) *Reworking China's Proletariat*, New York: St. Martin's Press.

Schram, S. R. (1973) 'Historical perspective' in Schram, S. R. (ed.) *Authority, Participation and Cultural Change in China*, London: Cambridge University Press, pp. 1–108.

Schuter, G. (2003) 'Democracy under one-party rule? a fresh look at direct village and township elections in the PRC', *China Perspectives*, (46). Online. Available HTTP: <http://chinaperspectives.revues.org/document256.html> (accessed 15 October 2009).

Scott, J. F. (2001) 'Protestant fundamentalism and globalisation' in Danks, C. (ed.) *Identity and Globalisation*, London: Routledge, pp. 5–28.

Selden, M. (1995) *China in Revolution: The Yenan Way Revisited*, Armonk: M.E. Sharpe.
Shambaugh, D. (ed.) (2000) *The Modern Chinese State*, Cambridge, Cambridge University Press.
Shanghai Daily (2009), 'Steel factory protest wins reprieve from takeover bid', *Shanghai Times*, 8 September 2006. Online. Available HTTP: <http://www.shanghaidaily.com/search/result.asp> (accessed 17 August 2009).
Shao Xiaoyi (2005) 'Negotiated salary system saves industry', *China Daily*, 24 February 2005.
Shao Zihong and Luo Weijie (2003) 'Yuhang jin ban fei gong qiye zhixuan gonghui zhuxi' (Almost half of the trade union chairpersons in Yuhang's private sector are directly elected), *Zhejiang Daily*, 5 September 2003.
Sheehan, J. (1998) *Chinese Workers: A New History*, London: Routledge.
Shen Jie (2007) *Labour Disputes and Their Resolution in China*, Oxford: Chandos.
Silver, B. (2003) *The Forces of Labour*, Cambridge, Cambridge University Press.
Solinger, D. (1999) *Contesting Citizenship in Urban China*, Berkeley: University of California Press.
—— (2001) 'Why we cannot count the unemployed', *China Quarterly*, 167: 671–88.
Somerville, Q. (2005) 'The rapid rise of China's sock town', *BBC News*, 29 September 2005. Online. Available HTTP: <http://news.bbc.co.uk/2/hi/business/4287398.stm> (accessed 12 April 2007).
State Council (1990) *Zhonghua renmin gongheguo xiangcun jiti suoyouzhi qiye tiaoli* (*Regulations on Township and Village Collective Enterprises of the People's Republic of China*). Online. Available HTTP: <http://www.jincao.com/fa/law24.22.htm> (accessed 30 October 2009).
—— (2004) *Laodong baozhang jiancha tiaoli* (*Regulations on the Inspection of Labour Safeguards 2004*). Online. Available HTTP: <http://www.jincao.com/fa/12/law12.52.htm> (accessed 10 November 2009).
State Council Information Office (2002) 'Zhongguo laodong yu shebao baipishu' (White paper on labour and social security in China). Online. Available HTTP:<http://www.china.org.cn/e-white/20020429/1.I.htm> (accessed 6 October 2009).
—— (2004) *China's Employment Situation and Policies*, Beijing: Xinxing Publishing House.
Tan Yingzi (2009) 'China's unemployment rate climbs', *China Daily*, 21 January 2009. Online. Available HTTP: <http://www.chinadaily.com.cn/bizchina/2009-01/21/content_7416242.htm> (accessed 15 October 2009).
Tang Wenfang and Parish, L. (2000) *Chinese Urban Life Under Reform: The Changing Social Contract*, Cambridge: Cambridge University Press.
Tao Junyi, Yang Guren and Jiang Jifa (2003) 'Jianzhu ye yu gongzi' (Wages in the construction industry), unpublished research paper, Zhejiang Provincial Federation of Trade Unions and Zhejiang Provincial Construction Trade Unions.
Taylor, B. and Li Qi (2003) 'An analysis of the collective contract system in China at various levels', paper presented at ICFTU conference on China and the WTO, Hong Kong, 21 November 2003.
—— (2007) 'Is the ACFTU a trade union and does it matter?' *Journal of Industrial Relations*, 49 (5): 701–15.
Taylor, W., Chang Kai and Li Qi (2003) *Industrial Relations in China*, Cheltenham: Edward Elgar.
Teiwes, F. C. (2000) 'The Maoist State', in Shambaugh, D. (ed.) *The Modern Chinese State*, Cambridge: Cambridge University Press, pp.105–60.
Thireau, I. and Linshan Hua (2003) 'The moral universe of aggrieved Chinese workers', *China Journal*, 50: 83–103.

Thompson, E. P. (1991) *Customs in Common*, New York: New Press.
Thompson, P. (1992) 'Disorganised socialism: state and enterprise in modern China' in Smith, C. and Thompson, P. (eds.) *Labour in Transition*, London: Routledge, pp. 227–59.
Walder, A.G. (1986) *Communist Neo-traditionalism: Work and Authority in Chinese Industry*, Berkeley: University of California Press.
Walsh, E. (1981) 'Resource mobilization and citizen protest in communities around Three Mile Island', *Social Problems*, 29 (1): 1–21.
Wang Fei-Ling (2005) *Organizing Through Division and Exclusion: China's Hukou System*, Stanford: Stanford University Press.
Wang Jiaoping (2003) 'Quanzong fu zhuxi Su Liqing jiu jiceng gonghui zhuxi zhixuan da jizhe wen' (Interview with ACFTU Deputy Chairman Su Liqing on direct elections), *Workers' Daily*, 25 July 2003.
—— (2005) '"2004 nian Zhongguo gonghui weihu zhigong hefa quanyi lanpishu" fabu' ("Bluebook of Trade Unions Rights 2004" released), *Workers' Daily*, 13 September 2005.
Wang Jinhong (2005) 'Gonghui gaige yu zhongguo jiceng minzhu de xin fazhan' (Trade union reform and the new direction of China's grassroots democracy). Online. Available HTTP: <http://www.usc.cuhk.edu.hk/wk_wzdetails.asp?id=4794> (accessed 20 September 2009).
Wang Kan (2008) 'A changing arena of industrial relations in China: what is happening after 1978', *Employee Relations*, 30 (2): 190–216.
Wang Lianxiang (2005) *Xin shiqi gonghui gongzuo (New era trade unions and their work)*, Beijing: China Workers Press.
Wang Tongxin (2008) 'Buyao ba bagong kan de tai mingan' (Don't be too sensitive over the issue of strikes). Online. Available HTTP: <http://www.chinawz.net/Article/china/all/200804/Article_58.html> (accessed 3 August 2009).
Warner, M. (2000) 'Whither the iron rice-bowl?' in Warner, M. (ed.) *Changing workplace Relations in the Chinese Economy*, Basingstoke: Macmillan, pp.3–14.
Warner, M. and Zhu Ying (2000) 'The origins of Chinese "industrial relations"' in Warner, M. (ed.) *Changing Workplace Relations in the Chinese Economy*, Basingstoke: Macmillan, pp. 15–33.
Wei Jianxing (2000) 'Renzhen xuexi guanche dang de shiwu ju wu zhong quan hui jingshen. Jin yi bu jia kuai xin jian qiye gonghui zu jian bufa' (Conscientiously implement the spirit of the Fifth Plenary Session of the Fifteenth Central Committee and speed up the organising and establishing of trade unions in new enterprises), Beijing Federation of Trade Unions. Online. Available HTTP: <http://www.bjzgh.gov.cn/jianghua/5_jianghua_13.php> (accessed 10 October 2005).
Wei Kailei, Yao Shujie and Liu Aiying (2008) *Foreign Direct Investment and Regional Equality in China*. Online. Available HTTP: <www.wider.unu.edu/publications/working.../rp2008-94.pdf> (accessed 18 August 2009).
Weil, R. (1996) *Red Cat, White Cat: China and the Contradictions of 'Market Socialism'*, New York: Monthly Review Press.
Wen Chihua and Qiu Lin (2007) 'Deng's achievements have lasting value'. *China Daily*, 16 February 2007. Online. Available HTTP: <http://www.chinadaily.com.cn/china/2007-02/16/ content_810681.htm> (accessed 22 September 2007).
Wen Dajun Dale (2007) 'Too much growth, too little development: the reality behind China's economic miracle', *Development*, 50 (3). Online. Available HTTP: <http://www.ifg.org/pdf/ChinaReality.pdf> (accessed 1 September 2009).

Wenling Federation of Trade Unions (2006) 'Xin silu xin jucuo xin tese nuli tansu hangye gongzi jiti xieshang xin jizhi' (New thinking, new tactics and new characteristics: working hard to explore new systems of sector-level collective wage consultation), 5 July 2006. Online. Available HTTP: <http://cmqfyc.acftu.org/template/10001/file.jsp?cid=311&aid=2127> (accessed 2 January 2008).

White, G. (1989) 'Restructuring the working class: labor reform in post-Mao China' in Dirlik, A. and Meisner, M. (eds.) *Marxism and the Chinese Experience*, New York: M.E. Sharpe, pp. 152–170.

—— (1993) *Riding the Tiger: The Politics of Post-Mao China*, Basingstoke: Macmillan.

Wong, M. (2006) 'Samsungisation or becoming China? The making of the labour relations of Samsung electronics in China', in Chang Dae-oup (ed.) *Labour in Globalising Asian Corporations: A Portrait of Struggle*, Hong Kong: AMRC, pp. 65–107.

Workers' Daily (1988) 'Jianshe duli zizhu, gaodu minzhu, zhigong xinlai de gonghui' (Build an independent, autonomous, democratic trade union trusted by staff and workers), 29 October 1988, in *ACFTU Eleventh Congress Documents*, Beijing: Economic Management Publishing House, pp. 148–151.

—— (2003) 'Wenling xieshang hangye gongzi wending laodong guanxi' (Wenling sector level wage consultation stabilises labour relations) *Workers' Daily*, 31 December 2003.

—— (2005a) 'Gongyun lunheng: yunyong jiti tanpan xietiao laodong guanxi' (Using collective bargaining to improve labour relations), *Workers' Daily*, 25 November 2005. Online. Available HTTP: <http://www.grrb.com.cn/template/10002/file.jsp?cid=0&aid=242403> (accessed 23 August 2008).

—— (2005b) 'Quanguo gonghui weiquan jizhi jianshe jingyan jiaoliu huiyi Yiwu zhaokai' (Conference to exchange experiences in establishing a national trade union rights work system held in Yiwu), *Workers' Daily*, 16 September 2005.

Wu Xiaoxian (2006) 'Yiwu zuidi xiaoshi gongzi 3.8 yuan' (Yiwu minimum hourly wage is 3.8 yuan). Online. Available HTTP: <http://www.jhfic.cn/news/2006-11-9/2006119101414.htm> (accessed 16 September 2009).

Wu Zhong (2007) 'China's cheap labor pool running dry', *Asia Times Online*. Online. Available HTTP: <http://www.atimes.com/atimes/China_Business/IF19Cb01.html> (accessed 1 September 2009).

Xia Xiaoyin (2005) 'Wenling gonghui: weiquan cong fensan xiang jihe kuayue' (Wenling trade unions makes the leap from upholding individual to collective rights), *Zhejiang Workers' Daily*, 12 July 2005.

Xinhua (2005) 'More unions adopt elections'. Online. Available HTTP: <http://www.china.org.cn/english/2005/May/128134.htm> (accessed 22 September 2009).

—— (2008) 'Yiwu launches first market credit index of China' Online. Available HTTP: <http://www.yiwu-sourcing-agent.com/news-events/yiwu-market/Yiwu-lauches-first-market-credit-index-of-China.html> (accessed 16 September 2009).

Xu Shi (2006) 'Shenzhen shi nei dafu tiaogao zui di gongzi' (Shenzhen city draws up plans for major increase in minimum wage), *Shenzhen Commercial News*. Online. Available HTTP: <http://news.xinhuanet.com/employment/2006-02/23/content_4217155.htm> (accessed 20 August 2009).

Xu Xiaohong (2003) *Chongtu yu xieshang: dangdai zhongguo siying qiye laozi guanxi de yanjiu* (*Conflict and Negotiation: Research into Labour Relations in Private Enterprises in Contemporary China*), Beijing: China Social Security Publishing House.

—— (2004) '"Ziran zhuangtai" de gongzi jiti xieshang' (Collective consultation on wages in the 'state of nature'), paper presented at the International labour Law Forum-Reform and Development Conference, Beijing: 26–28 February 2004.

208 Bibliography

Yao Kaijian and Chen Yongqin (2003) *Gaibian Zhongguo: Zhongguo de shi ge wu nian jihua* (*Changing China: China's ten Five-Year Plans*), Beijing: China Economic Publishing House.

Yeh Wen-hsin (1996) *Provincial Passages: Culture, Space, and the Origins of Chinese Communism*, Berkeley: University of California Press.

Yi Ming (2000) 'Lun weilai gonghui gongzuode fazhan qushi' (Future trends in the development of trade union work), *Trade Union Theory and Practice*. Online. Available HTTP: <http://www.fuping.gov.cn/fpzw/Article_Show.asp?ArticleID=867> (accessed 12 November 2009).

—— (2004) 'Lun weilai gonghui gongzuode fazhan qushi' (On the future work of trade unions). Online. Available HTTP: <http://old.fuping.gov.cn/fpzw/Article_Show.asp? ArticleID= 867> (accessed 15 October 2009).

—— (2007) 'Zhonghua quan guo cong gonghui lai wo xian tiaoyan hangye xing jiti hetong gongzuo' (The ACFTU investigation into collective sector-level contracts in Fuping county). Online. Available HTTP: <http://old.fuping.gov.cn/fpzw/Article_Show.asp?ArticleID=3125> (accessed 14 October 2009).

Ying Zhu (2002) 'Economic reform and labour market regulation in China' in Cooney, S., Lindsey, T., Mitchell, R. and Ying Zhu (eds.) *Law and Labour Market Regulation in East Asia*, London: Routledge, pp. 157–184

Yiwu Government Website (2008) Online. Available HTTP: <http://www.yw.gov.cn/ljyw/ywgl/csrk/> (accessed 12 April 2008).

Yiwu Health Bureau Website (2007) Online. Available HTTP: <http://www.ywwsj.gov.cn/wsxw/show.asp?docid=1535> (accessed 12 April 2008).

You Ji (1998) *China's Enterprise Reform: Changing State/Society Relations After Mao*, London: Routledge.

Yu Jianrong (2007) 'Social conflict in rural China', *China Security*, 3 (2): 2–17.

Yu Li (2004) 'Zhejiang Wenlingshi: laozi shuangying jinxing shi' (Wenling city, Zhejiang: A win–win for labour and capital), *Southern Weekend*, 23 September 2004.

Yuji Miora (2007) 'What is behind China's labor shortage?', *Asia Monthly*, August 2007. Online. Available HTTP: <http://www.jri.co.jp/english/asia/2007/08/china.html> (accessed 3 September 2009).

Zhang Honglin and Song Shunfeng (2003) 'Rural-urban migration and urbanization in China: Evidence from time series and cross-section analyses', *China Economic Review*, 14 (4): 386–400.

Zhang Wenxue (1993) 'Yiwu xiaoshangpin shichang yanjiu shehuizhuyi shichangjingji zai yiwu de shijian'(A study on Yiwu commodity market: the practice of the socialist market economy in Yiwu), Beijing: Qunyan Press.

Zhejiang China Commodities Cities Group Company Limited (2007) 'gongsi jianjie' (Company introduction). Online. Available HTTP: <http://www.cccgroup.com.cn/Active.asp?id=1> (accessed 12 April 2008).

Zhejiang Gongyun (2004) Issue One.

Zhejiang Workers' Daily (2005) 'Yiwushi gonghui shehuihua weiquan: "weiquan" cong geren dao zuzhi dao shehui' (Yiwu trade unions socialised rights work: 'upholding rights' from individuals to organisation to society), 4 August 2005.

Zheng Caixiong, Wu Yong and Guo Nei (2005) 'Rural dwellers to be granted urban rights, *China Daily*, 2 November 2005. Online. Available HTTP: <http://www.chinadaily.com.cn/english/doc/2005-11/02/content_489873.htm> (accessed 1 September 2009).

Zhou Qiong (2009) 'Quan shi geji fayuan shouli zhenyi anyuan tongbi shangshen 159.18%' (City courts process an increase in cases of 159.18%), *Caijing*, 14 January

2009. Online. Available HTTP: <http://www.caijing.com.cn/2009-01-14/110048077.html> (accessed 2 November 2009).

Zhou Yuqing (2002) 'Guanyu gonghui dangqian xuyao renzhen yanjiu de ji ge wenti (Several problems that the trade unions must seriously research), *Workers' Daily*, 3 September 2002.

Zhu Rongji (1997) BBC Monitoring Service, 9 August 1997. Online. Available HTTP: <http://www.monitor.bbc.co.uk/> (accessed 23 October 2002).

Zou Zhongzheng and Qin Wei (2001) 'Zhengfu, qiye, he jiating zai chengdu shi xiagang nugong de shehui zhichi wangluo zhong de zuoyong' (The role of governments, enterprises and families in social support networks of laid-off women workers), *Renkou yu jingji Population and Economics*, pp. 55–60, June 2001.

Index

ACFTU 1; appointment of officers 163; branch-building campaign 110; and BWAF 70; charity work 54; and collective contracts 47; and Cultural Revolution 65–6; and Democracy Movement 29, 31; and direct elections 169, 182; and First Five-Year Plan 62; and foreign pressure 168, 169; and ICFTU 1, 2, 31; and ILO standards 1; and labour disputes 101, 109, 110, 134–5; and labour law 5, 53, 55, 98; labour supervision and inspection committees 52; and labour unrest 55, 107, 182, 187; leadership purges 62, 65; as link between Party and masses 20; membership base 82, 110–11; and the Party 31, 38, 52–4, 62, 81; poverty relief centres 54; reform of 114, 115–16, 158–9, 169, 182, 183; and representing workers 133, 182; and restructuring of SOEs 81–4, 160–1; role in labour relations 54–5; and strikes 61–2, 65; and SWCs 30; top-down strategies 5; and Trade Union Law 35; and traditional custom and practice 52–3, 158–9; and xiagang 38
administratization 134
AFL-CIO 1, 187
All-China Federation of Trade Unions see ACFTU
All China Red Workers General Rebellion Corps 66
All China Women's Federation (ACWF) 141
Anti-Rightist Movement 2, 21, 65
April Fifth Movement 67, 68
arbitration: and black lawyers 102; committees 99–101, 109; and dispute resolution 48–9, 104, 139; and *hukou* 94, 95; law 95, 98; and mediation 151, 152
army 22–3, 41, 66–7, 183
autonomous trade unions 20, 31, 62, 65
autonomous workers' organizations 21, 23, 56, 69, 188

Beijing Faction 46, 99
Beijing Spring see Democracy Wall Movement
Beijing Workers Autonomous Federation (BWAF) 69–70
benefiting both labour and capital 54, 58
black economy 40
black lawyers 101, 102, 109
bonus system 28

capitalist class interests, eradication of 63
capitalist globalization 41, 44
capitalist labour relations 43
capitalist super-exploitation 88–109
capital rising and falling 58–62
Change To Win federation 1, 187
Chang Kai, Professor 46, 50, 53
cheap labour 89, 91, 188
Chen Ji 151, 152, 156, 157
Chen Youde 134, 135, 144–7, 149–50, 155, 156, 159
China Labour Education Centre (CLEC) 141–2
Chou Yang 64, 110
civil agency 102
civil servants, union officials 166
civil society 3, 6, 158, 186
collective action 93, 95, 101, 103, 110
collective bargaining 118–19, 132, 188
collective class interests 35–6
collective consultation, Xinhe town 114–32; analysis 129–32; legal

development of 119–21; methodology 116–17; results 128–9; vs collective bargaining 118–19; wage rates 126–7
collective contracts 35, 36, 47–8, 60, 119–22
collective dialogue 117, 119
collective labour disputes 99–101, 109
collectively owned enterprises (COEs) 28, 72
command economy era 1, 2, 6, 8; industrial relations under 11–25; labour unrest 57–68
commoditization of labour power 29, 45
Common Programme 58
communist neo-traditionalism 13, 14, 71, 72
Communist Party of China *see* CPC
compensation for workers 94–5, 108, 119, 153–4
compromise through mediation 151–2, 157
contracts *see* labour contracts
controlled migration to urban area 92
coordinators 73, 74
corporate social responsibility (CSR) 140, 141, 168, 169
cost of living rise 69
CPC: and ACFTU 31, 38, 52–4, 61–2, 81; and *danwei* 13, 18–19; and GMD 19; and labour unrest 62, 110; and post-liberation 57–8
cross-enterprise demonstrations 79, 81
'crossing the river by feeling for the stones' 25, 26, 41, 130
Cultural Revolution 2, 22–4, 65–8

danwei 11–19; and decent work 71–2; definition 11–12; dependency of workers 14, 71, 72; management of 17–19; role of trade unions 19–22; stability 15; wage system 15–17
Daqing, protests 77–8, 79–80, 81
decentralization 33–4
decent work 71–2, 88
Democracy Movement 28, 29, 31, 83
Democracy Wall Movement 28, 68
Democratic Reform Movement 18, 62
democratization of trade unions 18, 162, 164, 168, 180–1
Deng Xiaoping 24, 29, 34–5, 65, 68, 70
Department of Justice 145, 146, 148, 149, 157, 158
dingti 26
direct elections of trade union chairpersons 170–81
Director Responsibility System 26

dispute resolution 48–50, 60, 104, 107–9, 140
Document Nine 121
Dong Baohua, Professor 46
dual system of control 18–19
dual-track system 25–32

early reform era (1978–97) 68–71
economic reforms 2, 5, 24, 25–52
economism, union cadres 62
eight-grade wage system 15–16
elections, trade unions 160–82
employer-dependent enterprise unions 95–7, 102
employers and migrant labour 93–5
employment allocation procedures 27
employment security 15, 17, 28
employment structure 42–3
enterprise autonomy 25–6, 69
Enterprise Law (1988) 25, 26
enterprise-level mediation 48–9
enterprise-level party cells 19
enterprise-level trade unions 95–7, 98, 119, 165
enterprise managers 30
export promotion zones 35

Factory Management Committees *see* FMCs
famine (1958–61) 15, 65
fan xiang 43, 93
fencing 32
First Five-Year Plan 18, 62
Five-Anti movement 62, 63
FMCs 18, 19
food security 93
foreign capital 33, 34, 88
foreign direct investment (FDI) 1, 29, 31–2, 41, 71, 104
foreign-invested industry 42, 188
foreign ownership of enterprises 88
formal dispute resolution 107–9, 150–2
Four Modernizations 24–5
Foxconn 112, 113
freedom of association 1, 3, 7, 8, 185, 187
free speech 63
Fujian province 88, 137

Gang of Four 67, 68
gangs, place-of-origin 143
global integration of China 41, 45
globalization 41, 44, 57, 72, 97, 116, 188
global recession (2008–9) 93, 97
GMD 11, 19, 57
Gold Peak Limited 94–5, 103, 108, 119

212 Index

Great Leap Forward 2, 15, 21, 65
Guangdong province 71, 88, 101, 137, 140, 141, 159
Guomindang *see* GMD
guoying 2

Han Dongfang 24, 28, 69
health and safety 50–2
higher-level trade unions 52, 95, 134
hiring fairs 94
home town associations 106, 143, 167, 179
Honda 112, 113, 187
Hong Kong 88, 104, 121, 140, 141
household registration 12, 14, 92–5
Hu Jintao 46
hukou 12, 14, 42, 88, 92–5, 188
Hundred Flowers Movement 2, 63, 65
Hu Yaobang 32

ICFTU 1, 31, 79, 188
ID cards, confiscation of 94, 124
ILO 1, 35, 46, 71, 118, 130
indecent work 88
independent trade unions 4, 31, 88, 112, 115, 154
industrial reform 25–52
industrial relations 11–55; under command economy 11–25; policies 1–2; and reform 25–52; system 43–4; trade union law and practice 52–4
inflation 69
informal sector 43, 82
informal strikes 107–9
inspections, workplace 52
Institute of Contemporary Observations (ICO) 91
insurance 27, 51, 53, 92
International Confederation of Free Trade Unions *see* ICFTU
International Covenant on Economic, Social and Cultural Rights 1
International Trade Union Confederation *see* ITUC
international trade union movement: and ACFTU 29, 31, 158, 187–8; and lay-off disputes 79
intimidation 143, 144
Iron Man Square 78, 79, 80, 85
iron rice bowl 15, 26, 27, 28, 35, 69, 77–81
ITUC 1, 2

Jiang Qing 66
Jiang Zemin, President 5–6, 41

Jinhua City People's Congress (JCPC) 145, 146
job deposits 47, 94, 124
joint-venture enterprises 27, 33, 88, 188
'jump into the sea' 3, 28, 69, 83, 180

labour bureaux 27
labour-capital conflicts 46
Labour-Capital Consultative Conference *see* LCCC
labour-capital cooperation 61–2
labour-capital relations 118
Labour Contract Law (2008) 5, 46–7, 52, 98–9
labour contracts 27, 28, 44–8
labour discipline 59
labour dispute arbitration committees *see* LDACs
labour dispute resolution 48–50, 60, 104, 107–9, 140
Labour Insurance Regulations (1951) 20
labour law 1, 4, 5, 97–102
Labour Law (1995) 25, 30, 35–6, 43–4, 45, 48
labour legislation 41, 51, 52
Labour Mediation and Arbitration Law *see* LMAL
labour mobility 24
labour movement 37, 45, 55, 61–2, 77, 86, 108
labour relations 52, 54–5, 60
labour rights: individual 35, 36, 44; violations 135, 140, 151
labour rights centres 139–46
labour service companies (LSC) 27
labour shortages 104–6, 107
labour standards 46
labour turnover rates 15
labour unrest: in the command economy 57–68; and Cultural Revolution 67; migrant workers 87–8, 90, 98, 103; in the reforming economy 68–86; and state policy 63; in the state sector 56–86; and trade unions 5, 8, 20, 21, 31, 34, 55
Lai Rouyu 21, 22
land-use rights 93
lao-zi liang li 54, 58
Law on Safety in Production (2001) 50
Law on the Prevention and Cure of Occupational Diseases (LPCOD) 50
lay-offs 33, 36–41, 72, 73–7
LCCC 60, 62
LDACs 49, 100
learning from the peasants 23, 67

legal activism 97–102, 103
legal aid system 144, 146, 149, 158
Liaoyang, protests 78–9, 81, 85
liberation 57–8
Li Boyong 36
lifetime employment policy 8, 12, 17, 60
Li Lisan 20, 21, 22, 60, 61–2
Li Peng 29
litigation 107, 108, 109
Liu Shaoqi 60–1, 62, 65
LMAL 49, 50, 52, 100, 150
LNGOs 98, 101, 102, 109, 140, 141, 159
local labour bureau 90, 93, 102, 103, 105, 107
local private capital 88

management accountability 18
management autonomy 28, 37
Mao Zedong 17–18, 18–19, 22, 63, 65–6, 67
Marx, Karl 11
mass dismissals 76, 94
massization 162, 169
mass starvation 65
media: and ACFTU 54; and labour disputes 112, 149; and trade union elections 177, 178
mediation: and arbitration 151, 152; and compromise 151–2, 157; and dispute resolution 48–50, 156–7; law 95, 98; and trade unions 99, 109, 151–2, 153
Method on Election of Trade Union Chairpersons 162, 166, 178, 181
Migrant Employment Permit 93
migrant workers 87–113; constraints on 90–7; contracts 45; and labour rights centres 140–1; militancy 2, 4, 107–8, 132; off-farm employment 3, 5, 71, 88; as passive victims 8, 13, 71–2, 97, 104, 187; restrictions 93; rights 91, 103; strikes 66, 103–4, 108, 112; urban infrastructure projects 3
minimum wage 2, 54, 103, 112
Ministry of Civil Affairs (MoC) 141, 145, 158
Ministry of Labour and Social Security (MOLSS) 41, 47, 98, 119, 120, 121, 131
multinational corporations (MNC) 168, 169
mutual benefit 61–2
mutual cooperation between labour and capital 61–2

nationalization 20, 21, 59, 63
national labour law *see* Labour Law (1995)

new democracy 57–8
NGOs 82, 168
Ningbo Federation of Trade Unions (NFTU) 170, 180
Ningbo Opinion 180–1
non-pecuniary welfare entitlements 14, 17
normalization of strikes 103, 187, 188

occupational disease or injury 94, 108, 119, 153–4
Occupational Health and Safety (OHS) 51, 140, 141
off-farm employment 3, 5, 71, 88
oil workers 77–8, 79–80
one-man management 18, 19, 20
oversupply of labour 12, 89, 92

part-time trade union officers 96, 97, 167
pay-as-you-go social security system 40
Pearl River Delta (PRD) 46, 94, 105, 109, 117
peasants 3, 12, 23, 67, 71, 92, 114
pensioner sit-ins 72, 74, 80
pensions 22, 72, 76, 84
People's Liberation Army (PLA) 22, 66
petitioning, tradition of 73
phased redundancies 37, 38, 41, 42, 77, 78, 81
pilot projects 34, 114; direct elections 160, 167, 169, 170–81; enterprises 25, 26; labour contracts 27; and trade unions 8, 116, 187, 188; *xiagang* 37
place-of-origin networks 143, 144, 167
Planned Reproduction Certificate 93
Poland 31, 68
poverty relief centres 54
pre-reform industrial relations 2, 6
primary sector 42
primary trade unions 52, 135, 164, 166, 167
private capital 2, 3, 33, 71, 88
private ownership 88
private sector 17, 27, 36, 42, 44, 60, 88
privatization of SOEs 74–6, 77, 85–6
profit retention 25–6
prohibition of trade unions 22
protests, laid-off workers 40, 73–4, 76–7
Provisional Regulations for Primary-Level Trade Union Elections (1992) 172
public consultation 46
Public Security Bureau (PSB) 92, 93

qualified accountability 179–80

214   *Index*

Red Flag Army of Harbin 23
Red Guard organizations 66, 67
redundancies 37, 38, 41, 42, 77, 78, 81
Reebok 168, 182
re-employment centres 37–8, 39, 41, 82
reforms *see* economic reforms
Regulations Governing Resolutions of Enterprise Labour Disputes 48
Regulations Governing the Procedures for the Settlement of Labour Disputes 59
Regulations on Collective Contracts 120
Regulations on Household Registration 92
Regulations on the Democratic Management of Enterprises 113, 121
Regulations on the Inspection of Labour Guarantees 52
representatives' qualifications examination group 171
reserve army of unemployed 42, 91
residential registration 12, 14, 92–5
return to the countryside movement 43, 93
Revolutionary Committees 22–3, 66
reward system, wages 17
rights awareness 4, 103, 140, 141, 148
rural poverty 89
rural registration 93
rural surplus labour 24, 34
rural–urban migration 88, 89

sea elections 165, 174, 175, 177, 181, 187
secondary sector 42
self-employment 27
S Enterprise, direct elections 175–6
severance pay 47, 77, 79
SFTU 109, 111, 112, 159
Shanghai Faction 46, 99
shareholderization 85
Shenzhen 35, 71, 102
Shenzhen Federation of Trade Unions *see* SFTU
Sichuan 2, 25, 37, 123
skilled workers: migrants 103, 104, 105, 106, 125; woollen industry 124, 128
small- and medium-size enterprises 71
social contract 13–14, 57
social instability 37
Socialist Education Campaign 1963–4 65
socialist market economy 2, 5, 32–41
socialized rights network 147–50
social organizations 145, 147
social stability 33
SOEs: and enterprise managers 30; lay-offs (*xiagang*) 36–8; and profit retention 25–6; restructuring 32–3, 37, 72, 74–7, 81–6; wage system 16, 17, 28, 29; workers' standard of living 71, 72; and worker unrest 69, 71
solidarity among workers 74, 77, 79
Solidarność, Poland 31, 68
Southern Tour 29, 34–5, 70
Soviet Union 12, 160
Special Economic Zones (SEZ) 35, 71, 88
Staff and Workers Congress (SWC) 18, 30–1
Staff and Workers' Representative Congresses (SWRCs) 65
state-controlled media 59
state-owned enterprises *see* SOEs
state policies 3–4
state sector 42, 56–86, 88, 117
statistics, unavailability of 72–3, 100
street protests 106
strikes: and collective consultation 125, 126, 128, 132; and Cultural Revolution 66, 67; Honda 112, 187; informal 107–9; normalization of 103–4, 187, 188; and the Party 62; and SOE restructuring 76–7; strike waves 16–17, 18, 21, 63–4, 90, 112; and wages 103, 106; YICT crane operators 111, 187
student demonstrations 69, 70
suicides 112
Supreme People's Court 100

Taiwan 88, 104
Temporary Residence Permit 93
'ten lost years' 22–4
tertiary sector 42
The Yiwu Workers' Legal Rights Centre *see* YWLRC
Three-Anti movement 62, 63
three-in-one combination 27
Three Represents theory 6, 41
Three Years of Bitterness 65
Tiananmen Square 25, 27, 67, 69–70
TNCs 6, 45, 141, 188
top-down quotas 48, 121, 122
totalitarianism 13
township and village enterprises (TVE) 32, 33–4, 88
Trade Union Law (1950) 20
Trade Union Law (1992) 25, 35
trade union law and practice 52–4
trade unions: administratization 134; autonomy 20, 31, 62, 65; and Cultural Revolution 22–4; dependency on employers 95–7, 121, 133, 167, 182, 186; direct elections 160–82; and dispute

resolution 109, 115, 119, 133; and economic reforms 29–32; enterprise-level 95–7; labour relations system 52; reform 115–16, 158–9, 182; representation of workers 119, 133; rights centres 133–59; role in *danwei* system 19–22; safety production inspections 52; SOE workers and *xiagang* 38–41; union cadres and management 167; union cadres and members 165–7
transmission belt 20, 115, 116, 158, 180
transnational corporations *see* TNCs
Trial Method on Collective Wage Negotiation 121
tribunals 49

unemployment 24, 32, 37–41, 42–3, 63
union dependency on employers 95–7, 121, 133, 167, 182, 186
urbanization 2, 92
urban labour markets 24
urban sojourning 14
urban workers 2, 3, 17, 60, 71, 72

village elections 163, 165
VTUFs 123–4, 127, 128

wage arrears 94, 105, 124
wage reform 15, 28
wages and strikes 103, 106
wage system, *danwei* 15–17
Wal-Mart 111
welfare benefits 38, 40, 183
Wen Jiabao 46
Wenling City Federation of Trade Unions (WFTU) 115–16, 121, 128, 131
win–win agreements 115, 118
women workers 39, 60, 141
woollen sweater industry 123–32
workers, as passive victims 8, 13, 71–2, 97, 104, 187
Workers Autonomous Federations (WAF) 21, 28–9, 31, 69, 70
Workers' Representative Conference (WRC) 18, 62
Workers Support Centres (WSC) 82–3
working class: demography changes 71; militancy 2, 60, 61, 63–5; and revolutionary history 59; transformation of 6
workplace inspections 52

World Confederation of Labour 1, 188
World Trade Organization (WTO), membership 2–3, 36, 41, 44

XFTU 126, 127, 128, 130, 131
xiagang 3, 36–41, 42, 72
xiahai 69
Xinhe Federation of Trade Unions *see* XFTU
Xinhe town, collective consultation in 123–32
Xinhe Woollen Sweater Manufacturers Association *see* XWSMA
Xinhe Woollen Sweater Sector Trade Union *see* XWSTU
XWSMA 126
XWSTU 126, 127, 130

YFTU 134, 135, 142–59
YHFTU 169, 170–2, 179–80, 181
YICT 111, 187
Yiwu 133–59; case studies 152–4; development of Yiwu city 136–9; labour rights centre initiative 142–6; managing trade union rights centre 146–50
Yiwu City Federation of Trade Unions People's Mediation Committee 156
Yiwu City Legal Aid Centre (Staff and Workers' Section) 149
Yiwu Federation of Trade Unions *see* YFTU
Yiwu Model 151–2
Yiwu Workers' Legal Rights Centre 147
Yuhang Federation of Trade Unions *see* YHFTU
Yuyao (city) Federation of Trade Unions *see* YYFTU
Yuyao Opinion 172, 173, 174–5, 180–1
Yuyao Reference Opinion 172–3, 174–5
YWLRC 134, 135, 149, 151, 156, 158, 159
YYFTU 170, 172–5

Zhao Ziyang 25, 27, 31, 32
Zhejiang China Commodities Cities Group Company Limited (ZCCCG) 138–9
Zhejiang province 71, 88, 136
Zhengzhou, protests 84–5
zhigong 12
Zhou Enlai 67
Zhu Rongji 36

Taylor & Francis
eBooks
FOR LIBRARIES

ORDER YOUR FREE 30 DAY INSTITUTIONAL TRIAL TODAY!

Over 22,000 eBook titles in the Humanities, Social Sciences, STM and Law from some of the world's leading imprints.

Choose from a range of subject packages or create your own!

Benefits for you
- Free MARC records
- COUNTER-compliant usage statistics
- Flexible purchase and pricing options

Benefits for your user
- Off-site, anytime access via Athens or referring URL
- Print or copy pages or chapters
- Full content search
- Bookmark, highlight and annotate text
- Access to thousands of pages of quality research at the click of a button

For more information, pricing enquiries or to order a free trial, contact your local online sales team.

UK and Rest of World:
online.sales@tandf.co.uk

US, Canada and Latin America:
e-reference@taylorandfrancis.com

www.ebooksubscriptions.com

ALPSP Award for BEST eBOOK PUBLISHER 2009 Finalist

Taylor & Francis eBooks
Taylor & Francis Group

A flexible and dynamic resource for teaching, learning and research.

eupdates
Taylor & Francis Group

Want to stay one step ahead of your colleagues?

Sign up today to receive free up-to-date information on books, journals, conferences and other news within your chosen subject areas.

Visit
www.tandf.co.uk/eupdates
and register your email address, indicating your subject areas of interest.

You will be able to amend your details or unsubscribe at any time. We respect your privacy and will not disclose, sell or rent your email address to any outside company. If you have questions or concerns with any aspect of the eUpdates service, please email eupdates@tandf.co.uk or write to: eUpdates, Routledge, 2/4 Park Square, Milton Park, Abingdon, Oxfordshire OX14 4RN, UK.

ROUTLEDGE INTERNATIONAL HANDBOOKS

Routledge International Handbooks is an outstanding, award-winning series that provides cutting-edge overviews of classic research, current research and future trends in Social Science, Humanities and STM.

Each *Handbook*:

- is introduced and contextualised by leading figures in the field
- features specially commissioned original essays
- draws upon an international team of expert contributors
- provides a comprehensive overview of a sub-discipline.

Routledge International Handbooks aim to address new developments in the sphere, while at the same time providing an authoritative guide to theory and method, the key sub-disciplines and the primary debates of today.

If you would like more information on our on-going *Handbooks* publishing programme, please contact us.

Tel: +44 (0)20 701 76566
Email: reference@routledge.com

www.routledge.com/reference

ROUTLEDGE Revivals

Are there some elusive titles you've been searching for but thought you'd never be able to find?

Well this may be the end of your quest. We now offer a fantastic opportunity to discover past brilliance and purchase previously out of print and unavailable titles by some of the greatest academic scholars of the last 120 years.

Routledge Revivals is an exciting new programme whereby key titles from the distinguished and extensive backlists of the many acclaimed imprints associated with Routledge are re-issued.

The programme draws upon the backlists of Kegan Paul, Trench & Trubner, Routledge & Kegan Paul, Methuen, Allen & Unwin and Routledge itself.

Routledge Revivals spans the whole of the Humanities and Social Sciences, and includes works by scholars such as Emile Durkheim, Max Weber, Simone Weil and Martin Buber.

FOR MORE INFORMATION

Please email us at **reference@routledge.com** or visit: **www.routledge.com/books/series/Routledge_Revivals**

www.routledge.com

Routledge
Taylor & Francis Group

Printed in Germany
by Amazon Distribution
GmbH, Leipzig